I FIGHT FOR A LIVING

I FIGHT FOR A LIVING

Boxing and the Battle
for Black Manhood, 1880–1915

LOUIS MOORE

UNIVERSITY OF
ILLINOIS PRESS
Urbana, Chicago, and Springfield

Library of Congress Cataloging-in-Publication Data
Names: Moore, Louis, 1978- author.
Title: I fight for a living : boxing and the battle for black
    manhood, 1880–1915 / Louis Moore.
Description: Urbana : University of Illinois, [2017] | Includes
    bibliographical references and index. |
Identifiers: LCCN 2017015267 (print) | LCCN 2017023714 (ebook)
    | ISBN 9780252099946 (e-book) | ISBN 9780252041341
    (hardcover : alk. paper) | ISBN 9780252082870 (pbk. : alk.
    paper)
Subjects: LCSH: Boxing—United States—History—19th century.
    | Boxing—United States—History—20th century. | African
    American boxers. | Racism in sports—United States—History.
    | Discrimination in sports—United States—History.
Classification: LCC GV1125 (ebook) | LCC GV1125 .M66 2017 (print)
    | DDC 796.83—dc23
LC record available at https://lccn.loc.gov/2017015267

CONTENTS

ACKNOWLEDGMENTS

A special thanks goes to scholars inside and outside academia who helped shaped my work, took the time to read some drafts, or just kept me positive when things got hectic: Steve Riess, Patrick O'Connor, Mike Gallego, Dave Zirin, Derrick White, Johnny Smith, Adrian Burgos, and Matthew Klugman. I am grateful to Clarence E. Walker for mentoring me at UC Davis. I also thank my colleagues and friends at Grand Valley. The Amaya family in California and the Jones family in Cincinnati treated me like their own, especially Willie, who has always treated me like a son. Also offering continuous support have been my boys from day 1: Larry, Mark, "No Jumpshot" Todd, and Damion. Additionally, Eric Paul has supported me since grad school. My siblings have always supported me: Zoey, Zenobia, and my brother Lance, who taught me to love sport and be critical about everything. My mom, Mary, sacrificed everything to provide us with our needs, and encouraged me to pursue my dreams. And last but not least, a very special thanks goes to the three ladies of my life: my amazing wife Ciciley, who has always supported me, and my girls Amaya and Isla, who make my day brighter. A final thanks goes to mini-me, Grant, who keeps a smile on my face. Daddy loves you.

I FIGHT FOR A LIVING

INTRODUCTION

George Godfrey fought for a living. "I've got a wife and six children," he once told a reporter, "and I follow fighting as people follow any other calling."[1] Born in 1853 in Prince Edward Island, Canada, as a teenager Godfrey and his family left a life of segregation and poverty in the Bog district of his hometown and migrated to Boston for better economic opportunities. But like 80 percent of black men in Boston, Godfrey could only find menial work.[2] With little chance of economic advancement, in 1878 Godfrey joined the gym of the renowned black sparring master John B. Bailey, who had the reputation of being the best teacher in the country. Five years later, Godfrey won the Colored Heavyweight Championship after he defeated "Professor" Charles Hadley. Satisfied that he could make a living as a fighter, Godfrey quit his drudge job at a Boston meat market and dedicated himself full-time to his new craft.

When Bailey and Godfrey met in 1878, their meeting, and Godfrey's subsequent professional career, represented a generational shift in how black men viewed athletics. In antebellum America, Bailey and other athletes of his generation like Aaron Molineaux Hewlett and Patton Stewart—who owned middle-class gymnasiums in the Boston area and offered sparring lessons, gymnastics, and weight training—used their mastery of athletics, their fit bodies, and their eventual ownership of gymnasiums to prove that they, and by extension black men, were fit for citizenship. Hewlett, to be sure, momentarily tried to make a go out of a fighting career in the early 1850s, but quickly gave up what he considered a disreputable profession in 1855, when he had the opportunity to make a living as a sparring teacher and physical culture expert. Professional sports, on the other hand, were too closely associated with gamblers and other men in a sporting culture that rejected traditional norms about Victorian middle-class manhood.[3] Athletics, Bailey and others thought, should only be pursued for the purpose of health benefits, not financial gain. Plus, the overt racism one would experience made it nearly impossible to pursue a career as a professional fighter. Godfrey and his generation of athletes, however, saw sports as a means to employment and a way to assert their manly independence. Their economic livelihood and claims to equality rested on the mastery of their bodies, their ability to successfully compete in athletics, and the money they reaped from their athletic success. When Godfrey won the Colored Championship in 1883, there were already a few black men working as professional athletes, including a bevy of jockeys, Frank Hart the race walker, and notable baseball players including Bud Fowler and Moses and Weldy Walker. Out of this growing cadre of black professional athletes, the prizefighter represented the most recognizable figure. In 1884, for example, the *Boston Globe* observed, "Colored pugs are prevalent all over the country, the latest addition to the [Baltimore] Black Stars and [Cincinnati] Black Diamonds being [Boston] George Godfrey, who wants to do battle with Jake Kilrain, [Port Huron] C.A.C Smith, the Western Terror who was used as a shuttlecock by that other colored gentleman [Rochester] Mervin Thompson, and a 'Pop' Lewis of Chicago."[4] Each of these black athletes faced entrenched racism within their respective sports—the black jockey and the baseball player would be driven out of their professions—but prizefighting offered black men the best opportunity at full-time athletic employment because of the individualistic nature of the sport, the growing desire among men to see other men fight, and the easy access to fight. To succeed in the profession, a man needed his fists and the courage to face an onslaught of punches. Godfrey was the best of the lot.

Confident in his manly fighting abilities, for the right price, and under the right terms of conditions, Godfrey would fight any man: "I am not afraid to meet any one where there is a chance of making money," he claimed.[5] Full of racial pride, Godfrey even proclaimed he preferred fighting white men because they were "easier whipped." Successful black fighters like Godfrey publicly projected an image of toughness and manly confidence, a self-assurance derived from their disciplined body and rooted in a belief of black superiority. During an era in which black men faced increasing racial violence, a black fighter's public performance of manliness challenged whites' tolerance for what they would accept from a black man.[6] But in a sport where superiority had to be constantly demonstrated, and bodies were always on public

Boston's black sparring master John B. Bailey, standing in a fighting pose. Bailey owned his gymnasium for more than thirty years. Upon his death, George Godfrey took over. (1870, Library of Congress)

display, white pugilists did not always exude the same racial confidence as black fighters. To protect their claims to manly authority—and by extension the white race's claim to superiority—many white prizefighters hid behind the color line.

Like the racist job market that thwarted black economic advancement, the color line in boxing stifled black fighters' earning potential. Growing desperate for a fight, and tired of American racism, in November 1887 Godfrey floated the possibility of fighting in England. "I think I am a great fighter," Godfrey said, "but I can't do well in this country simply because no one will fight me." While exhibiting a common language of manliness in the sporting culture—all fighters of his generation used newspapers to conduct their business and challenge other men to fights—Godfrey's words attacked white American manhood. Very few working-class black men had the opportunity to publicly assert their manliness, physically challenge white men, and criticize racism. "In England" Godfrey claimed, "they do things in a different way. . . . If a man comes out with a challenge to fight, they do not let him spoil just because he happens to be colored. They always accommodate a man." Indeed, the majority of the top black fighters of his generation echoed

Godfrey's sentiments and traveled overseas for better racial treatment and for better paydays. But Godfrey needed a financial backer "with plenty of 'rocks'" to take him "across the 'big pond.'" Despite having a bevy of Boston friends, Godfrey never found a financial backer willing to front him money to embark on a career overseas.[7] He had to find work in America.

Although black boxers had to deal with unscrupulous white managers, financial backers, and athletic-club owners, black fighters saw themselves as independent artisans who controlled their own labor.[8] Some fighters settled for work quicker than others and fought for any price offered, while other fighters, like Godfrey, understood the growing consumer market in the athletic male body and keenly negotiated the terms of their work. A week after Godfrey pondered traveling to England, the massive Mervine Thompson challenged him to fight for $500. For Thompson, $500 would have been a fair price because he had not had a credible victory since he knocked out C.A.C. Smith (black) in March 1884. But Godfrey, the Colored Champion, believed he was entitled to more money than $500. He wanted to fight for $1,000. No black man had fought for that much money before, and most white men could not command that much loot either. A writer for the *Boston Globe* scoffed at his assertion of self-worth. "Godfrey," the writer suggested, "has been on a clamoring anxious seat for a long time, and he should accept this very liberal offer, as $1000 purses are not to be found every day."[9] Godfrey did not budge.

While Godfrey labored in Boston for a lucrative fight, across the country, in Denver, Colorado, McHenry Johnson clamored for a big payday too. Like most working-class black men, little is known about the "Black Star's" past. Reportedly born in 1859 in Baltimore, Maryland—it is not known free or slave—the "Black Star" first made headway in pugilistic circles in 1883 when he arrived in New York with the purpose of winning the Colored Championship. Quick and powerful, Johnson more than likely honed his craft by fighting in bare-knuckle contests in Baltimore's saloons and cellars. He impressed the sporting men in New York so much that a white financial backer, Theo Allen, backed Johnson for a $2,000 side bet for a contest against any black fighter—a significant upgrade from the $25 fights Johnson usually took.[10] Johnson never found a black opponent who had a backer willing to risk such a large sum of money. Most black men could not convince whites to financially support their careers. Soon, Allen stopped backing Johnson. He was on his own and had to raise his own money to fight, which meant the potential wages shrunk. Johnson momentarily headed to Ohio for better paydays, but quickly returned east for a coveted shot at Godfrey's championship. In May 1884, the two black bruisers engaged in a hotly contested four-round draw in Boston, but without a guaranteed purse, or a negotiated price for the gate receipts, neither man won any money from their $25 side bet.[11]

Collectively, black prizefighters represented a symbol of black mobility as they moved around the country or crossed oceans to find work.[12] Though all boxers had to be on the go to find work in the ring, some black men like Godfrey blended the sporting life with family life, while others, like Johnson, represented the colored sport, a loaded term denoting a black man's association with the undisciplined and undesirable sporting bachelor subculture. Historian Howard P. Chudacoff contends that bachelors created a distinct subculture where they constructed alternative ideas of manhood that often contrasted with those of Victorian culture. According to Chudacoff, "the emergence of what historians have called the sporting-male culture" was the most significant development of the bachelor subculture. In the sporting culture, "males received their identity from their patronage of various illicit pastimes involving gambling" and not that "in American cities they established themselves simply in contrast to 'respectable men' and included among their fraternity members from all social classes."[13] In this work, however, I will use the term *colored sport* to suggest a racial distinction among bachelors. While black men often risked their lives frequenting white sporting spaces, to avoid the dangerous racism and Jim Crow, colored sports created their own institutions at bars and billiard rooms to prove and affirm their manhood. The colored sport shunned most traditional Victorian norms about family that the middle class espoused, and believed their manhood was best understood in the hypermasculine sporting community. In this context, the black fighter moved to find work, make money, and broaden his manly image in a larger sporting context in saloons, newspapers, and the boxing ring. As scholar Davarian Baldwin has suggested, "the sporting life ran counter to visions of black and white reformers who believed that a strict work ethic and/or knowledge of the 'higher arts' were the solo routes to interracial understanding, self-reliance, and respectability."[14] The male social world of the colored sport is represented in the following description by a white writer: "They were holding forth yesterday afternoon in a long narrow room attached to an ill smelling joint bearing the euphonious name of 'Colored Young Men's United Republican Club'—Lou Simpson's club—in the front of which were seated an athletic club manager, a ball player and a few men who desired to get some 'feedbox information' before losing any money on the contest between Hank Griffin and Jack Johnson, scheduled for Friday night."[15] Though the white writer was seemingly mocking these black men, we can see in this piece these working-class black men rejecting norms of Victorian culture that suggested they put family first, and instead finding comfort and affirmation of their existence in this black-owned athletic club. The black fighter was the center of attention.

McHenry Johnson was one such fighter who felt he always had to be on the move proving his manhood. In 1886, for example, with the prizefight game slowing in the East, Johnson moved to St. Paul, Minnesota, where he joined top black fighters Henry Woodson (Cincinnati), Charles Hadley (Bridgeport, Connecticut), and Billy Wilson (Boston) who had all moved to the city within the previous two years to take advantage of the growing fight game. Three of these men, Johnson, Woodson and Wilson, owned bars. Woodson was murdered in 1887 in Chicago for sleeping with another man's wife, Wilson became one of the first black police officers in the city, and Johnson only lasted six months in St. Paul when legal troubles—he was arrested for selling liquor to local Native Americans—and a lack of fighting opportunities, pushed him out of the city.[16] Before he left town, he and Wilson engaged in a public spat to display their manly prowess. After a controversial ten-round rematch on December 2, 1886 in St. Paul that resulted in a draw, Johnson sent a telegram to the *St. Paul Pioneer Press* to protect his honor and devalue Wilson's manly reputation. Johnson wrote:

> Billy Wilson is still making cracks around the city that he can whip me. I would like it stated for once and all time that I am willing to meet Wilson upon a moment's notice for any amount of money. If he has no money to put up, I'll fight him for the $1000 purse offered by Mr. Ryan. This money will be put up the moment Wilson says he will meet me. If he don't care to have all the money go to the winner, I'll agree to have the purse divided—$800 to the winner and $200 to the loser. He certainly can ask for nothing fairer. I don't know that I can whip Wilson, but I am willing to risk my reputation as champion of the United States on the result.[17]

Despite a series of quarrels in the local newspapers over the next five months, the two never agreed on a satisfactory fight purse and thus never fought each other again. Looking for immediate work in the ring after his arrest, Johnson migrated to Omaha, Nebraska.

When Johnson arrived in his new city, the "Black Star" quickly introduced himself in the sporting community—usually at a popular sporting establishment—bragged about his pugilistic skills, and challenged all comers, black or white. His confidence and manly bravado were designed to catch the attention of other men. Understanding the growing consumer market in physical manhood, local newspapers were quick to report Johnson's public performances of physical confidence. Shortly after he arrived in Omaha, the *Omaha Bee* announced, "For some days past Mr. Henry Johnson, a pugilist, not a paper fighter, but one of those shoulder-hitters that some people have read of in days gone by, has been in the city. He has met many men in the ring, and defeated them, and as a consequence, 'Fistiana' has given him the name of the 'Black Star.'"[18] Sure, Johnson bragged about his skills, but could he back up his words? In other words, was Johnson a real man or a paper fighter? Paper fighters were not manly; they talked a tough game, boasted and bragged, but found ways to avoid battle. Within a week of his arrival, local white sports found an opponent to test Johnson's bold claims.

Every fighter has a puncher's chance, but in truth, the novice Elliot Edwards, "a coffee colored youth from South Omaha," had no chance against Johnson, a seasoned veteran.[19] In a fight that took place outside city limits, away from lawmakers, in the middle of a cow pasture, Johnson beat up Edwards with "paralyzing" uppercuts and hard body shots. Impressed by what they had witnessed, white Omaha sports fans placed a $500 forfeit at the *Bee*—a figure a future opponent had to match to secure a fight with Johnson—and challenged any black fighter for a $5,000 fight.[20] They found no takers.[21]

Despite the fact that Johnson "made many friends" in Omaha's sporting community, he could not stay long. In October the once-promising Omaha fight game had dried to a "low ebb."[22] Professional pugilists like Johnson, who never fought for large paydays, always searched for the next play. Johnson, like most black fighters during this era, was a meal ticket man, and fought to eat. He had to move. In December 1887, Johnson settled in Denver, Colorado, a bustling city of bachelor male culture that made it ripe for the fight game. After Johnson arrived, his manly boasting and sparring exhibitions convinced members from Denver's middle-class athletic club, the Crib Club, that Johnson was the best fighter they had seen, and they backed him for a $1,000 winner-take-all fight against George Godfrey. But their backing of the black bruiser went beyond benevolence for the white men in Denver. It seems that Johnson might have overstepped his bounds as a black man, but no white man could put him in his proper place. According to Godfrey, Johnson "had only been in Denver a couple of months before the match was made with me, and they say he went strutting around as though he owned the whole town. That is why they got me to go out and lick him." Most men accepted winner-take-all battles, but not Godfrey. If white men wanted a show, they had to pay. Godfrey, an astute businessman and a man who knew his worth in this dangerous business of boxing, countered with more favorable terms. From the $1,000 purse he wanted $150 travel expenses, a guaranteed $750 to the winner, and $100 for the loser.[23]

Beginning in the 1880s, changes in the rules of prizefighting that made the sport seem less violent, a shifting notion of middle-class manliness that focused on physicality, and a "commercial and consumer revolution" created a demand and financial incentive for prizefighters.[24] To supply their members with the manly shows that men now demanded, middle-class athletic clubs like Denver's Crib Club became boxing match-makers. Prior to these clubs' involvement, fighters had to find a financial backer willing to front their bets/stakes. The backer/fighter relationship limited the amount of money a fighter could make, because the fighter's potential earnings were based off another man's willingness to gamble. Athletic clubs, on the other hand, used the money they received from membership dues to bid for the best fighters. They also offered guaranteed purses. Denver's lawmakers, however, had not yet been convinced of the merits of fighting, and boxing remained illegal. The Crib Club had to host the Godfrey-Johnson fight outside the city limits.

Featuring fighters "built like the gladiators of old, with muscles of steel," and with "constitutions that have never been impaired by dissipation and disease," the Godfrey–Johnson fight for the Colored Championship consti-tuted the first significant contest between black fighters in America.[25] Free black men had been boxing each other throughout the nineteenth century in America—the first reported fight coming in 1822—but before the 1880s fights were few and far between and received little coverage.[26] The Godfrey–Johnson fight, however, "was the chief topic of discussion in pugilistic circles for a month or more," and the sports world "watched with interest all over the country."[27] Hyping up the contest, an officer of the Crib Club claimed there was "more newspaper talk over this contest than has been made about any one in America since the Sullivan-Ryan match some years ago." He also urged, "It will be a sight worth seeing" and bragged the fight would "go on record as one of the most remarkable matches ever made."[28]

Eventually, a boxer bites off more than he can chew. His desire to prove his manliness and to make more money ultimately gets the best of him. Such was the case for McHenry Johnson. Coming into the fight, Denver's sports community believed Johnson had key advantages over Godfrey—he out-weighed him 171 pounds to Godfrey's 168—and he had already acclimated to the altitude, unlike Godfrey, whom they expected to struggle because he "lived near the sea coast, and had never before attempted to do anything where the atmosphere is light." Godfrey, however, had a disciplined and well-trained body, a reputation as "one of the most scientific sparrers in the world," and was "capable of striking a desperately hard blow."[29] On the morning of January 25, the two gladiators, along with four hundred sports fans, hopped on the Utah and Pacific train in search of a suitable location to battle. When they found a place—an area with flat ground, open space, and away from the authorities—the train stopped, and the fighters prepared for battle. In the third round, "with a powerful swinging blow Godfrey heeled Johnson on the left jaw which so stunned him that he could not tell the referee from Godfrey. The Boston boy followed up his advantage and struck Johnson half a dozen blows in the face, knocking him over the ropes and completely blinding him."[30] "Why, when I hit Johnson [with] that new stylistic blow of mine," Godfrey recalled, "he went into a heap on the floor, where he remained unable to move."[31] The fight "grew into a bloody, brutal, sickening affair" until the referee claimed Godfrey fouled Johnson and declared Johnson the winner.[32] Luckily for Godfrey, the Crib Club acknowledged the referee misinterpreted the Queensberry Rules, and the club awarded Godfrey the $750. Johnson never fought in a meaningful fight again. Godfrey returned to Boston a fistic hero.

Satisfied with whipping Johnson, and with no credible black opponent in America to fight, Godfrey turned his attention to white men. In March 1888, Godfrey attended Jack Havlin's benefit in order to challenge any man in America for a $1,500 side: "I feel sure that if any one makes a bluff that he doesn't want to fight me now solely because of my color it won't go with the public. My challenge is open to any man in the business . . ." He also had a message for heavyweight champion John L. Sullivan, urging "I would be tickled if I could get on a fight with John Sullivan. There's a man whom I don't dread at all, and if I ever met him in a ring I would be confident of whipping him. I don't see what he ever did, anyway, to warrant making all the hullaboo [sic] about him that has been made."[33] Godfrey publicly embarrassed the epitome of white masculinity hoping it would draw Sullivan into a fight, but the racist Sullivan was too concerned with protecting his white privilege and white manhood. He did not fight "niggers," as he often said. Godfrey had to wait until August for his next fight, a battle against the recently arrived, West Indian–born Peter Jackson for the Colored Championship, and $1,400. Godfrey bit off more than he could chew.

What do we make of the public assertion of manhood by men like George Godfrey and McHenry Johnson? How did working-class black men use prizefighting to construct manliness? In what ways did their assertions of manhood challenge or reflect both traditional white notions of middle-class manliness and the black middle class's vision of masculinity? In other words, how did the black middle class and white society reconcile black fighters' emphasis on muscles, manhood, and money? It was a tough bargain to risk one's body to prove manhood, but black men across the globe took that chance. *I Fight for a Living* uses the stories of black fighters' lives, from 1880 to 1915, to explore how working-class black men used prizefighting and the sporting culture to assert their manhood in a country that denied their equality, and to examine the reactions by the black middle class and white middle class toward these black fighters.

For a black man, boxing gave him release from the daily indignities he suffered because of his race. It allowed him, in other words, to be a man. The great black prizefighter Archie Moore—the light heavyweight champion of the 1950s grew up in poverty in St. Louis—once reflected, "During the years of slavery and the years of economic exploitation that followed and still exists in some part, the Negro developed an escapist outlook. If nothing could be done about the situation, then why not go along with the way the wind blew?" These men, according to the champion Moore, were weak. Survivalist. But the fighter, Moore suggested, was different. Boxers believed in their manhood. "Fortunately there were a lot of colored men who couldn't accept that way of life. The great colored fighting men down through the years were among this group. Nobody gets into a ring to fight unless he believes in his manhood."[34] To believe in one's manhood was to be fully free.

By choosing the title *I Fight for a Living,* I am emphasizing the struggle for black working-class autonomy in the business of boxing and how these black men constructed their version of manhood in a racist society. The existence of the black prizefighter challenged the notion and portrayal by white Americans of the weak and emasculated battle royal boxer, representative of all black men. The battle royal, a popular a form of entertainment throughout the country, reinforced to white men the powerlessness of black men. The rules were simple: "Four negroes are put in the ring at the same time, one entering from each corner. The man who is on his feet after the other three are knocked out wins the purse; the limit of which, on a generous estimate, is usually about $10."[35] Indeed, $10 was a "generous estimate," because most winners could only expect roughly $1.50 for their services, a reminder of their worthlessness to whites. Sometimes, there was no escape from the embarrassment. To be poor and black in America was to be desperate and hungry. A man had to eat. Jack Johnson, who fought in a battle royal in Springfield, Illinois, explained his participation, saying: "I was hungry; my great ambition as the fight began was to eat; and I feared that if I did not win the fight,

I might not have an opportunity to eat."[36] Nobody knows what happened to those other nameless fighters he beat that night, but more than likely, they went home hurt, hungry, poor, and emotionally shamed.

To be sure, the battle royal became a comforting spectacle for white men, who had to confront the reality that black men possessed the same masculine physicality that white men claimed. This was racial medicine for a race of people dealing with the reality that their ideas of manhood and physicality rested on shaky ground. White promoters arranged battle royals as preliminary exhibitions to whip the majority white audience into a racial frenzy as they whooped and hollered at young black men forced to look like savages for white entertainment. "In the heyday of social Darwinism," historian Andrew M. Kaye writes, "the battle royal appeared to reflect the racial struggle being played out in the real world. Superior whites looked on as lowly blacks enacted a fight for survival among themselves." Kaye further notes that this "reassuring spectacle, in which only one child could win—and he too was more than likely doomed to extinction—captured the fate of weaker races and peoples."[37] "The spectacle of half a dozen gingers attempting to knock each other's heads off may not be according to the simple life doctrine," reasoned one white writer, "but it brings the smiles to the Caucasian brother just the same."[38] The black prizefighter, however, made white men cringe.

In this book, I make three interrelated arguments. First, I assert that prizefighting and the sporting culture provided black men a surrogate to the racist job market that had forced them into drudge labor. In other words, black fighters used their fists and well-trained bodies to position themselves as self-made men in a country that tried to deny their economic, social, and political manhood. Their status as full-time fighters, however, forced the black middle class to come to terms with this new assertion of black manhood that became a public spectacle that seemed more like disreputable leisure rather respectable labor. Second, I suggest black fighters publicly performed their manhood in a myriad of ways that were understood as manly in the sporting culture, and if they chose, simultaneously conformed to acceptable hegemonic middle-class manhood. The ability to be a "good fellow" and or a refined gentleman was an individual calculation by the fighter based on what culture would accept his assertions of manhood. Lastly, I argue that black pugilistic success on a national and local level shattered the myth of black inferiority. To protect white male authority, white writers used the press to depict black fighters as either Sambos or savages, and so-called progressive lawmakers restricted interracial fights in their cities and states as a form of white protectionism.

Central to this book is situating fighting as work. For black men, economic independence constituted an essential construct of manhood. In this context, manliness meant that a man had a good job and he could take care of his family. But the racist job market relegated black men to menial work and thus denied them a key component of manhood. Addressing these bleak economic conditions in 1901, black lawyer Adelbert H. Roberts pleaded, "We ask for no special privileges, we only demand the same chance of existence for earning a livelihood, for raising ourselves in the scale of manhood, as is accorded other people. Open the doors of industry to him, do not confine his employment to drudgery."[39] Commenting on this state of affairs, historian Martin Summers has written, "economic discrimination and the inability of most black families to survive solely on a male breadwinner's income militated against the patriarchal organization of the black household, further making it difficult to obtain manhood by dominant culture standards."[40] In the dominant white viewpoint—one blurred by social Darwinian thought—black men were less than men because they were not sole breadwinners. But prizefighting represented one of the few skilled jobs where a black man could earn the same amount of money as a white man. In 1892, for example, a writer claimed, "There are at least two professions in this country at which a colored man can win as much fame and money as a white man." He concluded, "They are jockeyship and pugilism. In these two walks of life the dusky brother has as much chance to win a fortune and the brightest laurels as any white man in the land."[41]

By focusing on fighters finding work, I build on scholarship about sports and working-class black manhood, especially the work of historian Theresa Runstedtler, who in her brilliant book *Jack Johnson Rebel Sojourner*, smartly places heavyweight champion Jack Johnson in the context of the black working-class manhood, and correctly notes that for black pugilists, "boxing was not just a better way to make money; it was a route to freedom and independence. . . . Black men often used the boxing industry as a means to escape from the discipline and degradation of menial work."[42] In other words, the sporting culture gave black men a platform to assert their manliness and prove themselves equal to white men. Runstedtler, however, sees Johnson and his contemporaries as "rebels" intentionally challenging a hegemonic notion of white manhood. But not every act was a challenge. Many of these fighters, as I will show, purposely molded themselves in the image of the middle-class, not so much as a challenge to white hegemony, but as an assertion of their own autonomy. They invested their money in business, bought suburban homes for their families, and openly discussed and displayed their roles as patriarchs.

In a nation that tried to deny black men their manhood, the black fighter looked for ways to publicly assert his manliness inside and outside the ring. When Godfrey returned to Boston after disposing of Johnson in Denver, using the widely read *Boston Globe*, Godfrey purposely presented a dual image of a sporting manhood and middle-class manliness. In his interview with the press, he first mentioned that after he arrived in Boston, he headed straight to his family, then he visited his successful boxing school for white middle-class men second, and lastly, he talked to the reporter about his fistic superiority.[43] Family, finances, and fists formed the foundation of his manhood.

The black prizefighter's assertion of manhood straddled the line between manliness constructed in the sporting culture and a performance of middle-class manhood. As scholar Davarian Baldwin notes, "The sporting sphere offered New Negro expressions of black ownership over body, behavior, and community through varying ideas about gender."[44] "[Jack] Johnson and other athletes not nearly as controversial," Baldwin argues, "represented a new modern position on race manhood somewhere between the archetypes of Washington's skilled trade laborer and W.E.B. Du Bois's 'talented tenth' professional/intellectual."[45] This "new Negro" mentality, I will show, started before Jack Johnson hit the Southside stroll. He was the latest, but loudest, of a long line of black fighters that led a fight to reimagine black manhood.

To put this new assertion of black manhood in context, this book builds on scholarship about the construction of black manhood at the turn of the nineteenth and twentieth centuries that have largely focused on the black middle class.[46] Martin Summers's *Manliness and its Discontents,* Kevin Gaines's *Uplifting the Race,* and Angela-Hornsby-Gutting's *Black Manhood and Community Building in North Carolina,* for example, have done a tremendous job in discussing how black men constructed their manhood based on the white middle-class ideas of Victorian manhood while also maintaining black agency. Summers describes this construction, noting, "when black men sought to organize households and institutions within the black community, such as the church, along the lines of patriarchy . . . they engaged in the same discourses that white men did—discourses that grounded manhood in, among other things, independence, citizenship, engagement in the marketplace, mastery over self and the environment, and patriarchy."[47] To position themselves as men, the black middle class relied on the politics of respectability as a surrogate to objective middle-class economic manhood. Grounded in an uplift strategy, black leaders wanted to show they had the cultural capacity to perform Victorian middle-class respectability. "For many black elites," Gaines suggests, "uplift came to mean an emphasis on self-help, racial solidarity, temperance, thrift, chastity, social purity, patriarchal authority, and the accumulation of wealth."[48] These black leaders also emphasized the importance of racial pride as their uplift strategy, "represented the struggle for a positive black identity in a deeply racist society, turning the pejorative designation of race into a source of dignity and self-affirmation through an ideology of class differentiation, self-help, and interdependence."[49] On this note, Hornsby-Guttings has demonstrated that in North Carolina, part of the uplift strategy was a performance of a communal manhood in which the black middle-class leaders positioned themselves as exemplars to uplift the race.[50] Looking to change black boys into respectable black men who would grow to challenge Jim Crow, "North Carolina's middle-class black men sought to rectify what they perceived as their generation's compromised public ambitions by instilling community-based lessons of self-pride, etiquette, and industry among boys and young men."[51]

Vital to their claim to manhood, however, was the denigration of the black working class, especially the colored sport. On the one hand, black elites used the black working class as a scapegoat to elevate the black elite's own claim of racial progress. The ability of the black middle class to acculturate, its member's thought, meant they had the cultural capital to succeed. On the other hand, the morals and manners of the black working class were perceived as working against the interest of the black race. Black elites believed the "offcasts" would continue to hold down the race. Concerned about urban black pathology, many middle-class black leaders asked the working class to avoid disreputable leisure like prizefighting. In 1883, for example, after Henry Woodson fought in Brooklyn, black newspaperman T. Thomas Fortune described prizefights as "brutal and demoralizing." Fortune also labeled fighters as "roughs" and argued their social status was "but a little higher than that of the poor captive slave sacrificed to the public amusement in the gladiatorial contests of the bloody licentious Rome." A few months later, Fortune begged "colored men to avoid patronizing them at any and all times."[52] "To such alarmists," Gaines notes, "the image of urban blacks and their forms of leisure signified the steady erosion of racial uplift ideals of service and upright moral conduct."[53] The values of the sporting culture were not compatible with racial uplift. But that thought would soon change. It had to. Though boxing remained disgusting, dangerous, and denigrating, black men had started to dominate the sport, especially in interracial battles. By the late 1880s, for the black middle class, black victories in the ring reinforced their belief in racial equality, because boxing was an exercise in merit and manhood, and the middle class openly celebrated black boxers, especially the champions who they hoped also had the community's best interest in mind. Sports mattered.

The increasing presence and domination of black fighters, however, openly challenged notions of white manhood. As early as 1890 it was clear black men dominated the prize ring. That year a well-known New York sporting man observed, "It looks as if the pugilistic fever which has raged so fiercely in this country for the past ten years is abating. The prominence darky fighters have assumed in the ring is contributing to this effect. . . . The shadow of the black man's fist is over the ring."[54] In other words, the ascent of black men in the ring coincided with the remaking of white manhood that emphasized the muscular body and physicality. Scholar Anthony Rotundo contends that the turn of the century constituted the time period in which white men were most concerned about remaking manhood, and "the male body moved to the center of men's gender concerns; manly passions were revalued in a favorable light; men began to look at the 'primitive' sources of manhood with new regard . . ."[55] Similarly, John F. Kasson has suggested that "in this period [white manhood] seems to have been undermined on a number of fronts and demanded constant work in new arenas to remain strong."[56] What caused this shift? Prior to the industrial revolution the ideal of middle-class manhood was constructed around men's participation and success in the market. A man's ability to be independent and take care of his family stemmed from his ability to discipline his appetites and succeed in the economic marketplace. Competing for jobs against women, ethnic working-class men, people of color, and an unstable economy challenged this construction of manliness. Because of this economic shift, white middle-class men "worried they had lost the manly authority their ancestors held in society."[57] To retain their dominant position in society, white middle-class men directed their attentions to the male body, tying manliness and racial superiority to physicality and primitiveness.[58] The emphasis on physical culture enabled white men to focus on their physiques, making the idealized male body both powerful and muscular. To reestablish their sense of manly authority, men joined gyms, lifted weights, and also sought forms of entertainment that displayed the powerful body. In brief, Michael Kimmel notes, the "doctrine of physicality and the body" replaced the financially successful "self-made man."[59] For white males, men like strongman Eugen Sandow and his muscular body became a symbol of white racial power, and "a sign of man's ability to make his way in the world against all adversaries, strictly on his own merits."[60]

In this celebration of the white male body, white fighters, especially heavyweights, became important figures of white male authority. Gail Bederman observes, "Late Victorian culture had identified that powerful, large male body of the heavyweight (and not the smaller bodies of the middleweight or welterweight) as the epitome of manhood."[61] With an emphasis on the powerful male body, and violent, yet controlled masculinity, white fans flocked to the fights. In 1910, for example, novelist Jack London told his readers that men "want to see fights, because of the old red blood of Adam in them that will not die down."[62] Descriptions of boxers' physiques were the norm in the press. Heavyweight champions John L. Sullivan and Jim Jeffries, with their massive muscular bodies, came to symbolize the strength of the white race.[63] In one of the few instances a newspaper used the word "masculinity" to discuss a boxer—they usually used manly or manhood—the writer described champion Jim Jeffries, remarking that Jeffries was an "untutored product of the working-class, elevated by the power of muscle, coupled with an instinctive dexterity, to the altar before which a majority of men bow . . ." The mountain of "Intense Masculinity," the reporter continued, was, "entirely human and masculine to the core."[64] Whites' claim to bodily strength and racial authority, however, was never as strong as they liked to have believed.

Notwithstanding a sharp racial color line in society, and a fear of black physicality, many white fans clamored for interracial contests as a proving ground for white manhood. "Despite the hatred of the colored boxer when pitted against a white man," a sportswriter quipped in 1902, "fight promoters and manages continue matching them, and undoubtedly will continue doing so as long as the sport remains alive." But "human nature," the white writer reasoned, "is a peculiar thing, especially with reference to race prejudice in pugilism." "When a crackerjack color fighter challenges a white man and the latter does not accept the den a cry will immediately be raised that the white man is afraid to fight. That is, the public abuses him for dodging the colored man, and when finally he is sandbagged into meeting the colored man. . . ."[65] It often proved a mistake. Great black fighters dominated their white competition, and whites feared that the manly confidence black men exhibited in the ring would trickle down to black men outside the ring.[66]

Entering into the ring with his muscular body, the black fighter forced white men to take notice of his manly physique. Black prizefighters keenly understood the growing emphasis whites had placed on the male body as a marker of manhood and authority. He developed his body with disciplined training habits that white men admired, thus suggesting the black body was not inferior. In 1885, readers of the *St. Paul Globe* read training tips from black pugilist Billy Wilson about how to remake their bodies. Wilson, whom the paper called "a young Hercules," told the *St. Paul Globe* about proper dieting, jogging, and sparring. He also told the reporter, "I do not smoke and I take no ale. I have never smoked, nor have I never drunk anything. I am in splendid condition and feel able to fight like fury." The reporter agreed and added, "His muscles are hard as iron."[67] In 1893 champion George Dixon claimed in his book *A Lesson in Boxing,* "In nearly every city where I have appeared I have been requested by gentlemen to give private instructions in the art of boxing."[68] Indeed, Dixon toured the nation teaching white men how to be men. With this enormous amount of racial stock placed on the white male body, the presence of black fighters with their manly muscles and fistic fury challenged any notion of white superiority.

Influenced by Michael Oriard's *Reading Football,* newspapers form the heart of my research and narrative. In his spectacular work, Oriard contends that sportswriters "had access to the most powerful media of the time, the daily newspaper and the large-circulation magazine," and with that weapon the press shaped the national narrative regarding the connection between football and masculinity and by doing so turned the sport into a popular spectacle.[69] Boxing and the celebration of the boxer as an icon happened along similar lines as the development of football. Beginning in the 1880s, every major newspaper carried information about fights and the lives of the fighters to their readers. A number of papers had circulation of more than 100,000, including *The National Police Gazette,* the leading sporting paper for boxing, which reportedly had a weekly circulation of 150,000 and an estimated readership of 500,000 across America.[70] In boxing, these papers reflected their readerships' feelings about race and manhood, as prizefighting represented an arena for racial dialogue, challenging or proving ideologies about manliness and racial superiority. The sporting press took what was private—fights in open fields, in lofts, bars, and arenas—and made them public for a wide readership waiting to consume narratives of manhood. In reporting on fighting and fighters, the press also made black men, who would normally be invisible to a white public, visible. The prizefighter was no longer a nameless black man deemed worthless and without value except for the exploited labor he could provide. In mass, black fighters were the most written-about black subjects in the media. People knew about muscled men like Walcott, Dixon, Gans, Godfrey, Langford, Johnson, Jeannette, Dobbs, and McVey, champions who had to be addressed as such, who traveled across the globe demanding they be recognized as equals in the ring and in society. In his 1897 book *Square Circle,* white boxing writer John B. McCormick (alias Macon) wrote, "The negroes of America should be staunch upholders of the ring, for it has done more toward enabling them to command the respect of the masses than even the ballot."[71] He added, "The negro race in the United States owes a debt of gratitude to the boxing ring which it should never forget or repudiate." McCormick insisted that in the ring blacks had "found 'equality' which is so much harped about in political platforms and speeches."[72] But the white press also looked at these men through racial lenses that coded the way they wrote about these athletes. Ring reports of these men's powerful and skillful capabilities challenged notions of black inferiority and docility, making white readership uncomfortable with the thought of black equality. Thus, to assuage anxieties, white writers had to bend the truth, tell a lie, and depict the black fighter as less than equal, all the while, through the fighter's actions, interviews, and his deeds, the black fighter publicly asserted his manly equality.

The black press is also essential to telling this story. Black writers used the fighter to counter narratives of race and racism while also critiquing class differences within the black community. During the nineteenth century, the black press existed to combat white racism, and also allowed blacks to define their own identity. Historian Martin E. Dann says the "Black press provided one of the most potent arenas in which the battle for self-definition could be fought and won."[73] Blacks used ownership of the press to assert their humanity while awaiting the legal protection of the law.[74] To prove themselves worthy of these rights, black editors had to prove black suitability. That is to say, in order to elevate the race, they chastised those individuals who lagged behind culturally, while simultaneously asserting their racial worthiness in comparison to those same blacks. After the demise of Reconstruction and the increasing "betrayal of the Negro" that was accompanied by escalating black migration, the black press became even more prevalent. During the 1880s, for example, 504 black newspapers were founded to protest the treatment of black people in America.[75] As the voice of the black middle class, newspaper editors identified and denounced the black working class, black migrants, and men in the sporting culture, including prizefighters, because of their supposed lack of preparedness for citizenship.[76] These same writers, however, used the power of the pen to uphold the prizefighter as an example of black advancement when his victories in the ring against white men, or his behavior outside the square-circle, fit a narrative of racial advancement.

And the black prizefighter used the press in ways that many black men, especially working-class black men, had not. Unlike his middle-class counterparts, the black pugilist used newspapers to advertise their physical prowess by utilizing a language that "sports" recognized and equated with manhood. By examining prizefight challenges from black pugilists and their interviews in the press, we see black men channeling the historical conflation within the black community between self-assertion and manhood.[77] With both local and national coverage, newspapers allowed a boxer to make a name for himself beyond his neighborhood or local sporting fraternity. For a black man, who had his manhood denied by legal and economic restrictions, the combination of prizefighting and the presence of the press, gave him an opportunity to assert his manhood in the ring with his physicality and in the press with his words.

To best capture these conversations about race and manhood, this book takes a thematic approach divided into two sections. The first section details how black men asserted their manhood through boxing and how the black middle class dealt with their presence. Chapter 1 explores the move from proletariat to prizefighting and looks at boxing as legitimate work as opposed to disreputable leisure. I examine why men fought and how the black middle class reacted to this new assertion of black manhood. Although the black middle class at first worried that the black boxer would embarrass the race, they came to terms with the existence of the prizefighter. He proved black discipline and determination and that if given a fair chance, black men could succeed in society. The second chapter moves beyond the ring and details how these sluggers straddled the line between sporting manhood and middle-class respectability. What did they do with their leisure time and money, and how did the white middle class react? These men used the trappings of their success to perform a construction of manhood understood by the middle class and the sporting class. Though the black middle class supported them in their financial and fistic success, they worried about a fighter's financial failure and how that would ruin racial uplift strategy. They quickly became symbols of failed black manhood. Chapter 3 examines black men in the white-controlled business of boxing. In a business that tried to squeeze everything it could out of these fighters, in what ways did black men class their freedom from a positions of powerlessness?

The second half of the book explores the various ways white fighters, writers, and politicians used racism to control the black fighters' assertion of manhood. Chapter 4 provides a detailed look at the history of the Colored Championship as a challenge to white manhood. George Godfrey, Peter Jackson, Bob Armstrong, Frank Childs, and Jack Johnson posed pugilistic threats to an ideology of white power partly supported by a belief in white physical superiority. White champions John L. Sullivan, Jim Corbett, Bob Fitzsimmons, Jim Jeffries, and Marvin Hart knew their pugilistic responsibilities to up hold the mantle of supposed white superiority. They refused to let black men fight for the championship. Tommy Burns, however, lifted the color bar, and promptly lost, causing great problems for a shaky white psyche propped up by physicality. Chapter 5 weighs in on white writers and how they used the time-tested tradition of turning the black body into a nonthreatening Sambo or the dangerous savage to assuage their white readers' fears. In other

AT LAST.

With no more white "boys" to whip the colored pugilist, must "do" his own. The race is getting there.

Cartoon sketch of two black boxers. The sketch shows the growing prominence of black fighters in America. (1894, *Indianapolis Freeman*)

words, despite the color line in boxing, white authority based on the physical always stood on shaky grounds. Manhood and power had to be proved, and the black fighter consistently defeated his white opponents in the ring. Thus the press turned these black fighters into stereotypical race characters to assuage whites' fears. Lastly, the final chapter concentrates on the connection between race, progressive reform, and prizefighting. As supportive reinforcements to rebuff the assertion of black manhood, cities and states across the nation legally abolished interracial matches. For black fighters, mixed matches allowed them to avoid being meal-ticketed men. Simply put, white people paid more money for mixed bouts. As cities and states banned these contests, they momentarily put black fighters out of work. Men like Joe Jeannette had to retire from boxing to avoid fighting the same tough black opponents for marginal money.

At its heart, *I Fight for a Living* is a book about black men who came of age in the Reconstruction and early Jim Crow era—a time when the remaking of white manhood was at its most intense, placing vigor and physicality at the center of the construction of manliness. It explores how the assertion of this working-class manliness confronted American ideas of race and manliness. While other works on black fighters have explored black boxers as individuals, this book seeks to study these men as a collective group while providing a localized and racialized response to black working-class manhood.

1

BRING HOME THE BACON

The Black Proletariat
and the Prizefighter

By the sixty-sixth round, the "Two Blowing Africans Contending for the Muscular Mastery" stood caked in blood. The combatants had battled for nearly an hour and a half when Cincinnati's Henry Woodson, the "Black Diamond," finally landed his knockout punch on Steve Williams, the black champion of Troy, New York. Williams, a thirty-year-old solidly built 5'9", 190-pound man, controlled the first thirteen rounds with constant movement and aggression, and though he knocked Woodson down several times, he could not finish his adversary; the pressure of growing up poor and black in Cincinnati had made the "Black Diamond" tough. Born a Kentucky slave in 1857, Woodson came of age in one of Cincinnati's most notorious areas, Little Bucktown, where his widowed mother ran a saloon that doubled as a house of ill repute. Occasionally, Woodson provided the muscle. Working at the saloon, Woodson had seen his mom's life threatened and had been shot. Steve Williams did not intimidate him.[1] During the last fifty-three rounds of their fight, the grown man from Little Bucktown overcame Williams's initial onslaught and "showed the Troy darkey that science is something better than slugging" and viciously beat his opponent.[2] "In the sixty-sixth round Woodson rushed at Williams, landing his left hand with the force of a pile driver on Williams' right cheek, sending him staggering to his corner. Williams could not respond when time was called for the sixty-seventh round, and Woodson was declared the victor. Williams was badly punished about the head."[3] Why would these two black men subject themselves to this type of physical punishment? Money. The $200 side bet Woodson won in his bout against Williams, plus portions of the gate receipts he received from the four hundred paying customers, earned him more than the year's worth of wages he would have made on the Ohio River.

In Woodson's Cincinnati, most black men struggled to make a living. Economist Nancy Bertaux noted, "when Cincinnati underwent the dynamic change from a preindustrial to an industrial economy, blacks' occupational status actually worsened."[4] Although white natives and immigrants battled each other for jobs, they remained solid in keeping blacks away from desirable employment. The menial work that most blacks could obtain was comprised of "job market leftovers" that whites did not want.[5] Feeling the sting of underemployment, in 1877 a group of black leaders in Cincinnati sought to buy federal land and establish a black colony in the West. In search of resources and recruits, they pleaded, "The condition of the colored laborer in the North is growing precarious." They told prospective investors, "trade unions are closing their doors against [the colored laborers in the North], and that all the avenues that lead to the mechanical industries and leading business are barred against him. . . . The future of the colored laborer seems to be covered with portentous clouds."[6] But a poor black man from Little Bucktown could not invest in a homestead. Instead, Woodson remained in a life of drudgery as he worked as a river man, a common black job on the Ohio River.

For a black man, life on a steamboat held little promise. For little pay, colored roustabouts did the most dangerous jobs. The fireman, Woodson's position, had to work every moment in fear for his life as he labored near intense heat and risked dehydration. If the ship caught fire, he was sure to die. River work, however, slowly disappeared as a "black job" as the city invested in modern railroads. In 1880, one-third of black river men were laid off. Between 1860 and 1890, the black workforce in the steamboat industry dropped from 13 percent to 2 percent.[7] The railroads did not come with job opportunities for black men. Through unionization and exclusionary practices, whites kept the better-paying skilled jobs and relegated blacks to porters, cooks, and other menial positions. In the end, racism and railroads pushed Woodson into the ring.

The "Black Diamond" started his new trade in 1882. With hardened muscles from his tough job, and the necessary grit to succeed in boxing, Woodson showed tremendous promise as a fighter. Within his first year of fighting, a *Cincinnati Enquirer* writer noted he was a "fine specimen of manhood," and observed, "he has for years been steamboating, but last winter began training in sparring. He is a well-scienced and powerful man, and will make his mark."[8] After making headway locally, in January 1883 he left for New York—with his white backer, Cincinnati sporting man James McVeigh—to battle "Professor" Charles Hadley for the Colored Championship. Although Woodson lost the match, his muscles, skills, and aggression earned him acclaim. After the Hadley fight, ex-fighter "Spring Heel Dick" observed that Woodson "never has been thoroughly taught in sparring, and, although a terrific hitter he lacks skill to go against such a man as Hadley, who is an old 'un." But "Spring Heel" left room for improvement and noted Woodson was "wonderfully quick with fine muscular development, and I honestly believe that he is a marvel. I or any one well posted could take him in hand and soon develop him into a splendid boxer."[9] He was right. By January 1884, the National Police Gazette considered Woodson "the best colored pugilist in the country."[10] This was high praise for a man who started at the bottom.

In the end, however, Woodson's battles with tough black foes like Billy Wilson, Charles Hadley, and McHenry Johnson, and his desire to prove his manhood in the sporting culture, took their toll on his body, and his ring prowess started to fade. By 1887, he was struggling to make a living in the ring. Woodson fought five times in St. Paul, Minnesota, between February and May and only managed to win one of those battles, a close decision over the forty-six-year-old Hadley, in which Woodson broke his hand. Still desperate for money after the Hadley fight, he competed in two more contests—he had to quit against McHenry Johnson and Billy Wilson thrashed him—before retiring.[11] Soon, everything ended. The man who grew up in the notorious "Little Bucktown," surrounded by pimps and prostitutes, finally lost his bout to the sporting culture. In September 1887, Woodson traveled to Chicago to provide muscle for his mother's new saloon. There, Woodson drank too much and fell in bed with an old flame from the past. As he slept in his room with his woman, a black porter from Chicago walked in on the two and murdered Woodson.[12] After hearing about Woodson's tragic death, instead of offering condolences, black newspaperman John Quincy Adams mockingly quipped, "The only question now is: Where will his next ring be pitched and who will be his next antagonist."[13]

Despite Woodson's tragic death, and Adams's insensitive comments, black fighters' presence had social implications for a race of men that had been barred from the market economy. In a larger context, success in the ring demonstrated that black men had the fortitude to succeed in the market economy. As one white writer observed, "Prize fighting, in the minds of most people is not a very noble occupation. But success in it calls for a constant attendance to business. To get to the top in that profession requires the hardest physical work and the strictest self-denial. One must indeed 'keep stepping,' or go backward." The writer continued, "This rule for success is not confined to prize fighting." "Those who 'keep stepping,'" he added, "are the ones who succeed in anything. It is only those who stop stepping that fail. The rule is a more imperative one than ever in these days when competition is so intense and the stakes are so high. To stop is fatal."[14] In other words, one could only succeed in the ring and the workplace through dogged determination. They had to "keep stepping," a term linked to race and class. For the above article, the particular sportswriter quoted Joe Gans's mother, who had telegrammed her son to "keep stepping" as encouragement to win a fight. In fact, Gans and his mother are also responsible for bringing the phrase "bring home the bacon" into the American lexicon, a clear reference that linked black menial work and money with subsistence living. After Gans beat Bat Nelson in 1906, he wrote his mother, "Your boy Joe is bringing the bacon and lots of gravy."[15] To "keep stepping" and to "bring home the bacon" pronounced black America's response to the daily racism they encountered in the job market and the interconnection between hope, work, and subsistence living. The phrases articulated aspirations that blacks' hard work would ultimately overcome racism.

By the 1890s, for a number of black leaders, the black fighter epitomized the hope of black America. Athletic success became part of black uplift strategy for economic and social equality. In an age where whites used social Darwinian thought to explain white market success and black economic drudgery, prizefighting became a proving ground for the black fighter and black spectator. In other words, success in the sweet science signified ideas of fairness and meritocracy. As one black writer wrote, "The pugilistic business is, however, indicative of something. It shows whenever a Negro is given a chance, to use the language of the street, he is sure 'to get there.'"[16] Race leaders' paradoxical thoughts about black prize fighters is best understood in the context of labor, race, and uplift politics. To be sure, race men struggled to come to terms with the reality that prizefighting represented legitimate labor and not a form of unruly leisure. Moreover, they worried that fighters' recalcitrant behavior outside the ring would hamper racial uplift if these pugilists continued to drift on a seemingly destructive path outside the ring. (This is discussed further in chapter 2.) These leaders, however, also understood something else about the meaning of black manhood and the manly art: The black prizefighters' fistic success represented black competence, work ethic, and grit and proved that blacks could succeed in the racist market economy if given an equal chance to compete in America and overcome white racism.

Cigarette advertisement featuring a white and a black bare-knuckle fighter. (1886, Library of Congress)

UP FROM THE BOTTOMS

For black men, prizefighting provided an opportunity to escape a life of drudgery. While most professional fighters, regardless of color, represented the proletariat of American and "sprung into world-wide notoriety from drudging obscurity through some sharp-sighted manager discovering their abilities," the depth of drudgery was drastically different.[17] As America's industrial economy continued to grow after Reconstruction, black workers saw their job opportunities shrink. As one Springfield, Massachusetts, man put it, "we are debarred from every avenue of work except the very menial. We cannot get a fair show in any line of work."[18] On this state of affairs, historian Rayford Logan concluded, "The failure of the tremendous expansion of American industry to change materially the essentially peasant and domestic service status of most Negroes is evident from the fact that in 1890, 88 percent and in 1900, 86.7 percent of all Negroes were still employed in these least remunerative and least dignified occupations."[19] The racial division of labor between black fighters and white fighters is clearly seen when comparing heavyweight fighters at the turn of the century. "It is interesting to note," a writer from the *Cleveland Plain Dealer* commented, "that many of the leading pugilists of the day started in the business with an uphill battle before them and received many hard knocks before getting to the top." But these men had to climb up different hills. Of the thirteen white heavyweights listed in a 1902 article about the fighters' past trades, their employment included careers as boilermaker, bank clerk, blacksmith, pressman, cooper, sailor, farmer, miner, horse-shoer, candy maker, miner, engineer, and plasterer.[20] This list included heavyweight champion Jim Jeffries, a boilermaker, the most privileged of the bunch. As one Los Angeles writer reflected, "With bright spots here and there, the home life of champion pugilists generally has been a checkered one, replete with incidents of dissipation and ribaldry. Not so, however, with the present holder of the toga. His home life continues along the same even tenor with no incidents or riotous living to mar its happiness."[21] Jeffries grew up in a mansion on a one-hundred-acre farm his family owned. In comparison, the notable black heavyweights of his generation Bob Armstrong (farm laborer and teamster), Frank Childs (railroad laborer), Hank Griffin (railroad laborer), Jack Johnson (stevedore), "Denver" Ed Martin (porter), and Sam McVey (farm laborer), were sons of ex-slaves.[22]

Martin and Armstrong, who were the only two black heavyweights listed in that 1902 article, made conscious decisions to fight their way out of poverty. Born in 1878, Martin "was picking up occasional quarters and half dollars doing odd jobs of one sort and another around the streets of Denver" before stepping into the ring. Martin's life of labor built his body for ring battles. "Being six feet and four inches tall and weighing considerably over 200 pounds, not an ounce of it superfluous, he was able to wrestle with some burdens that other men could not have handled and the rough work made him rugged and strong, brought his back to the breadth and firmness of that of a horse, made his legs like steel springs and the grip of his arms like the grasp of a vise." Dissatisfied with his life of drudgery, Martin hung around local gymnasiums during his leisure hours to exercise and study the manly art. "One day he put on the mitts with another dusky son of Ham somewhat shorter, but whose experience in manipulating the padded mitts was much more extensive," and after Martin handled himself well, "athletic club promoters learned about the big fellow and were told that he was strong as well as willing. Before long a chance was given him to show what he could do, and he made good in his first appearance."[23]

By the turn of the century, Martin was the most popular black heavyweight in America, but the color line meant he had to maintain a career battling some of ring history's toughest black fighters. Unfortunately for Martin, while top white fighters ducked him, great black fighters beat him. Vicious defeats to Jack Johnson and Sam McVey in 1903 derailed his rise to the top. In his first fight with Johnson, in February 1903, in what was the most important fight of Martin's career, he went twenty rounds with the future champ, but lost the decision. Martin used his long reach to throw his piston like jabs, but against Johnson, a defensive fighter and a fine counterpuncher, Martin's aggression played into the champ's hands. In the eleventh round, Martin got careless and "a hard jolt from Johnson's right, which landed on Martin's neck, sent the big fellow to the floor." Martin got up, but Johnson quickly pounced and continued to shred him with his sharp jab until the bell rang. For the final eight rounds, Johnson played it safe and coasted to an easy victory.[24] In his fight with McVey, a teenager from Oxnard, the "Oxnard Wonder" dug a left-right combination to Martin's ribs in the first round that sent Martin rolling to the floor in agony. Martin could not get up without assistance.[25] By 1904, Martin was a second-rate fighter just getting by on his name and trying to pick up meaningful meal-ticket fights. When he next fought McVey again in August 1904, Martin lived in Los Angeles "without a penny in his pocket or a money manager to fall back on . . ."[26] Martin beat McVey in August 1904, but two months later, Johnson knocked him out. Martin never had another credible fight. With few skills besides his fistic prowess and, in reality, facing a racist job market, Martin stayed in the business of boxing, training and finding meal-ticket fights, well into the 1920s.

Of the significant black fighters this study covers, only C.A.C Smith (a barber in Michigan) and Jack Blackburn (a barber in Indiana) held a skilled job before entering the ring. And only Bill Tate went to college (Alabama Normal). Otherwise, they were fish handlers, farm laborers, porters, teamsters, cabin boys, stevedores, and waiters, lines of work thought suitable for black men. Sometimes, the black fighter's nickname told one all he needed to know about the fighter's life of drudgery. For example, "Hock Bones," a popular fighter in Memphis, received his name because he was "picked off the street selling 'hock bones'" before turning to prizefighting.[27] Unfortunately, "Hock Bones" never climbed out of second-tier status in the Memphis fight scene and found himself relegated to fighting black men like Kid Congo or "Indian Joe," who, like Hock Bones, were meal-ticket fighters.

For some fighters, the racial violence at work pushed them into the ring. At industrial job sites, white workers saw black men as economic competition and often violently beat them to protect what they believed were their jobs. White Cleveland fighter Phil Brock—he was born Phil Slamovitz in Russia—got his start in the fight game by "whipping negroes." After being kicked out of school and then losing his job as a newspaper boy for fighting, Brock took a job at a livery stable, where he attacked any black person that came around his work. "Negroes never did look good to Phil and any smoke that showed around the livery stable was his target. He fought 'em all and he won all his fights." After seeing Brock in several of these racist attacks, the stable owner, Frank Thomas, convinced Brock to become a professional fighter. Unfortunately, the work world was full of Phil Brocks.[28] Sam McVey had to face such bullies. According to Billy Roche, McVey's manager at the time, Roche discovered McVey working at a livery stable in Oxnard, California. McVey "was a big, strapping, hard-muscled, colored man and had a way of defending himself against those who attempted to bullrag him."[29] McVey's white attackers clearly made a mistake. Although just a teenager at the time, at 6'2" and 220 pounds, McVey had already won eight fights in Australia while working as a seaman. After witnessing McVey's self-defense, Roche offered him an opportunity to fight professionally. McVey gladly accepted.

Knowing the desperation of black men, white promoters often searched typical black job sites to recruit hungry black men to serve as opponents. Jack Johnson remembered that early in his career he came to Pittsburgh, "without a penny to my name. I didn't even have enough to buy a plate of beans." With no job prospects on the horizon and no money in his pocket, Johnson looked for a free ride home back to Texas and headed to the slaughterhouses to sneak on a train. While at the station, a white man spotted the lean and desperate

Johnson and asked if he knew how to box, to which Johnson replied, "Are you telling me there's a way to make a little money around here?" The man told the future champ, "Fact is, we have a very strong, very well built man who has knocked out every man who's stood up to him. Do you want to put on the gloves with him?" Johnson asked, "How much money are we talking?" In terms that Johnson surely understood, the stranger replied, "I guarantee it will be enough to buy beans for a few weeks." The white promoter figured Johnson would get his head bashed in for the pleasure of the white audience, but despite the fact that Johnson lacked the time to train and the money to buy food, he dusted off his opponent and collected $75, a substantial payday for a meal-ticket fighter.[30]

To be sure, fighters faced a long road to the top to earn livable wages. Most were meal-ticket men. As Johnson said, "When you consider the relatively sizeable sums earned by top-ranked boxers, you might be led to believe that being a boxer is the ideal career. But, for every fighter who breaks through, how many are there who barely manage to scrape out a living? And all of them, champions and journeymen alike, experience hard times at the start."[31] Johnson knew hard times. In recalling the first time he saw Johnson in Stockton, California, one white promoter reflected, "I went out and [George Eckhardt] pointed to a long, lanky coon who was leaning up against the wall. The fellow looked like a hobo. He was about the shabbiest and most forlorn object I ever looked upon." Johnson was begging for a chance to fight, but the promoter would not put him in the show because there was a "complaint around the club about his having so many negro fighters on his string." Too many black fighters were getting paid to box. "We allowed the fighters in preliminaries the big fat sum of $2.50," the promoter recalled. "Jack Johnson needed the money: he was hungry and in rags, and begged hard to be put on."[32] But the white promoters ran Johnson off. He lost his meal ticket that day.

Johnson's words about his past poverty help us understand the economic choices of working-class black men as he articulated a race- and class-based understanding of his entrance into the prize ring. His dad, who was born a Maryland slave, could not read or write and worked as a janitor. Johnson's mother—born a North Carolina slave—held a domestic servant job. On his upbringing, Johnson remembered, "there were some hard times in our little house in Galveston, and as soon as I was big enough, my father took me on as his helper, as his work as a cleaning man kept him very busy."[33] This poverty pushed Johnson to pugilism: "The seed of discontent ripened fast within me and at the age of 12 I could stand it no longer. I laid awake one night thinking of the world beyond—of all that was to be seen, but more than all, of escaping the drudgery of janitorship [sic]."[34] Wanting more out of life than the assigned drudgery allowed for black men, the adventurous Johnson hopped on a freight train and left Galveston to find meaningful work. He tried various jobs, but in his early teenage years he realized prizefighting provided him his best hope, and he started fighting professionally at the age of sixteen. During the first eight years of his career, Johnson struggled to find fights and food; he even had to fight in a battle royal just so he could eat.[35]

He never forgot those days, and always made sure to remind the white press of where he came from. In his first autobiography, Johnson claimed his father, Henry, "was one of the strongest men, physically, I have ever known," but slavery deprived him of an education, fighting in the Civil War stripped him of his strength, and the racist job market took his opportunity to support his family. That Johnson's big, strong, strapping dad could only climb to the rank of a janitor ate away at the champ. Johnson recalled, "At the age of nine, I was already looking for ways to earn my living. I was not content pushing a broom behind my father; I wanted to get out and work on my own."[36] On another occasion he told a reporter, "I am glad that I had to rough it." He continued, "I have had money sometimes and others time have been broke. Now that I have fought my way into the championship, and to fortune as well, all my other experiences will count." In words that reflected his understanding of race and class, the champion added, "Corbett or Jeffries, or any of the other champions never had the hard times I had in my early life in the ring. They do not know what it is to have been in want."[37]

Johnson made the right career decision. Between 1908 and 1912, for instance, he made $196,000, or "$2,513 per round or an average of $833 per minute."[38] In 1913, Johnson also earned $5,000 for fighting "Battling" Jim Johnson (black) and $35,000 battling "white hope" Frank Moran in Paris. When adding $100,000 from the stage, Johnson had accumulated $327,000 in five years.[39] Columnist John E. Wray of the *St. Louis Post Dispatch* pointedly noted, "With nothing but nature's fistic gifts the poor stevedore has climbed in less than four years into the earning ability of captains of industry." Wray ended his article by romanticizing Johnson's rapid rise in the ring and remarked, "Few romances of fiction dare to build up a quarter millionaire here out of stevedore material in three and one half years."[40] Johnson's economic success allowed whites to uphold a tired trope of American exceptionalism while ignoring American racism. In other words, if a man worked hard, he could make it in America.

Black writers, invested in the bootstrapping business of racial uplift, also told stories about the hard roads of black boxers. As one black writer put it when Johnson won the heavyweight championship: "John A. Johnson, in his field, has set an example of persistence and courage in going to Australia for the title that every other Negro should resolve to follow. Pursue your object to the end of the world, if necessary, in order to accomplish it."[41] Thirty years prior to Johnson's fistic and financial success, however, the ascent of the black prizefighter in the 1880s put tremendous pressure on the black middle class to come to terms with a new assertive working-class manhood. By turning his leisure into his labor, the boxer rejected the traditional means of manhood and uplift that the middle class had previously prescribed. In their battle to uplift the race and secure civil rights, black leaders openly questioned the leisure habits of the working class.

FIGURING CLASS WITH RACE: LEISURE VS. LABOR AND THE BLACK PRESS

Looking to find meaningful work, Billy Wilson arrived in St. Paul, Minnesota, in November 1884 to take advantage of the growing fight industry in the city, a fight market that Thomas Jefferson, the leading black fight promoter of his generation, helped create. Wilson came with top-notch credentials. In June 1884, Wilson fought McHenry Johnson in New York, in a fight a local reporter noted as one of the best the city witnessed. For three rounds, before the police broke it up, the two black men tore into each other. In the third round, excitement was "at fever heat as the men faced each other and went into do or die" and the crowd screamed at each man to knock the other out. The police stepped in, declared it a draw, and that was that.[42] Shortly afterward, the city banned boxing, so Wilson traveled to Boston to earn money. Unfortunately for Wilson, racism in the ring restricted his revenue. Local white fighters chased him away. For Wilson, however, this violent situation tested and proved his physical manhood. According to Wilson, "Before I left Boston my endurance was tested. I was put in a room and nine men were sent at me, one after the other. One was big Mike Sullivan, and I reckon he can hit as hard as [Patsy] Cardiff. He hammered me all over the head, and at the end of two and a half hours I was still in the room, ready for nine more men."[43] When he arrived in St. Paul, Wilson immediately challenged C.A.C. Smith to a fight. He had to work. For a month, the two challenged each other in the press, but they never could agree on the terms of their contest. Although they were both black men, race got in the way. Wilson's white manager, Tom McAlpine, did not trust Smith's manager, Thomas Jefferson, a black man, to hold the forfeit money. The racial slight angered Smith and Jefferson, so they walked away from the fight. Wilson eventually left McAlpine for Jefferson, and had his first fight in St. Paul in March 1885 defeating "Professor" Hadley. The program organized by Jefferson featured a number of local black fighters including Louis Liverpool, Frank Wilson, The "Black Star" Jerry Murphy, Gilbert Murphy, Tom Murphy, Jack Caldwell, Charlie Page, and Bill Butts.

After Wilson's victory, Jefferson knew he had a star attraction in a city starved for boxing and wanted to bring in a top contender to test Wilson. On behalf of Wilson, Jefferson challenged a number of top white fighters, but only Mervine Thompson, who was passing as white, was brave enough to battle, while the other white fighters drew the color line. The match excited local white "sports" who believed that this was an interracial contest of physical manhood.[44] Leading up to the contest, fans bet more than $10,000 on the outcome. At 6 foot, 220 pounds, Thompson appeared a sure thing to whites. But the battle did not live up to the hype. More than 1,500 spectators witnessed Wilson knock out Thompson in the first round. Wilson took home $800.[45] After the Thompson fight, in June 1885, Wilson signed to fight the formidable Patsy Cardiff, "The Peoria Giant." The Cardiff–Wilson fight, a battle between "models of muscular physique," created so much excitement that promoters knew the police would not allow the battle to proceed in the city. The promoters arranged for the fight to take place in an undisclosed location up the Mississippi River, away from law enforcement's jurisdiction. At the St. Paul docks nearly one thousand fans boarded steamboats to go to the fight, and thousands of dollars exchanged hands as bets flowed freely on the boats and at the fight.[46] The fight lacked science, but made up for it with hard slugging and throwing. The London Rules of fighting, opposed to the more sophisticated Queensberry rules that forbid wrestling, governed the fight. Cardiff knocked Wilson down several times, and each time he jumped on him to ensure his opponent stayed down. Cardiff, the slight favorite, roughed up Wilson and knocked him out for good in the eighth round. For his victory he took home an estimated $2,000 while Wilson only received $55, which Cardiff collected for him out of pity.[47] Despite the fact that lawmakers tried to crack down on boxing, the sport's popularity continued to grow in St. Paul, mainly because of the abundance of black fighting talent in the city. These black boxers, however, became a nuisance for the black leaders trying to advance the race.

A week before the Patsy Cardiff–Billy Wilson fight, Samuel Hardy and John T. Burgett, founders of the *Western Appeal*, published their first issue on June 6, 1885.[48] By the end of the decade, the *Western Appeal* became one of the most successful black newspapers in America.[49] For racial uplift, the editors argued, blacks had to follow the professionals, not the prizefighters. For example, in 1885, Frederick Douglass Parker, the editor of the *Western Appeal,* complained, "We do not impress those that are interested in our welfare, with much favor if we instead of enlightening our minds with knowledge, and employing our hands with usefulness, continue to encourage the science of the manly art, and to worship the king of the green cloth, to the exclusion of everything else we will retard our progress in the right direction and cause a feeling of distrust to prevail against us. . . ."[50] A week later, Parker continued his battle against the working class's leisure habits. He noted, "There are [black] men in this city who have not done an honest day's work for years and yet they are allow [sic] to loaf arund [sic] and remain ilde [sic], creating, mischief, and corrupting the good standing of the race, the time has come for action and we insist on it."[51] Parker then pleaded with his black readers, "Let us purify ourselves, respect ourselves, respect our race, and you can demand respect and protection from others."[52] Parker's complaints about the black working class must be understood in context of class, leisure, and black migration.

Migration was central for fighters to find work, and black prizefighters traveled to cities like St. Paul that had growing black communities and a thriving sporting culture. In 1883, St. Paul was the ninth-ranked commercial and financial city in the United States.[53] As a port city on the Mississippi River, St. Paul offered job opportunities for blacks who wanted to leave the South. Most black migrant males were young and single and came from the Upper South. By 1885, 49 percent of blacks in St. Paul were southern born.[54] Owing to institutional racism, most black men worked as unskilled laborers and toiled in menial work in the shipping, railroad, or the hotel industries. "Service and menial jobs became synonymous with 'negro' work."[55] As the black migrant population increased, St. Paul became one of the top prizefight cities in the country. Between 1884 and 1887, notable heavyweights Henry Woodson, C.A.C. Smith, Charles Hadley, Billy Wilson, and McHenry Johnson moved to the city to fight. They joined notable locals Louis Liverpool, "Black Frank" Taylor, the "Black Pearl" Harris Martin, and Thomas Jefferson, a leading black Democrat and the sporting man responsible for recruiting the fighters to St. Paul.

Because of Jefferson's entrepreneurial skills and his ability to recruit black fighters to the city, he put on the best local shows and controlled local boxing for a year. By fall of 1884, prizefighting became the most popular sport in St. Paul. Jefferson also created his own touring combination of black fighters—the first of its kind in the nation—and he and his black fighters traveled around the Northwest and crossed the border to Winnipeg, Canada, to put on exhibitions.[56] The arrival in St. Paul of large numbers of working-class people, along with black prizefighters, however, posed a challenge to the cultural hegemony of the black elite, leading to intraracial contests over social, economic, and political ideas about racial representation.

The black editors' complaints about black leisure habits reflect their growing concerns about black pugilist's popularity in the city, and who would represent the race: the men of the ring or "respectable" men. In 1887, from January 1 to April 30, for example, more than fifty articles appeared about black prizefighters in the *Pioneer Press* and the *Minneapolis Tribune*. On March 28, 1887, the Harry Woodson–Billy Wilson fight attracted more than two thousand fans. By April, prizefighting had become so popular that the Olympic Theatre added an extra night to hold boxing exhibitions, in addition to their Friday night schedule.[57]

Black leaders also believed, and correctly so, that white writers used prizefighting to mock the aspirations of black men. In 1884, for example, while covering a Thomas Jefferson athletic combination, in an article entitled "Coon Hunting," the *St. Paul Globe* used the word "coon" fifteen times to characterize the black fighters. After the Cardiff–Wilson fight, Parker attacked the *Minneapolis Tribune* for using the word "Nigger," complaining:

> This is an age when all sober minded people lose Their gravity and drop in to levity cease from philosophizing and takes up the task of being funny, this is sad but true, this may be said of the Minneapolis Tribune they have been dealing in prize fights, and spelling nigger with two gg's for negro. Now Mr. Tribune we are not in favor of prize fights, neither are we given incite prejudice in the minds of intelligent people, we admire the zeal with which you give news to the public and we also admire the obtuseness of the negro who buys it, paying five American cents to see himself soundly abused and maligned, perhaps the Anglo African will learn some sense before the world come to and [*sic*] end.[58]

Parker asserted that only his paper would respect blacks, so blacks should spend their money on the *Western Appeal*. The black editors feared that the minstrelsy representation of the boxer in the press reflected on the race. The middle class opposed minstrel representations because the characterization assumed that only whites had genteel culture.[59]

Attending these black fights for whites was an extension of white voyeurism that had pushed these same white folks to attend the minstrel show. Despite the athletic display from these black bodies, most whites saw what they wanted to see, a "Desperate Coon" or a "Black Diamond" slugging away at another black foe. As sociologist Jennifer C. Lena suggests, "The voyeuristic gaze is a learned mode of appreciation that draws upon stereotypic notions of the 'other.'... Voyeurs mobilize preconceptions of experience, landscape and people to see 'exotic' others. They draw upon expectations of what 'typical black behavior' or 'the inner city' will look like, when encountered."[60] In regard to white voyeurism and boxing in the 1880s, the minstrel image of the boxer is best understood in the context of the trickster and the fake fight. A lot of fights involving black fighters throughout the nineteenth and twentieth centuries were often labeled as "hippodromes" or fixed fights.[61] I am not arguing that hippodrome is synonymous with black fighters, because white fighters were suspected of being involved in fixed fights too; rather, I am suggesting that the term carried a different connotation with the black pugilist. Owing to the "old darkey" images, whites naturally thought of black men as tricksters trying to pull a fast one on whites. If a fight did not meet the white fans' expectations—they expected little science and lots of hard punching—fans believed that black fighters had tricked them. The trickster as a boxer represented a conundrum to whites, because if their suspicions were true, the trickster outsmarted the white fans that expected blacks would only slug each other because blacks supposedly lacked science as fighters. In April 1887, the *Minneapolis Tribune* argued, "It seems that the colored pugilist who were meeting on the Olympic stage of late have got the science of deceiving the audience by slapping each other with the open hand down to a fine point." The paper continued, "To the audience it appears by the sound of the slaps that terrific blows are being struck; but it must be remembered that a slap with the open had does no injury and causes more of a sound than of a blow struck with the clinched fist." The *Tribune* predicted that after the previous evenings fight in which Harry Woodson quit with a broken hand against Billy Wilson, the audience had finally caught on. "Last evening will probably put a finishing touch to this kind of work which kills pugilism."[62] The *Tribune* had it wrong. The white fans kept attending black fights. The following week a sizable audience watched the "Desperate Coon" Julius Foster battle the "Black Pearl" Harris Martin. The next week they packed the auditorium for a thirty-eight-round fight between Martin and "Black Frank" Taylor. Two weeks later, fans traveled to Dakota County and paid $5 to watch a Wilson and Woodson rematch.[63] Race men hated the attention these ring men received. "Black Frank," "Black Pearl," "Black Dynamite," and the "Desperate Coon" did not represent the race.

For John Quincy Adams, who took over the *Western Appeal* in 1887, the fight over labor and leisure became a question of black manhood and convincing his black readers that pugilism was a performance of pathology, not professionalism. At times, Adams's criticism constituted consigning a question mark when referring to the phrase "manly art" in his editorials. Adams once complained, "The sporting element figures quite extensively in this part of the moral vineyard and the daily newspapers devote a large amount of space to accounts of sparring matches, prize fights and local 'scraps.' There used to be a time where it was considered very disreputable business, but at present the 'Professors of the Manly (?) Art,' are bigger than 'Ole Grant.'" In the same edition, Adams said, "Prize fighters, or pugilists, may be perfect gentlemen—and we think too much of our head to run the risk of saying they are not—but they do not very often belong to the Y.M.C.A, or teach in the Sabbath Schools. Neither are they generally advocates of temperance or members of church."[64] Adams reasoned that if black men spent their time training for fights, then they were not being industrious and taking advantage of the available job opportunities. Men engaged in "The 'manly art' (?)," Adams suggested, "had better spend their muscle in mauling rails."[65] But Adams, like other race men, would have a change or heart about labor, leisure, and fighting.

The arrival of Peter Jackson in 1888 changed the thinking of many race men about the meaning of prizefighting. Jackson, a West Indian–born migrant who labored as a seaman before becoming a boxer, migrated to San Francisco from Sydney, Australia, in April 1888 as the Australian Heavyweight Champion to challenge John L. Sullivan for his championship.[66] Despite the fact that Jackson never won the heavyweight championship—white champions Sullivan, Corbett, and Bob Fitzsimmons hid behind the color line—the black press "praised Jackson as a race hero of unparalleled proportions."[67] One of the first black newspapermen to understand the changing dynamics of manhood and race relations that placed intellectualism and physicality on the same plane was T. Thomas Fortune. Coincidentally, Fortune's recognition of Jackson's capabilities to help the race started after Jackson defeated his first noteworthy white fighter, Joe McAuliffe, on December 28, 1888, in San Francisco. Jackson's first major fight in America, a victory against Godfrey for the Colored Championship, barely registered in the black press. After Jackson knocked out McAuliffe, however, Fortune acknowledged the equality of intellectualism to physicality as they related to racial, social, and political power. He noted that sports "have taken the place in public im-

portance once occupied by the Senate, the lecture field, literature and art"
and that "the greatest of all contemporary idols is the boss slugger." He also
observed that Sullivan and white fighters Jake Kilrain and Charles Mitchell
were idolized in the white press as symbols of white manliness, and bragged
that a "new fistic wonder" named Peter Jackson gave blacks a representative
in this type of manhood. According to Fortune, "Great was the astonishment
therefore when the black man wiped the floor with the white man." Realizing the importance boxing played in American society he hoped Jackson
would "smash all the biggest pugilists in the two worlds."[68] In a sports-crazed
America, Fortune thought Jackson's championship status would give blacks
a claim to physical manliness and prove black equality beyond athletics.

For John Quincy Adams, Jackson's ability to beat white men brought out
his race pride. In March 1889, Adams pointedly suggested, "A few more victories, which only Men can win will probably convince some of our preju-
diced white brothers that we are MEN."[69] The following month, after Adams learned Jackson beat Patsy Cardiff in April 1889—the same Cardiff that
beat Billy Wilson four years prior in St. Paul—Adams gloated again. In the
Jackson–Cardiff bout, Jackson dominated his opponent in San Francisco so
severely that Jackson asked his white foe, "Do you want to quit?" As a local San Francisco reporter put it, "Jackson showed few signs of fatigue; his
opponent was well marked, but he had been hit so often he did not know
where he was hurt most." The reporter reflected, "From the beginning Jackson showed himself superior in every respect, and the great wonder was that
a man so insignificant in the manly art as is Cardiff should have sought to
earn fame and money by whipping him."[70] Writing like that, where it was
clear that racial superiority was demonstrated, captured Adams's attention.
Adams applauded, "The Colored people of the country are highly elated
over the success of Peter Jackson in fighting Patsy Cardiff to a stand still last
week. Jackson has demonstrated, that though he is a despised decendant
[sic] of Ham he is a man amongst men."[71] To be sure, Jackson was more than
a fighter. He was a man just like them.

Part of Jackson's appeal to the black middle class was that he embodied
the kind of manhood that black leaders could support. In other words, the
recalcitrant man of the ring could be redeemed. He dressed in fine clothes,
supposedly spoke multiple languages, and presented a public image of perfect
black manhood. For example, the Indianapolis Freeman reported Jackson was
a "very modest man and temperate in his habit."[72] One of the most important aspects of Jackson's personality was that he did not embarrass the race
like other sporting men reportedly had done. The Freeman observed, "Peter
Jackson does this generation a service by proving that a man can be both a

prize-fighter and a gentleman."[73] And after reading about a banquet black Philadelphians held in Jackson's honor, the *Freeman* commented, "PETER JACKSON, as far as we have been able to know him, is our kind of a man. Gifted with unusual strength, he is not a bully. Flattered and fawned upon him, he never loses his head. [Dined] and wined by the best people of his race, he bears his honors in a modest and dignified manner."[74] According to writer James Weldon Johnson, "Peter Jackson was the first example in the United States of a man acting upon the assumption that he could be a prize-fighter and at the same time a cultured gentleman."[75] Another black writer acknowledged, "Jackson, though a pugilist, is a gentleman, and is a credit to the manhood and skill of our race."[76] Frederick Douglass, the great black leader, also lionized the fighter, placing Jackson's picture on the wall next to Abraham Lincoln, Elizabeth Cady Stanton, and Charles Sumner. During an interview with T. Thomas Fortune in 1892, Douglass made sure to tell the editor about his photo of Jackson. After Fortune asked him about each portrait, Douglass said, "Don't forget Peter's picture," adding, "I consider him one of the best missionaries abroad."[77] At that moment Jackson was in England fighting various contenders, and according to Douglass representing the race properly. James Weldon Johnson remembered Douglass "used to point to it [Jackson's picture] and say, 'Peter is doing a great deal with his fist to solve the Negro question.'"[78] Douglass's acknowledgment of Jackson's physical prowess suggests that he saw the limits of blacks' assimilation strategy in regard to Victorian culture. Jackson's athletic success provided blacks with a new chance to fight for equality.

Jackson, and featherweight champion George Dixon, who became the first black champion when he defeated Nunc Wallace in 1890, epitomized the brawn-and-brain combination that some black leaders hoped would elevate the race. In other words, sports mattered. Boxing became proving grounds that blacks had the stuff to succeed. By the 1890s, as part of their uplift strategy, black writers combined the best qualities of the intellectual and the athlete to characterize the race. In fact, 1890 represented a banner year for blacks in America, and black accomplishments allowed black leaders to advance their brawn-and-brain theory with confidence. That year Dixon defeated British boxer Nunc Wallace for the bantamweight championship, Du Bois delivered the commencement speech at Harvard University, and black jockey Isaac Murphy won another major racing event. The black press combined these events as proof of black equality. In April 1890, after observing that "physical culture is becoming a favorite diversion with the Afro-American," the *Indianapolis Freeman* concluded, "The Negro must grow in brawn as well as brain." The editorial noted, "Brain and brawn will tell" and "with our men of broad intelligence and statesmanlike qualities upon the floor of Congress, our champions of muscle winning victories in the squared ring and green diamond, and the avenues of trade opening wider and wider daily, the Negro race promises to be in at the finish."[79] Later that year, an editorial in the *Cleveland Gazette* quipped, "Will someone tell us what this country is coming to? Young Afro-Americans are winning prizes at colleges, riding winning horses in leading races and winning world's championships in the pugilistic arena. There are other avenues in which we have excelled in the past year. Isn't all this an indication of progress?"[80] In July, T. Thomas Fortune wrote a full-page article on Isaac Murphy and noted, "In the pulpit, in the schools and the colleges, in journalism, in the law, on the turf, in the prize ring, in all the life of our civilization, the Afro-American is acquitting himself as 'a man and a brother.'"[81] A few months later, Fortune made another pointed observation in an article entitled, "In the College and the Prize Ring," and argued that blacks had been outperforming whites in colleges, proving that blacks had the brain capacity to succeed as a race. While college students provided the brain, George Godfrey, Dixon, and Jackson had the muscle. Through athletes' bodies, Fortune claimed, "We shall yet convince the Anglo-Saxons that they are not the monopolized salt of the earth and sea." He closed his thought by saying, "may the best man win."[82]

Black writers' words about "ability," "holding their own," "skill," and "may the best man win" spoke to the language of labor and meritocracy and suggested black men had what it took to succeed in the market economy. Writing about black advancement, Professor P. H. Murray, the editor of the black newspaper the *St. Louis Advance,* declared "by redundant vital force and intellectual vigor individuals of the race have reached the topmost round in various lines of skill and learning—from Peter Jackson to Frederick Douglass, from George Dixon to Clement Morgan. . . . Courage, music, art, oratory, science, invention and genius have each woven a garland for some Negro's brow."[83] Taken from this perspective, the ring represented a rejection of racism and whites' characterization of the inferior black worker. If given a fair opportunity, the black press reasoned, then the black worker would succeed.

To be sure, the celebration of leading fighters of this era mirrored the adulation of leading black jockeys. Outside Peter Jackson and George Dixon, the most celebrated black athlete at the time was Isaac Murphy. Murphy was the most successful in terms of winning races and earning money, and his named graced the black press more than any other black jockey in history. Like fighters, Murphy and other leading jockeys earned the ink in the black press, because "they represented more than material wealth." As historian

Katherine Mooney contends, "Murphy did not just have money. He had poise, and he had unmistakable style both in and out of the saddle. And those qualities drew the attention and adulation of black audiences just as surely as his wealth or success."[84] Moreover, Mooney makes the point that these jockeys came from southern poverty and their success gave hope to those poor black boys and men from similar positions who dreamed of making it out. In Murphy, Mooney mentions, blacks saw "with rigorous training, talent, and luck, [Murphy] had made himself a symbol of unshakable dignity and inspiring possibility."[85] The major difference between the pugilist and the jockey, however, is the fact that the fighter, despite racism, got to keep fighting, while Jim Crow eventually knocked out the jockey, leaving the fighter as the leading black athletic figure.

By the turn of the century, the black middle class used prizefighters as a teaching tool to motivate the black working class, and black champions became race heroes because of their dogged determination defeating discrimination. Celebrating Dixon's prowess, in 1900, a writer for the *Colored American* argued, "There is no sentiment involved when white men do business. . . . Why was Dixon followed, admired, feted and given a man's consideration? It was a matter of business, pure and simple." The writer continued, Dixon "had something—prowess—that somebody wanted. Somebody could benefit themselves by dealing with him and they came to him. When the Negro can put up the best fight, build the best steamship, make the best wagon, raise the best cotton and corn, turn out the best butter, write the best book, design the best house, perform necessary service in a better and quicker manner than any other class—in a word, when the Negro proves that he can and will survive and compete with the best—his hour of recognition will come." Once blacks proved they were the best workers, he added, "Money will come with it. Other privileges now denied will follow in its wake." The author concluded, "The Caucasian race owes us nothing but fair play. We must make our own opportunities and improve them."[86] After Gans beat Bat Nelson in an epic forty-two-round battle in 1906, one black newspaperman reasoned, "Gans has won his laurels from knowing how to 'deliver the goods' and not by tricks or favor, and is placed among the worthy of his race."[87] Observing the same fight, a writer for the *Broad Ax* asserted that, "The one great lesson to be drawn from this memorable prize fight is simply this, that if fifty or one hundred Afro-Americans would have the courage to stand up, face to face, and fight those who are opposed to the advancement of the race along civil and political lines, the same as Gans fought Nelson, they would revolutionize the public sentiment of the world."[88]

In many ways, the black prizefighter and the celebration of his feats embodied Booker T. Washington's racial uplift strategy in which he urged blacks to move beyond the oppressive color line, work hard, succeed at their profession, and save money to convince whites that black deserved civil rights. Washington, and by extension the newspapers he controlled, even found time to celebrate the occasional prizefighter. In October 1907, for example, Washington's *Colored American Magazine* praised Gans for his victory over Jimmy Burns (white) in Los Angeles and claimed Gans "won a great victory for the race" and also suggested, "success in any line of commendable endeavor in the same manner helps to lighten the burden resting upon our entire people." The magazine added, "The sporting world, in connection with its treatment of Joe Gans has taught a useful and practical lesson to the American people. The sporting world has treated Joe Gans with more fairness in helping him win this victory than the religious, educational, philanthropic and political forces have ever shown a member of our race." The writer ended his hopeful message saying, "All these forces could learn a lesson in fair play from the sporting world in this instance."[89]

In fact, during the peak of Gans's career, Washington used Gans's success and popularity as a model for black workers to follow. Washington once told a black congregation in Philadelphia to "learn a lesson from Joe Gans," and reminded them of the fighter's fearless attitude toward the color line. After Gans beat Bat Nelson, Washington remarked, "Nervous people ran to Gans and asked him if he wasn't afraid of the color line but to all inquiries he only answered, 'Put every dollar on me.' And he won he had faith himself." Washington finished his assessment encouraging the audience: "If he had only moaned about his downtrodden race, and gone around with the same old whine, the same old backache, the same old tale of woe and hard luck, would he have won or would he have been supported?" Washington answered his own question: "One exhibition of accomplishment will do the race more good than all the indignation meetings you can hold from now to doomsday."[90] Confidence, success, and merit, according to Washington, would allow blacks to prove their usefulness to whites.

In this same line of uplift thought, Washington also praised Jack Johnson and linked the champion to a black economic uplift strategy. During a 1909 speech in New York, Washington told a black audience, "Success is what counts. Success, despite race or color, will make the man on top respect you. What the world wants is success. Hold up your successes; don't herald your gloom." He then asked the audience, "You remember when a certain member of your race went to Australia to do a job; warnings were sounded that the color line would be drawn. The question was hurled at him: 'Aren't you afraid in that white man's country?'" Washington answered his own question, "Now, suppose he had gone to Australia crestfallen, saying that he was a negro and much oppressed, would he have won? It is a Godsend that he did win. It shows to the negro race what determination will do."[91] Washington took this train of thought further and equated Johnson's championship to black economic pursuits. "The time has come when a negro must get a commercial, business and economic footing, and get it in this generation or fail in ever getting it. Commerce, the dollar, draws no color line. The man who produces what somebody else wants will get the trade." Washington was not alone in this line of thinking that linked Johnson's success to black determination. One writer noted Johnson "set an example of persistence and courage in going to Australia for the title, that every other Negro should resolve to follow. Pursue your object to the end of the world, if necessary, in order to accomplish it."[92]

In this era, however, Washington's political rival, W.E.B. Du Bois, did not entertain the thought that the prizefighter could represent or serve as an example of racial leadership and advancement. These fighters did not belong to the "talented tenth." In this line of respectable thinking about leadership, however, Du Bois advocated for physical education in black schools as a way to teach the importance of health and discipline derived from athletics. In 1897, for example, Du Bois urged black southern colleges to train black students in athletics to build up their bodies and develop the complete man of brawn and brain. He also added, "There does not stand today upon God's earth a race more capable in muscle, in intellect, in morals, than the American Negro."[93] Although the prizefighter displayed the necessary discipline to have a fit body, his professionalism—Du Bois was a proponent of amateur athletics—and his connection to the sporting culture were problematic. But overall, by the turn of the century, despite the brutality in the sport, as long as fighters behaved as respectable black men outside the ring, for Washington, Du Bois, and other black leaders, sports made sense. There were winners and losers with well-trained disciplined bodies, and the winners worked the hardest despite discrimination. But what happened when the black boxer did not meet the expectations of respectability?

2

RACE MAN OR RACE MENACE?

Pugilists, Patriarchy, and Pathology

Frank Erne did not have a chance. When Joe Gans fought on the level, not many fighters did. Although Erne had beaten Gans in their first bout—a nasty cut on Gans's eye from a head butt forced him to quit—nothing would stop Gans this time. He had come too far from the days of battle royals to face defeat now. On May 12, 1902, Gans, the greatest counterpuncher of his generation, so slick in the ring they called him the "Old Master," came out of his corner the aggressor. Erne was not ready for what awaited him. An unexpected right-hand lead to Erne's ear wobbled the champion. Then Gans flipped a sharp jab that shot through Erne's guard and bloodied his nose. He rushed in with another quick left, followed by a right to the jaw, and the champ crumbled to the canvas. Fight over! In one minute and forty seconds in the first round, Joe Gans, the poor kid from Baltimore, won the lightweight championship. "I did not expect to win so quickly, but I believe the end would have been the same had the fight gone much farther."[1] For his work, he won $3,500. Now it was time to party.[2] Joe Gans was good at that too.

Seemingly all of black Baltimore had jammed the streets to celebrate their fistic hero. Dressed in Maryland's state colors of black and gold, the poor denizens, the colored sports, and race men blended together. During the festivities some boasted loudly, while others stood quietly and took in the moment. The parade of hacks carrying the participants stretched two scores deep, the colored sports in the procession coolly smoked their cigars, a black band played "Hail to the Chief" and "See, the Conquering Hero Comes," and Gans, impeccably dressed, sparkled in diamonds. When the parade finished, the leading black social clubs tendered Gans a dinner. At two dollars a plate,

Joe Gans, "The Old Master,"
shows off his boxing pose in a
studio photo. Gans is considered one of the best fighters of
his generation. (1898, Library
of Congress)

the price kept the poor denizens out, but inside the building, colored sports
and race men celebrated.[3] At a time when the politics of respectability kept
the sporting class and race men at odds with each other, Gans's presence
brought the two factions together.

With diamond stickpins, elaborate canes, and flashy clothes, Gans epitomized the term "colored sport." "Joe Gans dropped in a few days ago," a
black Nashville writer reported, "Joe looked like a Bermuda millionaire in
his fur-lined coat and diamond studded tie."[4] He looked the part and played
the part. A year and a half prior to his championship victory, Gans teamed
up with Chicago's leading black gambler, John "Mushmouth" Johnson, and
fixed his fight against Terry McGovern. Gans, who started as a 3–1 favorite,
took a dive and brought colored sports with him to swim in the pool of easy
money. According to one report, "colored men had received an advance tip
and bet freely against Gans, with whom their sympathies would naturally be.
'Mushmouth' Johnson is said to have made up a pool on McGovern. A number of west side saloonkeepers lost money to colored sports on the knockout

proposition."[5] The *Chicago Daily News* claimed, "The negroes around Johnson's place were close-mouthed and expressed utter ignorance. It is said that here Gans leaned back in his chair while playing poker a night or so before the fight and exclaimed: 'Boys 'eres a chance to make your fortunes. Bet on McGovern.'"[6] In Denver, New York, and Baltimore, cities where Gans had ties to the sporting community, colored sports also hit big.

The greatest pound-for-pound fighter of his generation took a lot of chances, but he rarely weighed the risks. By 1906, he had squandered $100,000 and hit rock bottom. "I have made about $100,000 but all I have left to show for it is a couple of houses in Baltimore. The rest went backing sure things in the race tracks—dope right from the stable—the can't-loose [*sic*] kind, you know. Every man in this business is going to get his sometime."[7] Like a true sporting man, however, he took it all in stride and quickly rebounded. How? He bet on himself. A few months after he lost all of his money, Gans took an advance on his entire $11,000 purse for the Bat Nelson contest, and he let it ride. He won the fight, the money, and returned back to black Baltimore for another glorious celebration.

The majority of the black fighters of this generation, by virtue of their profession, spent a considerable amount of time in the sporting community. A colored sport like Gans proved his manhood in a myriad of ways, including in how much money he spent, what kind of chances he took, and his ability to take care of other sporting men. In other words, he had to be a good fellow and impress his brothers in the sporting community. It was nothing for Gans to bet hundreds on a craps game and thousands at the tracks. "I used to rush to the race track right after every fight and throw my earnings away on the ponies," Gans said. "The last time I got trimmed for $15,000 in a few days. I had given all my money to my mother to take care of, and I had to go to her for $15,000."[8] That was the life of a good fellow. Good fellows seldom banked their money; instead they carried their roll of cash with them, ready to bet on horse races, play card games, shoot dice, or pay for rounds of drinks. But as fast as he could throw his combinations in the ring, and toss his money at a game of chance, the successful pugilist could transition to perform a role of manly patriarchy.

Black fighters' construction of manhood straddled the line between Victorian respectability and sporting manhood.[9] In other words, many tried to emulate their middle-class brothers. As part of the black-middle class' strategy to prove their equality, race men grounded their manhood in thrift and patriarchy. Speaking to an audience about uplift, one black speaker pleaded, "the elevation and ennobling of our race never can be accomplished through mass meetings, conventions and leagues—it can only be effected through the economy and zeal of the masses of the race in the acquisition of wealth." In the context of racial uplift and economic thrift, the home became a platform to prove racial parity. Historian Kevin Gaines suggests, "elite blacks celebrated the home and patriarchal family as institutions that symbolized the freedom, power, and security they aspired to." Gaines added, "Through their frequent tributes to home and family life, African Americans laid claim to the respectability and stability withheld by the state and by minstrelsy's slanders . . ." Thus the black family was "a sign of the race's triumph over their ruinous impact of slavery. . . ."[10] Seen from this perspective, if the pugilist could avoid the perils of the sporting world, and live up to the ideals of the patriarch, he could properly represent the aspirations of the black middle class.

Despite spending their leisure time in the sporting culture, when they had a chance most black prizefighters publicly placed themselves as economically responsible patriarchs. They wanted to prove that their manhood went beyond their physicality, on the one hand, and was not solely rooted in the disreputable sporting culture, on the other hand. Prizefighters talked about investments, bought businesses, purchased homes for their families, and discussed their patriarchal role with the media. After Gans defeated Bat Nelson, for example, he used his winnings to buy a hotel in Baltimore. Named the Goldfield Hotel after the location of his fight with Nelson, Gans spent $40,000 buying the property and used $30,000 of winnings from his next fights to outfit the interior.[11] His hotel was the crown jewel of black Baltimore and stood as a symbol of race pride. Gans learned from his past gambling mistakes and publicly discussed his newfound economic discipline. He once told a black reporter, "I have earned $81,000 in the past sixteen months, and I haven't thrown it away. I've got a good hotel and the best café in Baltimore, and I own every bit of it. It's mine. . . . I've put my money in property, where it'll always make a living for me."[12] When he died two years later, his estate was valued at $45,000, which included the Goldfield Hotel worth $30,000 that he left to his wife, a house he left to his mother, and $2,000 in diamonds, a fact the black middle class did not miss and celebrated in the press. Gans was one of them, but he was also a good fellow.

To be sure, most black fighters lacked the education and refinement to perform Victorian respectability full-time; thus placing faith in prizefighters as examples of racial uplift and black equality included inherent risks for the black middle class. Prizefighters came from the sporting community, where alternative notions of manhood reigned supreme. The sporting culture was a world of pimps, prostitutes, and players, where manhood was proved through deeds and actions understood within that context. Although race men celebrated black fighters as manly examples of hard work, black leaders quickly abandoned the boxer when they realized that many black pugilists did not consistently uphold the middle class's respectable politics. Thus, great fighters who proved black superiority in the ring became ostracized figures in a battle for racial uplift if they failed outside the ring.

PUGILISM AND PATRIARCHY

The idea that a prizefighter could exemplify respectable patriarchy seems odd. After all, the very nature of his business epitomized the colored sport. Before he entered the ranks of prizefighter, when he finished his day at his menial job, if he did not patronize the colored sporting club he spent his leisure time at the all-male social spaces of gymnasiums, honing his skills in hopes of turning propensity for pugilism into a profession. Once he became a professional fighter—a decision that shunned his participation in the traditional labor market—he spent his time in male social spaces like taverns, training camps, and arenas, where very few women were allowed. As part of his job, he migrated from city to city, riding the rails, staying at hotels, and ingratiating himself in the local sporting community. For the most popular fighters, hundreds and sometimes thousands of men cheered him at a train station or the local hotel, or congregated at his training camp to fawn over his manliness. How could the black prizefighter be a patriarch if he lived the life of a colored sport?

If married, to reconcile their family life with the realities of the ring and the sporting culture, some fighters traveled with their spouses and children. Hank Griffin traveled with, trained with, and took his family in on the boxing business. At 6'4" and 175 pounds, Griffin, a Los Angeles–based fighter, was one of the best heavyweights at the turn of the century. Lean but muscular, and a very crafty boxer—they called him the Black Bob Fitzsimmons—Griffin started his career in 1890, at seventeen, battled in sixty-one bouts during his career, and only lost a handful of those affairs. He beat Jack Johnson once and fought two draws with the future champ. Throughout the Los Angeles area, he doggedly demonstrated his manly discipline and trained in front of the public so onlookers could see his determination while sparring, hitting the punching bag, running at the beaches, or rowing a boat. Although Griffin kept his kids away from the Los Angeles sporting clubs, like Lou Simpson's United Republican Club, he often incorporated his family in his rowing routine, a task that did not require him to be around the social male culture of boxing. "Hank Griffin finds a long, hard row in the inner harbor about as conducive to muscle building as anything he can do," a reporter noted. "It has been his custom to take Mrs. Griffin and all the little Griffins, three in number, along with him on these jaunts . . ." During one training session, however, his son almost drowned when he fell out of the boat, but Griffin jumped in and saved him.[13] Days later, and still drained from the incident, Griffin stepped in the ring with heavyweight champion Jim Jeffries for a four-round exhibition. Although the larger Jeffries physically punished and pushed around his foe, Griffin never took the count and lasted the full four rounds with the champ.

Los Angeles's black community appreciated Griffin's efforts inside and out-side the ring. Less than a month after his battle with Jeffries, right before he went into the ring with "Denver" Ed Martin, local black citizens gifted Grif-fin a belt with red, white, and blue stripes, and big white stars. He was their ideal representation of citizenship and manhood. Before the gong, Griffin made a speech thanking the black community and promised he would not let them down. But on that night, he could not back up his words. Martin manhandled him over seven rounds. In the seventh and final round, Martin drilled him with several uppercuts that left Griffin limp. Instead of letting him fall to the canvas, Martin held him up and punished him more. A blow to the heart ended the fight.[14] Miraculously, Griffin recovered from that beat-ing and bested Jack Johnson the next month.

Griffin was more than a fighter. He also operated a boxing business with his wife. In 1903, they opened a boarding house for fighters in Monrovia, California, where he trained other fighters, including Sam McVey, and his wife cooked the meals.[15] His business lasted a year until the fight game dried up in Los Angeles, and Griffin went on the road, joining a sparring exhibition with ex-champ Bob Fitzsimmons. Something happened to his marriage—it is not clear if his wife died, they separated, or he left her—and Griffin remarried while on the road. He met his new wife while on tour in Jackson, Michigan, and the couple, along with his kids, lived there for two years before moving to Ann Arbor. Although Griffin engaged in the occasional fight and sparring exhibition, he quit the ring because his wife "didn't like the fight thing."[16] He eventually opened up a sparring academy in Ann Arbor and taught local college students the rudiments of the ring. The couple also ran a successful black hotel, the Griffin Hotel, until his untimely death in 1911. After Griffin passed, the local Ann Arbor press noted, "Griffin had the respect of many people in this city, both of his own race and among the white people, for he was always courteous and obliging and he had a excellent reputations in every way."[17] In other words, he showed the respectability and patriarchy the middle class valued.

Like Griffin, Joe Jeannette preferred patriarchy to being the good fellow. Jeannette, a Hoboken, New Jersey, native, was one of the greatest heavyweights of his generation. As a youth, in hopes of saving money to attend veterinarian school, he worked for a coal company breaking in horses, but the allure of money made in the ring changed his career plans.[18] Because top white fighters avoided Jeannette throughout his career, he had to spend most of his time battling other talented black fighters like Sam Langford, whom he fought eighteen times. He also traveled overseas to find better paydays, and when he made those trips he took his family. Discussing Jeannette's popularity in France, American cyclist Floyd McFarland noted, the "Parisians are crazy about negro fighters. They are idolizing Joe Jeannette now and are ready to patronize the fighting game to the limit."[19] While Jeannette entertained the crowds with his physical manliness inside the ring, he performed middle-class patriarchy outside the squared circle. White athlete R. L. Baker observed, "Jeannette is a fine fellow, and thought very well of by everybody here. He has a white wife and two children, runs a fine motor car, but is in no way arrogant or flashy. When not boxing or training," the writer noted, "Joe is with his wife and kiddies, or looking to the gardens surrounding his pretty home in the suburbs."[20] Jeannette was also one of the few black fighters of his generation to find financial success after his career. In 1919, ex-fighter Young Peter Jackson—a sailor in the Navy at that time—told a reporter, "Joe saved his money, and I think he is about the richest of the colored fighters. He has a family and spends most of his time at home."[21] Five years later, in 1924, Jeannette purchased property in New Jersey, spent $30,000 on renovations, and built his house and a gas station, and opened a gymnasium on the land. He also ran a Cadillac limousine service for funerals and weddings and became an example of black economic uplift.[22] As late as 1947, at the age of sixty-seven, Jeannette still ran the business.[23]

To be sure, white writers were not always willing to celebrate black patriarchy unfiltered. To assuage white anxieties about the challenge of the black self-made man, writers often crafted the black fighter's words to resemble childlike Sambo dialect. Take, for example, how a white reporter rephrased Sam Langford's discussion of his patriarchy in a 1914 interview. He transcribed Langford's words, writing, "You see, I'se now 28 and dis fightin' am one tough game. I likes to fight all right, 'cause I likes de money. But now I'se got about enough coin salted down to quit an' settle down on a little farm I'se got back near Boston. I'se got a wife and baby and I done just started the youngster to school and now I want to quit kickin' around and go back home to be with my wife an' kid." When the white writer asked Langford how much money he made, Langford reportedly replied, "Ma wife looks after de coin, and I does the fightin'. Whenever I gets my share of de receipts after a fight I always makes tracks for my ole friend, de Western Union and ebery cent of day money goes direct to Mrs. Langford in Boston. And what does she do with it? Why, she banks it of course. You didn't think she totes it around in her stocking, did you?"[24] Despite the fact the paper chose to quote Langford in Sambo dialect, what we see in Langford's words is his proclamation of his patriarchy through fiscal responsibility and financial control. The interview allowed Langford to situate himself as an accountable and attentive authority figure. During his career, he bought three homes and invested in a poultry farm.[25]

While the white American press often failed to show positive acts of black fatherhood, we know that Langford was a publicly loving father. In 1912, during his sojourn to Australia to participate in the fight game, Langford had his wife (Martha) and four-year old daughter (Charlotte) visit him. Upon his family's arrival, an Australian newspaper reported that Langford "jumped for joy when he saw his household of two straining over the rails to single him out from the waiting crowd, and the joy soon became contagious." Langford told a reporter, "I'm sure I wouldn't be more pleased if I beat Jack Johnson and won a fortune than I feel right now."[26] In another article, a local reporter captured Langford at play with Charlotte as he bounced her on his knee and spoke glowingly of her. "She likes the boys better than the girls," Langford bragged. "Funny, ain't it but she's just the cherry kid, I tell you." Langford also joked, "I call her Tom because she likes the boys," and added, "She's a winner everywhere she goes."[27] For whatever reason, very few athletes, black or white, had been captured in this fatherly fashion.[28] Sadly, for Sam, although he made at least $300,000 in his career, he struggled to hold onto his earnings, and he spent the last thirty years of his life a broke and blind charity case and died in a Boston nursing home. According to Jeannette, "He made lots of money, more than I did, but he spent it fast or gave it away. He always said what good was money except to spend or give it to somebody."[29] Before he died in 1956, Langford told a reporter, "I spent most of it having a wonderful time. And I don't regret it."[30] He lived the life of a patriarch and a good fellow, but the latter won.

Black fighters publicly discussed their patriarchy and economic thrift to push back against the racism they faced in society. They wanted to be seen as a self-made man, and not the Sambo caricature whites viewed him as. In one account, Gans noted he and his family "were poor people. My mother, when I was a little boy, had to work hard. My father didn't do much to support the family, and my mother took in washing and did other things. She got me two or three suits of clothes a year, of course, and was always anxious to have me go to school and learn something." To provide for his family, Gans worked as an oyster huckster, making $6 a week, but that was not enough to lift them out of poverty, so he chipped in money with coworkers, and they bought a pair of boxing gloves for $5. After his first big money fight—he beat Kid McPartland for $5,000 in 1897—Gans gave his winnings to his mother so, "she never had to do any more hard work after that. I always looked out for her, even when I was down to a hard thin dime."[31]

In her effort to ensure that her husband was not just remembered as a colored sport, Gans's wife wrote a powerful letter to the *New York Age* about the man she loved. First, she wanted to clear the air about Gans's finances. "Joe is no millionaire," she claimed, "but he has, thank God, saved enough so that his family need not want after his days are ended." She also pleaded that his fans not throw him a benefit, as was customary among the sporting fraternity to help a poverty-stricken boxer. "I feel that you will be interested in knowing that neither Joe nor I would for a moment countenance a benefit of any sort and in his dying moments he feels a thrill of pleasure in knowing that he has cared for his loved ones so that they will not be forced to look for charity from anyone else." Mrs. Gans emphasized, "You will be doing Joe and his family a big favor if you will emphasize this fact most strongly."[32] Gans did not waste his money as a colored sport. He was a real man, not a menace to his race, and race men recognized and applauded that fact. He was one of them.

Likewise, Jack Johnson used the press to construct an image of his masculine responsibility. Johnson had a keen understanding of how the media portrayed him as an irresponsible sport—he purposely fed that narrative through his flashy clothes, cars, and jewelry—but he also wanted to craft an image of respectability and prove he was a self-made man. As early as 1903, for example, we see Johnson straddling the line between colored sport and patriarch, as he easily moved from being a good fellow to a good man. Explaining to a Los Angeles reporter about how and why he spent his winnings so fast, Johnson bragged, "I always like the very finest clothes, and I generally wear them. So I bought some new togs. And I put a few hundred in diamonds and gave 'em to my wife. I like diamonds and so does she." "Then if you're in my profession," Johnson added, "you've always got to have your hand in your pocket when you meet the crowd in the bar—and all that sort of thing counts way up, you know. A hundred a week won't near last a first-class boxing man." Demonstrating his sporting confidence, Johnson showed no worries about making more money: "I'm going to try mighty hard to cut a clean thousand out of my next fight with McVey—and if I do, you bet I'll soak it away!"[33] After Johnson beat McVey, however, instead of blowing all his money, he traveled with his wife back to Galveston to visit his family. As one reporter wrote, "Jack brings back a big wad of the needed coin and says he proposes to make his old mother independent for life, and so she will have some of the benefits from his success in life."[34] Johnson's trip home, however, was one of the last times he went back to Galveston to visit his family. In 1909, his mother reflected, "It is six years since he was home, but he never forgot us. He always says it would be better for me to have the money he would spend making the trip than to see him, so he writes and sends me the money. He has done well by us."[35] Three weeks after Johnson arrived in Galveston in March 1903, he came back to Los Angeles with his good friend, Joe Walcott, to watch Walcott battle Billy Woods and to celebrate their birthdays with the local colored sports. The Los Angeles media, of course, took

A well-dressed Jack Johnson posing for a photo in his trademark attire. (1909, Library of Congress)

the opportunity to mock Johnson's actions. In a supposed conversation he had with a cigar store owner, Johnson reportedly asked, "Now, Mistah Hookstratten, ah was bohn in Galveston Mahch thuhty fuhst, 1878. How old does dat mek me, now?" When asked if he was kidding, the Colored Champion reportedly replied "Ah'se not kiddin' no sich thing. Ah'se tahkin' business." Johnson refused to pay for his cigar and invited all the surrounding sports in for a drink of wine.[36] To the white press, he was nothing more than a black man-child.

Because whites insisted on portraying Johnson as a man-child, Johnson attempted to publicly craft an image of respectability. When he dictated his life story, Johnson denounced the sporting life and assured a white writer, "Now that I have fought my way into the championship, and to fortune as well, all my other experiences will count. I am going to hold on to what I have—not in a stingy manner, but I am not going to be foolish like a good many other fighters have been." Johnson claimed, "I used to gamble at race tracks, and I liked shooting craps, but I have no more time for either diversion." The champion continued, "the race-track is dangerous and crap-shooting is a game for a fellow who works for wages." To clarify that last part—one that was seemingly an attack on the working class—Johnson added, "I mean that the weekly wage man sometimes is lucky enough to get a bunch of money at one time which he would never get by saving. It's a bad business anyhow."[37] In another instance, while preparing for his fight with Jim Jeffries, Johnson gave a talk at a New York YMCA, entitled "Manliness," in which he told the black audience, "Sobriety, application and again sobriety, are cardinal requisites for success in life, with devotion to one's aged mother as a close fourth." He also told the captivated audience, "Learn to use your hands and not fall over your feet, and your social success will follow." The champion's suggestion about "social success," however, irritated one southern writer who argued, "some one ought to take a shotgun to any fool negro who springs that 'social success' talk."[38]

For Johnson, part of portraying the "good family man" meant proving he made thrifty economic investments to support his family's financial needs. As champion, he invested nearly $200,000 in property. Johnson claimed he learned from his days of poverty that he never wanted to be hungry again. "With me the remembrance of those bean days is very keen, and I am investing the money I won in purses and am still earning on the road. . . . Since I fought Burns and won the championship I have been pretty careful of my fortune."[39] Most of his investments went to buying real estate in Chicago's South Side. In 1909, he purchased an $11,000 building, which prompted a black writer to proclaim, "that eleven thousand dollar Chicago real estate investment of 'Jack' Johnson's last week, would indicate that he intends to 'side-step' the heartrending poverty fate that overtook poor Peter Jackson and George Dixon."[40] Jackson and Dixon died broke because they lived the sporting life. In 1912, Johnson also purchased a $25,000 mansion in Lake Geneva, Wisconsin, for his wife: "I desired to give Mrs. Johnson a Christmas gift which would please her and I believed that a nice home would be the best kind of a gift." As an added investment he bought a thirty-acre farm near the property, where he planned to breed cattle, noting, "I am tired of the fight game and am going to turn farmer." When discussing cattle breeding, Johnson told a reporter he wanted to "breed a cross between the buffalo and the Texas Hereford to try to get a better beef animal. That will prove a good investment I am sure."[41]

During this time period studied, no boxer better represented black middle-class patriarchy than George Godfrey, the colored champion from 1883 to 1888. Though a member of the sporting community where booze flowed freely, Godfrey "did not destroy his manhood with intoxicants," and, in fact, while most colored sports spent their time at the bar, he "spoke against the saloon, worked against it, and voted against it." Godfrey once told the *Boston Globe,* "I don't drink any 'booz,' you see, but eat three square meals every day, and four if I'm hungry. My digestion is perfect. I can digest a wooden toothpick."[42] He also used his home and family as a point of emphasis to showcase his respectability.[43] For example, while negotiating terms of conditions for his fight with Jack Ashton, Godfrey told a reporter, "I have a family to look out for and I must get something for them to live on should any accident take me from them." While he prepared to battle Joe Choynski for $5,000, Godfrey claimed that he wanted "that $5,000 for the education of his children and their future." To spend more time with his family, he outfitted his "elegantly furnished" home with workout equipment.[44] According to one writer, Godfrey was "better than most of the class with which he associated." Another reporter noted, "Godfrey would rather train at his home than elsewhere, for he is more contented and does not have to worry about his family." Other than the gym equipment there was "nothing in his house that would indicate it was the home of a prize fighter."[45]

Godfrey also invested his winnings wisely. He owned $40,000 in real estate, and he lived in "comfortable circumstances pecuniarily, owning quite a block of real estate in Chelsea, Mass." Godfrey even shared his economic strategies with his fellow fighters. Peter Jackson once told the *San Francisco Chronicle:*

> I feel since getting acquainted with George Godfrey of Boston that I have made several great mistakes in my way of conducting my affairs. While Godfrey was here we talked several times about the pecuniary phases of a boxer's life, and he often urged the wisdom of banking or investing the proceeds of matches as soon as they were received. His argument was that, during the golden days of a boxer's life, he would have friends in plenty, and if taken sick would receive the best of care, but if permanent disability should come and the boxer be compelled to seek other employment, no one would hold out a helping hand . . . [46]

Unfortunately for Jackson, he did not follow the plan Godfrey prescribed. Jackson died in poverty in 1901.

Godfrey had the discipline and determination to represent the race. One black writer suggested that boxing was "strictly business" to Godfrey and bragged that with each fight Godfrey bought "a house with the proceeds of every victory."[47] Godfrey was a man to emulate. On another occasion, the *Cleveland Gazette* claimed, "Godfrey tells stories how he built his house, and other tales that mark him a man who would succeed in every thing where push and tenacity count, and deserves all his good fortune. He has had a hard row to hoe, but has stuck manfully to his aim."[48] Twenty years after his death, a black writer recalled, "he was perhaps one of the most thrifty of the colored fighters. He worked in a butcher shop in a Boston market during the day and trained at night. He also worked at night on the foundation of his home."[49] But most black fighters were not like Godfrey. While they strived to be both a pugilist and a patriarch, the allure of the sporting community kept pulling them. After all, they more readily found the acceptance of their manhood and their equality in the sporting community.

THE GOOD FELLOW

Joe Walcott came from nothing. At the age of nine he left Barbados, hopped on a schooner, and worked as a cabin boy to earn a living. On the ship, Walcott had to learn how to fight for protection, and to keep his job, he learned how to cook "slum," a concoction of the leftover food the guests did not want. But this line of work did not suit him. As a teenager, he quit the ship and made his home in Boston. His ability to cook slum landed him employment, but his propensity to land a punch earned him a career. Each day after work, Walcott headed to a local gymnasium for sparring lessons to round the rough edges off his fighting skills.[50] At 5'2", with muscles the size of a heavyweight, his ferocity and prowess caught the attention of George Dixon, who brought Walcott on as a sparring partner. Soon, Walcott would be one of the best fighters in the world and one of the highest-paid pugilists.

At the peak of his career, Walcott represented an anomaly for the white press. Here was a man so dark, muscular, and relentless in the ring, writers labeled him the "Barbados Demon." He was physical manliness personified; Walcott was one of the top fighters in the world—he won the welterweight championship in 1901—but white writers marked his darkness and power in the ring as supposed uncivilized savageness. Pound for pound, no fighter hit harder than Walcott. In 1900, for example, as a welterweight, he knocked out Joe Choynski, a light heavyweight, and a 4–1 favorite. For the white audience, the fight was a racial nightmare. "The white man was hopelessly beaten before a minute of the first round had passed. But Choynski was game and stood the gaff like a hero." The fight continued as Walcott whipped Choynski until the seventh round, when Walcott knocked him down three times. After the first knock down, "the White man's burden at that moment looked as if it might crush him," but Choynski rose for more punishment. Before the final blow, "Walcott crept up to him with a grin that looked almost inhuman and started in to finish the helpless victim."[51] To put this victory in perspective, the following year, Choynski knocked out Jack Johnson.

In the ring, Walcott was the demon, but the "Demon" mastered so-called respectable manliness too. In 1903, with his wife, four kids, and stepmother, Walcott purchased a $6,000 home, outfitted it with training quarters, and raised his family in a wealthy white neighborhood in Malden, Massachusetts, on Belmont Street next to the millionaire rubber manufacturer E. S. Converse. For race men, Walcott's home signified a sign that their plan of economic racial uplift worked. Of course, his white neighbors wanted him to move. He did not budge.[52] Walcott tried his best to reconcile the ring with his respectability and used politics as his platform. In 1904, for example, he ran for the mayor of Malden. Although the white press mocked him, this was no joke. The previous year, Walcott led the Walcott Republican Club and organized the four hundred black voters in Malden, and for this mayoral campaign he planned to spend $2,500 of his own money. As part of his campaign he promised, "the town will be an open town, but respectable, and poor men and colored gentlemen will get a show." He also wanted to lower taxes because, as he said, "I own two houses in the burg and I want lower taxes, and rascals turned out of office." He added, "I'm against dynamite, and want lives of children protected." The champ continued, "I'm for a new city hall. I'm for recognition of colored people."[53] Did Walcott really have a shot at winning? History will never know, because a week after he announced his bid for mayor, Walcott accidently killed a man at a black dance hall. While everyone partied that night, Walcott and a group of colored sports, including Nelson C. Hall, lounged in the corner as the champion showed the crew his new revolver. As he displayed the gun, he accidentally pulled the trigger, which sent a bullet threw his right hand and into the heart of Hall, who instantly died.[54] The champion survived the incident, but with a wounded hand his career was virtually over. The money stopped flowing, and without his large fight purses he could no longer survive his penchant for the sporting life.

A decade after the shooting, Walcott wandered the streets of Boston, broke, and a tragic tale of so-called Negro pathology. In 1913, in an article entitled "They were Good Fellows When They Had It," white writer Hal Coffman described the pitiful scene of seeing a broken Walcott: "Ten years ago—in Los Angeles—I saw Walcott training for his fight with Billy Woods. At that time Joe had money—lots of money—diamonds—big diamonds—and everything he wanted." After Walcott shot himself in the hand, Coffman claimed the ex-champion "went the pace harder than ever and now is a common sight wandering around Boston, but instead of a crowd of admirers telling him what a great fellow he is, no one seems to have time for him anymore."[55] With no job prospects, Walcott left Boston to work on a schooner. When Walcott's ship docked in New York in 1916, white writer Paul Purman told his readers, "He was a good fellow when he had the coin. That tells the story of Joe Walcott, perhaps the world's greatest welterweight in his time, who slipped into New York a few days ago as a stoke on an Australian liner." Purman continued, "Penniless, down and out, ragged, a pitiful figure he made as he crossed the plank and made his way to the places he used to haunt as a popular hero." How did he lose his money? According to the writer, "Drink, women, dice—they draw the picture of downfall."[56] Walcott spent the next twenty years of his life a broke charity case. White writers, however, never looked at the individual failings of a fighter as the failings of an individual.

For whites, a black pugilist's inability to save money proved black pathology: a reflection that blacks—especially those black men who were the most visible in the country and thus came to represent the "Negro problem"—did not have the necessary culture or discipline to succeed in society and prove manly patriarchy. In his racist thinking, one writer observed, "It seems to be an unfortunate trait with the colored fighters that they have not sense enough to lay up a little of worldly goods against the coming of old age.

Practically every one of them has been an object of charity at some time or other. Contrast these negro boxers with the average white scrapper of the same skill and prominence. While the colored man grovels in poverty the white chap toils in the lap of luxury."[57] Great white fighters including John L. Sullivan, Terry McGovern, Sandy Ferguson, and Jake Kilrain went bust, but white privilege meant that the media treated their failure as representative of the individuals and not their race. In his take on black fighters, former fighter Jack Skelly (white) observed, "It seems to me that most of the black champions make a bad finish in this fickle world of ours. . . . They have nearly all fallen by the wayside, and soon go down and out." Although Skelly admitted white fighters' financial failures, he believed the inability to save money and live up to manly responsibility was innate in black men. "Too much money and luxury seems to sap all the vitality of the black gladiators. They do not thrive on champagne, hot birds, silk underwear, automobiles and other high rolling stuff," Skelly observed. The ex-pugilist ended his racist rant reflecting, "It's a well founded fact that however strong as a negro boxer may be, he's usually weak in the top story. This does not seem to be so with most of the white fighters, for I know many who have retired from the ring years ago and are today successful business men, holding responsible positions throughout the civilized world."[58] On a similar note, another white writer concluded, "poverty, it appears, is a traditional nemesis of our great colored prize ring champions. With, hardly an exception, one after another, despite the immense sums their powers gained them, have faced the great Reaper absolutely penniless." That white writer blamed black boxers going broke on bad business decisions and "an unwholesome desire for drink."[59] With so much discussion about black prizefighters, pathology, and poverty, the black middle class had to take note.

Black leaders believed the race could not rise if prizefighters like Walcott, George Dixon, and Jack Johnson continued to drag them down. Thus, blinded by uplift politics, race men often fell into the trap of blaming and scapegoating the supposed individual failures of a black fighter for what plagued black America, while momentarily choosing to ignore social, economic, and political discrimination. Denigrated in Paul Lawrence Dunbar's popular novel *The Sports of the Gods,* the saloon was the hub for the bachelor lifestyle and black pathology, and, according to the middle class, led to the downfall of many young colored men and women, especially new urban migrants. For black fighters, other than purchasing a home, buying a saloon constituted the most common investment. Notably, Henry Woodson, McHenry Johnson, Billy Wilson, George Dixon, Joe Gans, Peter Jackson, Joe Walcott, Jack Johnson, and Sam Langford invested in saloons. All of the establishments failed. In their quest to uplift the race, black leaders worried that whites would view black saloon patronage and ownership as proof of black pathology. In 1889, for example, black newspaperman John Quincy Adams of St. Paul—who had to compete with black saloon owners like boxer Thomas Jefferson, who used his saloon to run the black Democratic Party—complained, "It is a misfortune to both races, that the white people are so constantly forced to witness and learn of the bad conduct of the saloon-loafers and criminals of the Colored race and that they take such pains to keep themselves from witnessing the decent and creditable performances of the intelligent virtuous and industrious ones."[60] Fifteen years later, black leaders in Los Angeles asked the police to shut down two prominent black saloons, the Republican and the Manhattan Clubs, the main hangout for colored sports and black prizefighters. When the police did not immediately oblige, J. J. Neimore complained to the *Los Angeles Times,* "These places are a disgrace to the colored race in Los Angeles. We do not know why they are permitted to do business." He also argued that the clubs destroyed the black family, and stated, "Colored boys have too many temptations in a city like this, and it is not any easy matter for a father to keep them from evil. But with such dens open to them and frequented by members are more than doubled. It is the duty of the police to close those places, even if they have to resort to the same methods they used at the Manhattan Athletic Club." Invoking his class status, Neimore claimed, "I know I speak for the respectable portion of the colored population of the city when I say that such places should not be tolerated in any city no matter who keeps them."[61] In his newspaper, the *California Eagle,* Neimore further complained, "There is no need of these dives, they promote neither happiness nor wealth; they produce sin and only sin."[62] For race men, denigrating the colored sports became a way for the middle class to prove black respectability and show whites that they were conservative and deserving of social equality.

In the context of race, the ring, and recalcitrant behavior, George Dixon was the first fistic hero to move from fame to infamy in the black press. Dixon, who won the featherweight championship in 1890, had lost nearly $100,000 in earnings by 1896. Although he continued to earn more money throughout the decade—he made roughly $250,000—he continued to spend his money as fast as he made it. "No instance seems more pathetic than the career of George Dixon," recounted one white writer. Lack of responsibility and "'carelessness' which embraces that 'good fellow' stuff" did him in.[63] According to champion Bob Fitzsimmons, Dixon "couldn't seem to make money stick to him anyway he got it. He bought everything in sight and was a 'good fellow' all the time."[64] In 1900, a nearly broke Dixon gave a candid interview about his money troubles and reflected on his lack of financial responsibility. Dixon, who had "a few hundred dollars" at that time, and a $6,000 house in Boston, said "I lost my money by gambling, playing the races, leading a fast life and by lending my money to friends." "I was a good fellow," he continued, "I guess, with my money, but, as all good fellows generally see a day when they need a dollar, I certainly have seen that time very often."[65]

In 1903, Dixon went back to England to earn some necessary money. Within a year he had made $7,000 and vowed to save his earnings. In a statement Dixon admitted, "I used to be a fool when I was younger and careless. I never used to know the value of money. It was like nothing to me. But I have tasted the bitter pangs of poverty and know what it is to be hungry." Unfortunately for Dixon, these joyful feelings did not last long, and in 1905 he came back to the States penniless.[66] On his deathbed, Dixon sadly admitted: "The men who followed me in the days of prosperity can't see me when I am close enough to speak to them."[67] Joe Gans supposedly reached out to Dixon and invited him to live in his Baltimore Hotel, but according to Dixon, Gans "was advertising his show when he said that," and only wanted publicity. The homeless Dixon added, "his hotel would sure look good to muh right now."[68] Facing death, Dixon only had one friend, the racist John L. Sullivan. Sullivan claimed, "between the white and the black bluffers, Dixon is getting the con good and strong, and it isn't putting any meals under his belt nor any overcoats on his back. . . . If Dixon had even the interest on the stacks of stuff he put into the pockets of some of his 'friends,' he wouldn't be wondering today where his next highball is coming from."[69] In 1908, at thirty-eight years old, Dixon died a penniless alcoholic in New York City.

Because Dixon was one of the most popular black figures in America, for the black middle class, the financially failed fighting figure became an example of failed manliness. Their critique of the once-celebrated Dixon's downfall fit a familiar narrative of the black middle class trying to appease and prove their equality through uplift and economic responsibility, and the working-class and colored sports often became a scapegoat for this strategy. In 1902, the *Colored American* asked, "How many young men in the heyday of prosperity will be warned by the improvidence of George Dixon to save up a few pennies for the rainy day that is sure to come?"[70] In another issue a writer bemoaned, "to-day George Dixon is practically penniless and unnoticed. Had his money been safely invested, he would have been in his retirement, independently wealthy." "Young men," the writer warned, "'make hay while the sun shines.' Don't live up to all you earn. Store up your substance for harvest days are over when the chilly blast of age comes athwart our pathway."[71] Six years later, when Dixon lost his final bout to the sporting culture, black writers once again reminded their readers of his failures. The *Nashville Globe* lamented, "It might be well to live high when you are making plenty of money, but at the same time one would do well to save a little to care for one's self during his last days."[72] Similarly, the *Iowa State Bystander* said, "this is a great object lesson for young men today." The paper noted that all the money Dixon won "has only this particular effect upon the race, that the race is producing a good man as the best, but upon the other hand if his energy and same amount of labor had been applied in [the] same worthy direction ultimate results would have been lasting." The writer further warned, "Ill gotten gains seldom profit much; evil associates and whiskey will ruin any man. It is a shame to see some of our young men and girls going crazy after the minstrel show and the sporting business, neither ought to receive our approval."[73] The paper's last warning about shady associates, whiskey, and minstrels, was an indictment of the colored sport.

Like Dixon, Jack Johnson went from a celebrated prizefighter to a denigrated pariah. In a well-told story, the massive black middle-class disapproval of Johnson started as a reactionary response to white backlash to Johnson's social behavior. These fears swelled up after Johnson opened his controversial Café de Champion in July 1912 and found himself under government investigation for violating the Mann Act (the white slavery law) in October of that year. During Johnson's legal troubles, Chicago's city council urged Mayor Carter Harrison to revoke Johnson's liquor license and resolved, "Johnson has brought burning shame to the fair name of Chicago." Alderman Ellis Geiger claimed, Johnson "scandalized and outraged all decent citizens of all races. His depraved and immoral character stands as a menace to good public morals, righteousness, and decency. He has disgraced his race, and his alleged calling."[74]

Among the black community, Johnson's court situation quickly reverberated outside the "Windy City." Booker T. Washington argued, "Chicago is at present witnessing a good example of the result of educating a man to make money, without due attention having been given his mental and spiritual development. It is unfortunate that a man with money should use it in a way to injure his own people when those who are seeking to uplift his race and improve its condition. In misrepresenting the colored people of the country, he harms himself the least." He closed his remarks saying, "It only goes to prove my contention that all men should be educated along mental and spiritual lines in connection with their physical education. A man with muscle minus brains, is a useless creature."[75] In Philadelphia, G. Grant Williams, of the *Philadelphia Tribune*, reasoned, "It is unfair for whites to try to class all colored men with Johnson. . . . Yet, with all of his faults, Jack Johnson is the champion of the world, and unlike the whites, we condemn him for his bad traits and give him credit for his good ones. We appreciate his physical ability, but not his mental or moral weakness, and we want it understood that all colored men are not like Jack Johnson is alleged to be." Williams also urged, "Johnson does not represent our better class, therefore, he is not to be considered socially, but when it comes to the prize ring he is king of all races . . ."[76]

But Johnson also had his defenders. Several black leaders, including Ida B. Wells and W.E.B. Du Bois, believed that the attack on the black boxer constituted a larger assault on black people and that whites used Johnson as an excuse to release racism. Concerned that whites would blame all blacks for Johnson's actions, black leaders in Chicago held several meetings to discuss their fallen hero. As more southern black men migrated to the city to seek work, and also find comfort in the sporting culture, it was important for the black middle class to demonstrate that Johnson—a southern migrant—was an anomaly. One black reverend urged, "Every man, colored or white, who acts in a way or conducts his business in a manner as to injure public morals, and who persist in doing so after having been warned to detest, should be tried by the courts, and, if found guilty, punished; and whether he is convicted or not, he should be ostracized by all who believe in common decency and good morals."[77] In November, Wells called a meeting of leading black Chicagoans to discuss how to proceed with Johnson's problems. In the end, two thousand citizens signed a resolution that acknowledged "the sensational exploitation of charges against Jack Johnson great injury has been done to the civic, industrial and business relations between colored and white citizens of Chicago," and appealed "to the public for the presumption of innocence which is every man's due . . ."[78] And in 1914, after the court found Johnson guilty of violating the Mann Act and Johnson was in Europe, on the run from the law, Du Bois used his position in the NAACP and editor of their national magazine, *The Crisis,* and jabbed at the notion that whites had a problem with Johnson's sexual and marital affairs but not his race: "Of course some pretend to object to Mr. Johnson's character. But we have yet to hear, in the case of White America, that marital troubles have disqualified prize fighters or ball players or even statesmen. It comes down, then, after all to this unforgivable blackness." But Johnson's support in the black middle class could not defeat the politics of respectability. Despite understanding that whites used Johnson as a weapon to attack black folks, many in the middle class tried to distance themselves from the champ.

In 1915, after Jess Willard defeated Johnson, to correct the menace's so-called mistakes, black writers continued to insist that Johnson was a racial anomaly. Lester Walton of the *New York Age* concluded, "Although the prevalent belief exists in this country that the caliber of a man is determined by the color of his skin, those of education and culture and who are real Christians, not hypocrites, know that CHARACTER, after all, counts most." He further added, "I do not regard the defeat of Jack Johnson by Jess Willard as a calamity to the Negro, but merely an incident. If the white citizens view it as an event of great satisfaction, let them be happy in the thoughts and perhaps in their jubilant frame of mind they will treat the colored brother with more fairness and go about with less envy and race hatred."[79] Believing that Willard's victory would change how whites treated blacks, in Philadelphia, Williams argued, "We feel it is for the best Jack Johnson has met defeat." Williams and other race leaders must have been relieved by the *Philadelphia Record*'s willingness to acknowledge that Johnson was an individual and not a reflection of black people. The *Record*'s white sportswriter acknowledged, "Johnson was the man who caused the drawing of the color line, for it was not because he was a Negro that the people disliked him, but simply because he was Jack Johnson. He was disliked by colored people, as well as by whites." Williams agreed, and claimed "Johnson's personality shut him out from all races and he ostracized himself." In the end, the one-time symbol of race manhood quickly became a race menace.

3

BLACK MEN AND THE BUSINESS
OF BOXING

On September 25, 1894, Bobby Dobbs sat stewing inside a Boston jail. His crime? As a black man, Dobbs tried to assert his autonomy in the white-controlled business of boxing.[1] Just a few months prior, in St. Paul, Minnesota, Dobbs signed a contract with the white sporting man, Ben Benton, who had promised Dobbs big-money fights. But things did not go as planned. Instead of getting a fight with a notable boxer like Billy Meyer, Austin Gibbons, Joe Walcott (black), or the lightweight champion Jack McAuliffe—matches that would have yielded Dobbs his highest career earnings—Benton had Dobbs sparring at the local fair in Eastport, Maine. Benton provided Dobbs with room, board, and travel expenses on the condition that Dobbs would pay him back out of future earnings. The longer Dobbs stayed in Maine, however, the more debt he would accrue. If Dobbs had to wait for big-money fights, then Benton would receive a bigger piece of Dobbs's next fight purse. Dobbs had spent the first four years of his career managing his own affairs, keeping most of the money he had earned in the ring, and thus, he had grown impatient with Benton's ineptness and exploitation. Dobbs maintained that the moment Benton had him "hustling for himself" to survive in Maine, Benton broke their contract, so Dobbs emancipated himself and lined up a fight in Lynn, Massachusetts against John Butler (black).[2] But Benton did not like Dobbs's assertion of his freedom. In the business of boxing, no matter how skilled the fighter, white managers believed they had the right to control their black fighters. The day before Dobbs's scheduled fight with Butler in Lynn, Benton had Dobbs arrested for breach of contract. The Boston court sided with the white manager. Dobbs signed a poor debtor's oath—he owed $300—and left for the fight game in Philadelphia. He had money to make.[3]

Dobbs's career coincided with a transitional period in prizefighting, as boxing changed from a sport controlled by white financial backers to a business run by white managers and white-owned athletic clubs. Only a handful of black financial backers, managers, and athletic clubs existed. No matter the era, if a black man wanted to find work, he stood at the mercy of white men. Dobbs knew this racial reality all too well. While fighting in St. Paul in the spring of 1894—Dobbs moved to the city in 1893 after California momentarily banned boxing—Dobbs lined up a big-money fight against the English lightweight champion Stanton Abbott. The two fighters signed the customary articles of agreement and planned to battle for $800. But Dobbs was a black man, and in the business of boxing, black men always had an extra opponent to contend with: racism. After he learned of Dobbs's skin color, Abbott withdrew from the fight. The English fighter would not risk his reputation—he had a potential $10,000 fight awaiting him in San Francisco—by losing to a black man. Although local white sporting men shamed Abbott for his cowardice, they understood that he had a racial right to draw the color line.[4] What could Dobbs do about this situation? White men had all the power. Dobbs complained and waited for the next foe Benton lined up. With the promises of more lucrative fights, Benton eventually took Dobbs to Maine.

To find work, black fighters like Dobbs constantly migrated.[5] During the course of his career, Dobbs reportedly battled in more than one thousand contests across America and Europe. Four years into his career, by 1894, Dobbs had fought in Salt Lake City, and Ogden, Utah; Denver, and Pueblo, Colorado; Omaha, Los Angeles, San Francisco, Sacramento, Cincinnati, St. Paul, Philadelphia, and Bangor, Maine.[6] After the Boston ordeal, he lived on the East Coast for the next three years, fighting and teaching sparring lessons, mainly in Scranton and Philadelphia, Pennsylvania. In 1902, Dobbs opened one of the first black gyms in Baltimore. Many of the city's leading black residents flocked to the new gym to transform their bodies. The *Afro-American Ledger* observed, "He has some of the finest citizens as pupils and his place will be a success" and the newspaper noted that the hundreds of blacks that joined his gym "have been inspired by the magnificent specimen of muscular development printed in the pages."[7] But Dobbs was a black man in a racially restrictive line of work and, thus, he always had to be on the move looking for his next play. Within a year, he closed his gymnasium and moved to Europe.

In fact, Dobbs spent the majority of his career in Europe (1897–1899 and 1904–1916). As Theresa Runstedtler has noted, Europe provided a black fighter respite from American racism, and the majority of top black fighters ventured overseas.[8] In Europe, Dobbs traveled around the continent and operated several gymnasiums and promoted and fought in the first official prizefight in Berlin; Dobbs even taught German soldiers how to box on horseback and learned to speak German and Hungarian.[9] When he returned from England in 1899, wearing "a long paddock coat, a light colored suit, a golf hat and his shirt was of red material, dotted with white . . . two big diamond rings adorned his fingers and he carried a large English cane," he told a group of black supporters, "I was treated like a prince, and everybody made it as pleasant for me as they could. They certainly like a black man over there; that is if he acts right and behaves himself."[10] Dobbs brought "four trunks, five grips, and about a dozen suits of clothes, hats, overcoats and suits." He also told the large crowd that cheered his return, "The trip has done me a world of good . . . I made about $10,000, not counting the money I spent for living expenses and buying clothes in England."[11] In 1904 Dobbs returned to England, and wrote back home to invite more black pugilists to earn a living. In his recruitment letter to the *Indianapolis Freeman*, Dobbs wrote, "if you know of a good young lad that can fight at 124 to 126 pounds, write and let me know who he is and what he has done, if he is a good one, I will

Bobby Dobbs, who spent most of his career overseas to avoid American racism, teaches a German man how to box on horseback. (1913, Library of Congress)

send for him, if he would like to come, and I can get him some money."[12] Baltimore boxers Young Peter Jackson and Harry Lyons followed Dobbs. In fact, Dobbs did not want to go back home. Living in America meant fighting constant racism, a point Dobbs emphatically made to the *Chicago Defender* in 1916 when he complained, "America is no place for him as the race man is treated like a dog."[13]

To understand blacks' role in prizefighting we must understand the role race and racism played in the business of boxing and black men's quest for manhood within this racially restrictive business. In a business where white men sought to control every facet of the sport, Dobbs and other black fighters constantly sought control of their own affairs. Black boxers migrated to find freedom and mobility. If a black fighter deemed his manager inadequate, he would fire him and move on to the next manager. When American racism became too heavy to bear, many black fighters traveled overseas. Despite the tight grip whites had on boxing, black fighters tried to carve out a space of manly independence. These men understood the central importance of their black bodies in the business of boxing and used that knowledge to get the most from the sport, their manager, and athletic clubs.

WHITE BACKERS AND BLACK HONOR

C.A.C. Smith had his own boxing school and barbershop in East Saginaw, Michigan, when he decided he wanted to fight fulltime. At six feet tall, Smith had a muscular body and weighed around 180 pounds when trained. Well-schooled in the manly art, the "Michigan Thunderbolt" reportedly had his first official prizefight in 1869, at the age of seventeen, recording a victory over Jim Whalen in a bare-knuckle contest in Pittsburgh. Smith had another fight that year and one more in 1870, but for the next decade, instead of turning to prizefighting to make a living, he chose the respectable and steady income of a barber.[14] To supplement his income, and to keep his skills sharp, he taught sparring lessons in the rough and tumble timber town.[15] By 1880, however, he changed his mind. It is hard to tell why he wanted to fight fulltime. Was it the money, or was it the fame? Perhaps both? But the money was not guaranteed, and these fights were winner takes all. Most men who fought sought recognition from their peers, or in other words their manhood, spreading across the sporting community. So in September 1880, Smith wrote to the most important sporting press in the nation, the *National Police Gazette*, looking for a fight. When he announced himself to national sporting culture for the first time, he challenged, "I am ready to meet any colored pugilist in

America in a contest with hard gloves for $250 a side, Queensberry rules, with or without gloves for $500 a side. George Taylor the lightweight champion preferred." In 1880, most fans in New York considered Taylor the best black boxer in the business, so it made sense that Smith selected him. The bigger the name, the more money, but Smith outweighed his potential opponent by more than fifty pounds. Boxing's weight classes required men fight on fair terms. There was no honor in defeating a noticeably smaller fighter. The *Gazette* suggested that instead Smith challenge "Dangerous" Jack Lawson of New York or George Brown of Chicago, black fighters more his size. Smith found no takers and continued to fight locally.

Because he had never lost a fight, and nobody wanted to battle him, Smith deduced that meant he was the colored champion. Hoping to confirm this point, so he could cement his reputation in the local sporting community, Smith wrote back to the *Gazette* in 1881 asking for their verification of his championship status. Instead of confirming his status, the *Gazette* shamed him: "CAC Smith is no champion. He might be the champion of his village or town but he is not known outside of those parts."[16] It was simple: If he wanted to be "known outside of those parts" he had to fight outside of those parts. But if he wanted to fight, he had to find somebody willing to front him financially. For that, he needed a reputation. Smith also had to find a white backer. In March 1883, he left his wife behind in Port Huron, Michigan, and migrated to New York, the fight capital of America, where he could find fighters and financial backers.[17] He hooked up with a backer, and immediately challenged any black boxer to a $1,000 contest.

Throughout most of the nineteenth century, most men, regardless of race, could not earn a living boxing. Guaranteed money that came from filling arenas with paying customers was uncommon.[18] Instead, fighters made their money through side bets, or what were prearranged figures the contestants agreed to wager. Of course, these working-class men, especially black men, did not have their own money to bet—at least not enough to make a fight worth their risk—so they had to tap into sporting culture and find someone to back them. For a percentage of the profit, financial backers—usually a local gambler—guaranteed these bets, which could range from $25 to $1,000, but the risk all depended on the backer's willingness to gamble. If he lacked confidence in his fighter, the backer would not bet a huge stake. Very few black men acted as financial backers—New York's Ed Nail was the only well-known backer—thus, if he wanted to make a living fighting, the black fighter had to give up financial control to a white backer. In New York, white sporting men like Theo Allen, Richard K. Fox, Hugh Reilly, and Frank Stevenson were the leading fight backers. All four men, at some point, claimed they would back their black boxer for $1,000 fights. But their fighters never fought for $1,000. Ultimately, two white backers—each fighter had to have a backer—were not willing to support their black fighters for $1,000. When it was time to wager on a black fighter, most backers would not risk more than $200.

Although black men like Smith lost their economic autonomy to white financial backers, by issuing fight challenges in newspapers—in other words calling someone out—black fighters had an alternative way to assert their manhood outside the ring. While most local papers supported challenges, if a man wanted a national name he had to go to the *Police Gazette,* a paper with a reported circulation of a half-million readers.[19] The paper also boasted an international readership. For instance, in 1888 when Professor Graves, a black pugilist in Colon, Columbia, read in the *Police Gazette* that Peter Jackson was the black champion of the world, he immediately sent in a challenge to Jackson and claimed that he was the black champion of the Isthmus and the West Indies. Graves claimed that the *Police Gazette* was widely read in that part of the world and wanted readers to know that he, not Jackson, was the best black fighter in the world.[20] Jackson paid no attention to Graves. Black fighters who lived outside New York used telegrams to arrange matches, while local fighters went to the *Police Gazette* offices to place challenges. The telegrams included a list of possible opponents, the type of fight the boxer wanted, and the amount of prize money he wanted to fight for. The *Police Gazette* published these request, and it was then left to the challenged fighter to respond to the call. A fighter had to respond, because his honor and manhood were at stake.[21]

To be sure, in an era in which many of the top white fighters avoided black pugilists, black fighters often challenged other black boxers to establish their reputations. These challenges were not about pathology or self-hate. These were about business and manhood. They developed out of the need to earn a living where a fighter's reputation made him more money. The more prestige the pugilist had in the press, the more money he could get from a financial backer. In addition, his reputation was an acknowledgment of his manhood. His peers had to believe he was tough and that he could back it up. This was about honor. And having honor carried considerable weight in the sporting community. These telegrams from black fighters reveal how these working-class black men had mastered the language of the fighting market. Through studying these challenges, the historian can hear a once-muted voice assert their ideas of manhood that often stood in stark contrast with those of the black middle class.

For the black fighter, having a fight challenge printed by a mainstream newspaper earned him respect among his peers. He was a symbol of true manhood, because he was willing to risk his body and reputation against a man he had just shamed. He also gained social status by risking large amounts of money. Being a "newspaper fighter," however, was only half the battle. Men expected the boxer to back-up his words with action or risk being called a coward. Being a coward in the sporting culture meant losing the social recognition and respect that came from his trade.[22] For example, after black fighter Pop Lewis refused to fight Henry Woodson after Woodson accepted Lewis's open challenge to fight any black man in Ohio for $500, the *Cincinnati Weekly Enquirer* remarked, "Pop Lewis, the alleged Chicago pugilist, is evidently a newspaper fighter. After inserting his bold challenge to the Black Diamond in Tuesday's *Enquirer* he has acted the part of a coward."[23] Lewis, the coward, lost his honor and was never heard from again in the business of boxing.

Honor played a central role in the concept of manhood and prizefighting. In this heteronormative male world, honor meant, for whites and black boxers, protecting one's name both inside and outside the ring.[24] According to Bertram Wyatt-Brown, "Honor is essentially the cluster of ethical rules, most readily found in societies of small communities, but which judgments of behavior are ratified by community consensus." He further suggests, "it cannot be too strongly emphasized that honor is not confined to any rank of society; it is the moral property of all who belong within the community, one that determines the community's own membership."[25] Elliott Gorn has pointed out that during the mid-nineteenth century, "toughness, ferocity, prowess, honor, these became the touchstones of maleness, and boxing along with other sports upheld this alternative definition of manhood. The manly art defined masculinity not by how responsible or upright an individual was but by his sensitivity to insult, his coolness in the face of danger, and his ability to give and take punishment."[26] For boxers during the mid-nineteenth century, fighting for money and the bragging rights of their neighborhood were important, but "the real battle was for peer recognition, for a sense of distinction that made a man first among equals in the small male cliques of working-class society."[27] By the 1880s these "male cliques" included a diverse fan base beyond the neighborhood, which meant that matchmaking expanded from the local saloon to a national and international stage, especially with the popular sporting newspapers the *New York Clipper* and the *National Police Gazette* doubling as matchmaking repositories.

When C.A.C. Smith posted his challenge in 1883 to all black fighters, it earned him the attention he sought. His manly assertion offended Henry

Woodson, the "Black Diamond" from Cincinnati, who had issued his own challenge. Like Smith, Woodson recently migrated to New York to earn his living fighting and had recently knocked out the Irish American fighter Soap McLaughlin in the seventh round.[28]

The Woodson–McLaughlin match should be noted as one of the first instances, if not the first, in which a major American newspaper contrasted the racial differences between athletic white and black bodies, recognizing that the muscularity of the black body severely challenged white notions of manliness and physical prowess. The *Brooklyn Daily Eagle* described Woodson's body; writing "[Woodson] astounded everybody with his splendid development. He peeled a very Bronze Hercules. The muscles overlapped each other on chest and ribs, like the plates of an ancient piece of armor. . . . His neck was firmly set and as finely proportioned as the Apollo Belvedere." His white opponent, however, had a "finely formed and immensely muscular" body, but it looked "rather beefy than fined down" when compared to Woodson's.[29] Black muscles thoroughly defeating white muscles in the ring would soon be a point of concern for Americans, but with only a handful of black fighters, and middle-class white Americans still coming to terms with the manliness and the muscular body, Woodson's black body did not challenge white authority as Jack Johnson's body would twenty-five years later.

Most importantly, Woodson's triumph over McLaughlin changed his career. According to the *Cincinnati Enquirer*, his local paper, Woodson was "on top again," and he promptly challenged all black heavies to battle for $1,000 a side, champion George Godfrey preferred. Smith, who read Woodson's challenge in the *Police Gazette*, did not want to pass up this opportunity to make money and create a name for himself, so he quickly traveled to Albany, New York. When he reached the city, he started boasting to local sportsmen that he traveled to New York just to whip Woodson. The *Detroit Free Press* told readers, "Smith went to Albany and commenced training, and from that city reports of his wonderful prowess reached New York, dimming the luster of the Diamond, who has backed squarely out. Smith telegraphed home yesterday that he is going to say 'dassent' to the New Yorker, and make him fight."[30] Woodson caught word of Smith's boasting and immediately took to the press to lament his frustration and assert his manhood. He could not let Smith publicly question his manliness. Woodson had to defend his honor. He wrote:

> Sir—having learned that Smith, the colored heavyweight pugilist of Port Huron, Mich is making a sensation at Albany, N.Y., stating that he came from

Michigan expressly to fight me, I am ready to fight Smith or any other colored pugilist at anytime according to the rules of the London prize ring for $500 a side and the colored heavyweight championship of America. If Smith's backers mean business, let them forward $250 to Harry Hill, who will suit me for the final stake holder, and I will cover the money and arrange the match anytime at the Police Gazette office. Now, if Smith is not blowing, he will put up a forfeit and arrange a match.[31]

Newspapers across the nation, and most importantly the *Police Gazette,* reprinted the dispute, which placed the pressure clearly on Smith to respond. Both men lacked their own money to fight for a significant stake, and had to rely on white men to work, but now they both had a reputation in the press. While Smith and Woodson carried on in the press, Smith also challenged Boston's George Godfrey, the recognized colored champion, for the title. Because Smith had a recognizable name, Godfrey had to fight. Godfrey agreed, signing a $100 forfeit for a $300 fight.

A fighter could never renege on his word. If he said he was going to fight, men expected him to fight. The forfeit money fortified his commitment. He could never give away the forfeit money without fighting. If he reneged, his reputation would take a serious hit. In May, Smith arrived in Boston ready to fight Godfrey, but according to rumors, Godfrey went to Smith's headquarters to watch him train, and noticed Smith's size and skill and forfeited the fight. Godfrey claimed an illness kept him away, but he and his backers still lost $100 dollars and the potential earnings from the fight. Godfrey lost more than his money, however; he lost his honor. On two occasions the *Police Gazette* noted that Godfrey feared Smith. The *Boston Herald* said "a few days ago a brawny, broad-shoulder, heavy-weight boxer named C.A.C. Smith, who is unmistakably of African descent, reached the city from Wisconsin in expectation of meeting a well-known boxer of this city named Godfrey, and deciding with him the question of superiority with gloves. Godfrey said he was a sick man, and declined to fight, very much to Smith's disappointment."[32] Even Smith called him a coward, telling a friend, "I frightened Godfrey to death. He forfeited to me."[33] Luckily for Godfrey, he had another sporting code working in his favor; a champion could only lose his title in the ring. He still had something people wanted to fight him for.

Godfrey's avoidance of Smith made the "Michigan Thunderbolt" the new black sensation. He had arrived. Although not a champion, the national sporting community recognized him as the top black fighter. The *Police Gazette* observed, "Any pugilist who will go to Albany, NY, and defeat Smith, can break all the sporting men who are booming the colored champion." The paper also noted, "Smith made such a great impression among the sporting men of Albany" that they "offered to back him to box Mace, Slade or any other pugilist, and they claim that he is a match for Sullivan."[34] This is a telling statement. White financial backers realized they could make money off black bodies.

Smith's white benefactor, Hugh Reilly, was one of the first white men to recognize the potential in marketing the black male athlete for white public consumption and personal financial gain. He knew the best way to get a financial return on their investment was to pit Smith against a credible white opponent, with the biggest prize being John L. Sullivan. White backers were not going to gamble huge stakes to see black men fight. To get the racist Sullivan in the ring, Reilly challenged, "If Sullivan can stop the colored giant he is welcomed to the gate receipts."[35] In hopes of making a fight, Smith boldly showed up to Sullivan's exhibitions prepared to battle, and reportedly went to the champion's house to arrange a match. Sullivan did not budge.

If honor in the ring was important, why did Sullivan avoid Smith? Race trumped honor. Honor had no social significance if white men had to treat black men as equals.[36] In Sullivan's world, Smith and other black fighters were never his equals, and fighting them would be an acknowledgment of racial equality. While Smith quickly rose to the top of the ring's ranks, events that summer that challenged his honor brought the "Michigan Thunderbolt" crashing down.

As quickly as white financial backers supported their black fighters, they would just as easily turn their backs on them. No black boxer had the same financial backer for more than a year. In June 1883, for example, Smith and Reilly had an argument over money—Reilly claimed Smith owed him $500— and Smith, believing he should keep a larger chunk of his fight money he had earned in the ring, refused to pay. To seek revenge, Reilly tried to publicly smear Smith's name. If a fighter developed a reputation as a coward, backers would no longer support him, and without financial backing, the fighter would be out of a career. In June, Reilly posted a challenge in the *Police Gazette* on behalf of Smith to fight any black man for $500 to $1,000 at a boxing exhibition at Harry Hill's saloon, in New York. When Henry Woodson appeared ready to battle, Smith, who knew nothing of the challenge, was nowhere to be found, which angered paying spectators who expected to see a battle. They labeled Smith a coward, just as Reilly planned.[37] To earn his respect back from sporting men who shunned him for being a supposed coward, Smith wrote to the *Police Gazette*—the most important newspaper in the sporting community—and informed readers that he did not know about the match and that he never sent a dispatch that his wife was sick.[38] With his explanation, Smith momentarily avoided the embarrassment of being a coward. He also found a new backer, Richard K. Fox, the owner and editor of the *Police Gazette*.

After saving face in print, and finding a backer, Smith also had to fight Woodson and settle their conflict. On July 17 in Troy, New York, Smith whipped Woodson. With his long reach, he kept the "Black Diamond" off balance and spent three rounds peppering him with both fists. Smith's showing impressed local white sporting man, Peter Curley, so much that he told Smith that he could use his theater for free and charge admission for his sparring exhibitions. Scientific sparring exhibitions were easy money compared to bare-fisted bouts with the "Black Diamond." But Smith still had one major problem—Hugh Reilly was still mad at him and continued to use the press to shame Smith publicly. After the Woodson affair, according to the *New York Sun*, Reilly told the press he had "a very poor opinion of the colored pugilist. He says that, while Smith has plenty of science, he is absolutely without pluck, and would break through a brick wall sooner than meet Sullivan in the ring."[39] He shamed him by questioning his honor.

Being labeled "without pluck," a coward, or known to have a yellow streak, were terms that applied to both black and white men, but for black fighters those words had a different racial connotation. The popular black-faced minstrel shows of the burnt cork had scorched in the minds of whites the idea of black docility, and white fans always questioned a black man's toughness. Thus, in the manliest of all sports, black pugilist started with an inferior tag and spent their careers fighting that racial stereotype. The only way a fighter could prove otherwise was to fight. Fight like a man.

Unfortunately for Smith, Reilly was right. He lacked pluck. In August 1883, Smith damaged his reputation during a match with the Canadian champion Jack Stewart, a man he had previously bested. Smith, who entered their battle "with a great reputation for strength, skill and science as a boxer," left the ring known as a coward. Instead of being a man and fighting, in the second round Smith "beat a retreat, first by a step backward, and then, when followed up, breaking ground and actually running away."[40] He then committed another manly sin. He quit. Months later the *Police Gazette* ridiculed Smith, observing, "If he possessed courage he would be the colored champion of America."[41] In March 1884, in Cleveland, after Mervine Thompson subdued Smith, Thompson questioned his toughness, "He [Smith] is about as cowardly a man as I ever met. If he would stand up as Jack Stewart did, I could have whipped him in one." The following week, Smith quit during his fight against the black pugilist Tom Robinson, of Springfield, Ohio.[42] The two men originally agreed to split the gate 60–40, but after Smith's unmanly actions, Robinson took all of the money without a protest from Smith. Things continued to get worse for Smith. A year later, in 1885, he had a scheduled fight against Morris Hafey (white) to take place on January 5, 1885, 150 miles from St. Paul, Minnesota in Fergus Falls.[43] Smith failed to show for the fight, and the white fighter Ed McKewon labeled Smith a coward in front of the audience. For his part, Smith argued that he was an innocent victim of a scam and did not want to ruin his reputation by being involved with a "hippodrome." He also acknowledged that he knew he would be labeled a coward for avoiding the fight, but it was worth the risk, and blamed his financial backer Tom Jefferson (black) for changing the terms of the contract without consulting him. Sports did not believe Smith's claims.[44] Although he kept fighting, by 1885 his reputation was damaged and he could not earn a living in the ring.

Near the end of his life, while working as a barber in Chicago, Smith tried one last time to publicly protect his honor. Hugh Reilly believed his race gave him the perpetual privilege to profit from Smith and had been exploiting Smith's name without his fighter's consent. In 1898, Smith learned that another black fighter, Amos Lavender, a pugilist from Albany whom Reilly also managed, had been using Smith's name and ruining Smith's reputation. Lavender, whom Smith defeated in 1883, started fighting under the name C. C. Smith, the "Thunderbolt." Smith went by C.A.C. Smith the "Michigan Thunderbolt." This fact has even confused boxing historians who do not make the distinction. But C.A.C. Smith knew the difference and told the press his story. Fed up with the faker, Smith, who was working as a barber in Chicago at the time, wrote the *Buffalo Courier*: "Dear Sir—Please allow me a few lines to let the sporting public understand that I am not in the ring . . . although my name is used, and by a man who seems to have no honor about him. What a queer brain he must have to insist on using my name, C.C. Smith." Smith also suggested Reilly had been stealing his name since their dispute in 1883. In his final words, Smith argued, "I feel as though I should have justice in this matter. I don't want to have my name used, as there is only one C.C. Smith, and I claim to be that man, and I will take any step that there is in the law to stop the use of my name."[45] Unfortunately for Smith, Reilly and Lavender kept using his name, earning money, racking up losses, and ruining Smith's legacy.[46]

Regardless of a fighter's color, he had a disadvantage in his business arrangement with his financial backer. The prizefighter assumed all of the physical risks and had to share the financial profits. Plus, side bets were winner-take-all fights, so if he lost his match, he stood at the mercy of the fans and their willingness to take up a collection. Until the late 1880s, the inherent financial and physical risks in fighting reduced the number of competitors. But once fighters had better financial options, like gate receipts and guaranteed purses, more and more men chose fighting as a profession.

CARVING A SPACE IN WHITE-OWNED ATHLETIC CLUBS

At 10:30 at night, both men toed the scratch. The white crowd in San Francisco was ready to see the two black gladiators. On one side stood Charley Turner, of Stockton, "an ebony hued gladiator, beside whom Peter Jackson would have looked pale." At 144 pounds, the two-fisted fighter had a decided advantage over his 140-pound opponent, Wiley Evans, a California migrant who was a "dark mulatto, very powerful in the arms, chest and back, and having splendid legs." For seventeen hard-hitting rounds, the welterweights threw feints and combinations trying to take their man out in this finish fight. While Turner showed more class, Evans, always a game fighter, had a knockout punch that most guys his size lacked. In the seventeenth round, however, Turner found his opening. In what Evans thought was a low blow, Turner got his man to drop his hands and complain to the referee. With Evans's hands down, Turner followed with a blunt blow beneath the ear, and dropped him for good. "Turner stepped lightly to his corner, and the distressed and badly punished mulatto was carried to his dressing room." On that night, these two second-tier fighters fought for $1,000, the most two black non-heavyweights had fought for up until that point. What explains this change in finances? The white middle class.

Changes in rules—moving from the brutal London Rules to the more ordered Queensberry Rules—padded gloves, three-minute timed rounds, and clean boxing—and, most importantly, a shift in white middle-class thought on manliness and the male body, made the once-grotesque sport of prizefighting seem more acceptable. This development also came with a change in white middle-class attitudes, from patrons and political officials, about leisure and public entertainment in which more white men willingly went to boxing shows in legally sanctioned spaces.[47] In 1892, for example, after commenting on the grotesque nature of the Sullivan–Corbett championship match, a Los Angeles writer observed, "there is something in all of us, birds and humans alike, I presume, that makes a combat full of intense and enthralling interest."[48] And as novelist Alfred Henry Lewis commented in 1910: "We need a gladiatorial class. It reflects itself in the swelling stamina and courage of a people."[49] In other words, the prizefighter provided white men the perfect prescribed performances for a race of men that needed manly entertainment as a reminder of their dominance and a boost in confidence that they were still manly specimens. This need for manly entertainment resulted in paying customers and guaranteed money for the fighter.

The increase in fight purses coincided with the development of middle-class athletic clubs, but the advent of the athletic club also represented the white middle-class takeover of boxing. Scholar Jeffory Clymer suggests that the athletic club was an extension of the market's control of the worker. He argues, "Exactly at the moment that boxers became paragons of individualistic virtue for the emerging professional managerial class, boxers' own agency and control was undergoing a rationalization that was similar to the organizational impulses that eclipsed male corporate employees' sense of masculinity in the increasingly bureaucratic and routinized work place."[50] Despite the grip the clubs had on the fighters, there was an opportunity for the black fighter to earn more money.

Although white clubs and white managers tried their best to control black fighters, the club's entrepreneurial spirit also enabled the black boxer to prosper. These clubs competed with each other to attract the best talent, so the black boxers pitted clubs against each other to obtain the best offer. In the late 1880s and early 1890s, for example, San Francisco—one of the leading fight cities in America—had four successful clubs that bid against each other for fights. Coincidentally, during the late 1880s and 1890s, San Francisco became a popular destination for black fighters across the country, because the clubs usually offered the best prices. The Peter Jackson–George Godfrey fight for $1,600 on August 24, 1888, in San Francisco represented the largest purse two black fighters battled for in the 1880s. For winning the fight, Jackson received $1,200 and Godfrey earned $400 plus travel expenses in the loss.[51] After Jackson defeated Godfrey, a San Francisco athletic club posted $6,000 for Jackson to fight "notable" white fighter Joe McAuliffe and brandished the possibility of a $20,000 purse for a fight with Sullivan.[52] In 1891, when Jackson battled "Gentleman" Jim Corbett to a sixty-one-round draw, they fought for $10,000.[53]

Even a second-tier black fighter like Charley Turner could expect to earn $800 to $2,000 for a fight in San Francisco. In seven fights in the city, between 1888 and 1892 Turner, who was one of the top fighters on the coast, fought for a total of $8,050. He went 4–3 in those fights, winning $3,000 for his services.[54] The price these clubs paid for a fighter like Turner reveals the economic impact athletic clubs had on boxing. Six years prior, in 1883, June Dennis, the "colored" lightweight champion of the Pacific Coast, fought for

$50 a side at a local theater.[55] But the clubs represented a great paradox for black boxers: To make this type of money, Turner and other black fighters had to endure the inherent racism in these white-owned spaces.

Most athletic clubs had white ownership and white patrons that created a hostile work environment for black fighters. White fans called black fighters "niggers," "coons," and even threatened to kill black fighters, especially in interracial contests. One reporter noted, "On the night of the fight as soon as the colored boxer puts up his hands voices from all parts of the house can be heard advising the white man to knock the negro's head off."[56] In 1891, champion George Dixon recalled that in Boston, "it is not many years ago since I first stepped into a ring in this city, but even then a colored man would be considered crazy if he went to fight a white man outside of a clubroom. He would surely have been killed, or brutally injured, if he made the least attempt to win."[57] Early in Joe Gans's career, white fans in Baltimore had subjected him to taunts of "kill the nigger," but as champion he refused to put up with their racial jeers. In 1906, Gans lectured his hometown Baltimore fans about racism, and complained, "You people don't encourage your boxers properly. If you would, you could have another champion coming up. If a German gets in the ring and gets wobbly from a few punches you shout, 'Kill the Dutchman.' If a Hebrew is getting his you scream to 'Kill the Jew.' If it's a chocolate, well, I'll leave it to your imagination what you yell."[58]

Like Gans, black fighters did their best to fight racism in their workplace. In 1884, Henry Woodson and McHenry Johnson boycotted their planned exhibition at Billy Madden's New York club because Madden barred their black friends from entering the establishment. Woodson and Johnson, according to a black writer, demonstrated "that they posses [sic] manly natures and hearts as well as sturdy arms and fists."[59] Four years later, in 1888, George Godfrey declined a $1,000 offer to fight a white opponent in New York, and cited, "I do not recall an instance of where a colored man went up against a white man in Gotham and was fairly treated. There is a prejudice there among the sporting people against the colored race, and I firmly believe that they would 'kick' against me on principle."[60] On another occasion, after Godfrey read that Jack Ashton (white) wanted to fight in Providence, Rhode Island, Godfrey asked, "How long is it since they had a good old-fashioned lynching down in Providence?" "Don't you think they are itching for one now?" He claimed that even with a Gatling gun he would not fight Ashton in Providence. Instead, Godfrey insisted on battling in Boston, or in the West. Godfrey fought for a living, but not for his life.[61]

The most powerful symbol of a black fighter asserting his autonomy in the workplace occurred in 1892 when, just a few months after Homer Plessey filed his famous anti–Jim Crow case, George Dixon momentarily knocked out Jim Crow in New Orleans.[62] As a stipulation of his contract for the $7,500 championship fight against Jack Skelly—he also had a $5,000 side bet—Dixon required the New Orleans Olympic Club to integrate the stadium and reserve seating for black fans. With Dixon's urgings, the club integrated for the first time and set aside one thousand seats for black fans. Roughly three hundred black men supported their champion and screamed loudly when Dixon knocked out Skelly in the eighth round.[63]

Understanding the magnitude of Dixon's demonstration, black writers celebrated his victories over Jim Crow and Skelly as victories for the race. A *Cleveland Gazette* writer cheered, "Dixon has given a favorite Dixie prejudice a terrible black eye." He also boasted, "It is all right to see one white man whip another in the south, but to pay one's dollars and a number of them, too, to see a Hamite 'whip the stuffing out of' a white man, even if he is a northerner, and then give the former an ovation, is something more than the average southerner can or will stand."[64] In the *Western Appeal,* John Q. Adams, who had previously argued that blacks should not attend the fight because he believed the sport brutal and the Olympic Club racist, changed his tune and taunted, "there are cases in which an Afro American is a better man than a white man."[65]

Owing to the violent nature of Dixon's victory and its potential racial implications, however, the white New Orleans press urged white clubs to bar interracial matches. The *Times-Democrat* reasoned it "a mistake to match a negro and a white man, a mistake to bring the races together on any terms of equality, even in the prize ring."[66] Afterward, athletic clubs in New Orleans banned interracial contests. After the New Orleans clubs' decision, the *Cleveland Gazette* retorted, "We thought the sight of one of our race pummeling the face and body of even a northern white pugilist would be more than they could stand, and our readers can now see how correct our estimate was."[67] Dixon did not fight in New Orleans again and, in fact, he never fought in the Deep South after that match.

BLACK-OWNED ATHLETIC CLUBS

Up until 1915, black men only operated two boxing clubs that could be categorized as middle class, and the majority of black-owned clubs, the ones that generally escaped the view of the local press, were working-class black clubs that catered to the colored sports. Distinguishing the clubs as middle class is a judgment of the club's ownership, the club's facilities, and how the owners geared their business to attract middle-class patrons. The first black middle-class club, the Orleans Athletic Club, opened in 1892. Although the club was the second wealthiest black social club in the nation, little is known about the club's venture into boxing except for a few promotional pieces from local newspapers. Operated by middle-class lawyers J. Madison Vance and Walter Cohen, the club had an eight hundred–seat arena attached to the facility, as the black owners looked to tap into black consumer dollars in a boxing-crazed city.[68] In their most successful fight, they promoted the battle for the Interstate Championship between Chicago's Bob Harper and New Orleans' Joe Green for a title that excluded the prefix "colored," in a match that featured two of the best black middleweights in the nation.[69] The Orleans Athletic Club also timed the fight to coincide with the middleweight championship bout between Bob Fitzsimmons and Jim Hall at the New Orleans Crescent City Club that took place two days before the Harper–Green affair. The proprietors might have been trying to prove a point about race and equality, or just cashing in on the prizefight buzz in the city.

Harper came into the fight as one of the most recognizable names in the sport. In Chicago, Harper's boxing finances improved as a result of local black fighters demanding more financial support from white sporting men. In 1890, Chicago's black fighters, including Andy Mills, Billy Piper, and Shorty Ahearn, complained about racism and asked Chicago's leading boxing promoter, Parson Davies, to create a colored championship. These fighters believed that if they could market themselves as champions they could command more money in their fights. Davies obliged, and he made a gold medal for the lightweight and middleweight colored championships in Chicago. When Harper defeated Andy Mills for the middleweight championship, his victory gave him instant name recognition, and he received a number of challenges from notable black fighters across the nation, including Wiley Evans of California and Joe Green of New Orleans.[70] In 1892, Harper knocked out Evans, in what the *Tribune* called "as pretty a contest that has been seen here in many a day."[71] This victory eventually led to the interstate championship fight with Green in New Orleans. In a thrilling forty-seven-round contest, Green knocked out Harper. This was the club's last major fight. Harper went back home and worked as an instructor for Chicago's Colored Athletic Club (CAC.)[72]

Unlike the Orleans Athletic Club's middle-class leadership, the black gambling fraternity in Chicago operated Chicago's black athletic club. Ownership included A. J. Scott, who had a financial vice empire reportedly worth $250,000. By 1892, the club hosted weekly exhibitions and battles that featured Bob Harper, Alex Ahearn, Fred Dempsey, Andy Mills, Al Miles, Ike Rivers, and George Williams.[73] Despite the class differences between the Orleans and Chicago Colored Athletic Club, both institutions folded in 1893 with the coming of the economic depression.

The following year in Chicago, one of the leading fight clubs was an illegal club run by Willis Woodson, the "Black King." During the economic depression (1893–1897) that coincided with the beginning of the "good government" reform movement in Chicago, in which boxing was momentarily banned, the "Black King" ruled the "Westside." The police knew his place as the "toughest" in the area. On a regular basis there were fights, stabbings, and shootings. Because he paid police for his protection and helped local aldermen get elected, authorities never bothered him. Although many blacks suffered during the depression, Woodson was reportedly worth $100,000. In his two-story building he counterfeited money, ran craps games, sold opium and liquor, operated a dancehall, and hosted prizefights twice a week. However, the "Black King" let his prosperity and political protection go to his head, and he stopped bribing local politicians. An 1897 report stated, "Before the downfall was fully accomplished Woodson renewed his allegiance to the Aldermanic sponsor and the latter tried to give him a list out of his troubles, but it was too late. Under the present administration (Mayor Swift) and encouraged by the civil service which makes them secure in their places despite political attacks, the police refused outright to longer tolerate the man or his methods."[74] Once he lost police protection, patrons stopped coming to his establishment, because they had to fear being arrested. In 1901 he died of consumption, financially broke.[75] Others learned from his mistakes, and knew they had to have the right mayor in charge.

As black migration increased, working-class black sporting clubs became more omnipotent in the black community. The men who ran the clubs realized their black male clientele provided political power; thus, the combination of black migration, segregation, and vice had an unintended consequence of giving some black sporting men political power.[76] In cities such as St. Paul, Chicago, and Los Angeles, the black "sports" used their ownership of saloons and proximity to the black working class to control black votes, and reap the benefits of their political efforts. In Los Angeles, for example, at the turn of the century, the black sporting saloon became synonymous with prizefighting, and black club owners in the City of Angels used vice and boxing to gain political power.

Black sporting clubs in Los Angeles first gained political power after the 1898 mayoral election. The United Republican and the Manhattan Club had formed in previous elections to legally run vice operations. In California, political clubs had to register with the state, but once they did, the clubs received the privilege of selling members alcohol without a license. Prior to the 1898 election, a small but politically important bloc of middle-class black voters left the Republican Party, and sporting black men filled the power void.[77] By October, during the 1898 election campaign, Lou Simpson's United Republican Club became the largest black political club in southern California. The club held daily meetings that attracted local candidates, including Republican mayoral candidate Fred Eaton.[78] Not everyone was amused by the connection of the black sports with the Republican Party. After one political meeting, the *Herald* quipped, "The club is called the Central Republican club, although as the meeting was held in the notorious Manhattan club rooms the mistake in the names is perhaps natural. The Manhattan club is a resort for

The *Los Angeles Herald* mocks the black-owned Manhattan club. At that time, the club used boxing as a front to some of its illegal activities. (1898, *Los Angeles Herald*)

negro prostitutes, a poker den, and prize fights are pulled off occasionally."[79] Helped by the great efforts made by the black social clubs, Republican Fred Eaton won.[80]

The black clubs reaped the benefits of their political engagement until they challenged the city's comfort with interracial sex. After the election, the police cracked down on liquor infractions but let the black clubs operate with impunity. This irritated white saloon and restaurant owners, who complained to the Finance Committee that the police did not enforce the law. Their complaint that "two of the toughest joints in the city are clubs formed by negroes, at which whiskey is sold at all hours without license" reached the mayor, but neither he nor the police chief took any action.[81] City officials, however, were more worried that the black clubs challenged the notion of white sexual purity than the fact that the clubs illegally sold liquor, and lawmakers told police to arrest all the white prostitutes who frequented the club. Labeling this type of interracial vice "interzones," historian Kevin Mumford has argued, "These interracial relations on the margins remain central to understanding the character of modern American culture."[82] White women like Mabel Brown, who as one headline suggested, "Loves Blacks," were barred from these establishments. After three prostitutes got into a fight and were arrested in front of Lou Simpson's club on June 20, the *Los Angeles Times* complained, "Both [clubs] are sinks of iniquity, where the drudges of society of both sexes and all colors congregate nightly to indulge in unbridled vice." Six months after the election, the police moved to close the clubs to protect the purity of the city. On June 24, the police raided Simpson's "resort for men and women of the lowest classes of all nationalities" and arrested sixty-nine people, including Simpson. Detailing the racial dynamics of this raid, the *Herald*'s headline read "Raid of the Coons." The *Los Angeles Times* argued Simpson's place would have been raided if "officers on the beat had not been held in restraint by a higher power."[83] The newspaper wanted to print a member's list to discourage politicians because "many of the candidates for office at the last city election visited Simpson's dive and inscribed their name on the membership roll," and the press noted that "at least one of the present Councilmen and one of the present Police Commissioners were so enrolled, not to mention persons who have held even higher offices."[84] City officials had brief cause to celebrate, because they temporarily restrained wide open vice and interracial sex, but the black clubs found new life in the 1899 California boxing law.

To continue to run their businesses, the United Republican Club and the Manhattan Clubs both filed papers as legal athletic clubs. This allowed them to host fights and sell alcohol as private clubs without a liquor license. Despite the fact they used boxing as cover for vice, the two clubs were serious about promoting fights. By 1900, the Manhattan hosted weekly fights featuring meal-ticket black fighters and, at one point, even hosted a battle royal for their racially mixed audiences' delight. In that shameful show, future welter-weight champion "Dixie Kid" Aaron Brown defeated his black opponents.[85] In February 1900, the *Los Angeles Herald* reported, "There seems to be a dearth of fighters. True, the Manhattan club is to hold contests every Friday night, but the bouts are of minor importance. The fights are well enough as long as they last, but the men are seldom in condition to remain anywhere near the advertised number of rounds." A week later, however, the paper suggested the Manhattan "has of late somewhat improved, both as to the general character of the place and as to the standard of the contests."[86] By the end of 1900, Los Angeles had developed into a top-tier fight city in the West, and the black athletic clubs had outperformed the white-middle-class owned Los Angeles Athletic Club. In fact, in December 1900, the LAAC stopped hosting box-ing matches, because the club could not put on quality fights to satisfy their white patrons. Once the LAAC closed, black clubs controlled boxing in Los Angeles. With the black clubs in charge, and the boxing game growing, the city's potential as a fight town caught the eye of San Francisco fight promoter J. R. Kennedy, who noted, "There is plenty of room for good boxing matches in Los Angeles. . . . The attendance at the small [black-owned] clubs has demonstrated the fact that the public is interested in the sport, and I believe the proposed club will be welcomed."[87]

In the midst of the increasing interest in local boxing, and the city becom-ing a much-touted location for fighters to perform their trade, in March 1901, the United Republican Athletic Club hosted its most successful fight. The fight, a scheduled twenty-round interracial affair between locals Jim Tremble and black fighter Billy Woods, attracted four hundred people to the United Republican Club and demonstrated that "the boxing game has a strong hold on the sport loving public," but white patrons also complained that the club was a "veritable death trap . . . there was no such thing as a passageway, and the ventilation was abominable." The United reaped the financial windfall of their success, but the fight also highlighted the problems white patrons had with the black athletic clubs. The *Los Angeles Herald* contemplated that if whites were forced to attend the black clubs, "the better element, which was out in large numbers, will not spend another evening in such discomfort."[88] The close proximity in which the clubs operated, the illusion of equality they afforded blacks, and the missing comforts in the eyes of the white patrons meant the existence of the black athlete clubs could not continue. Something had to change.

To get rid of the black athletic clubs, city officials cited health concerns to temporarily close the United and Manhattan Clubs. In Los Angeles, according to historian Natalia Molina, health reformers had a "long tradition among city health officials of tracing any blemish on the pristine image of Los Angeles—including all forms of disease and any manner of disorder—to the city's marginalized communities."[89] On March 15, 1901, quarantine officer G. L. Berg closed the Manhattan and the United Republican clubs after ruling that local black shoe shiner, "Pegleg Dick," who had a scheduled fight at the Republican Club, had smallpox. Berg closed both clubs despite having no proof "Peggy" would have contact with the audience and despite the fact that the scheduled contest was at the United Republican Club and not the Manhattan.[90] Ten days later, the city attorney ruled that the Republican and the Manhattan clubs, "two of the most disreputable places in the city," had to close their doors for good.[91] Lou Simpson, who owned the Republican Club, argued that the police were out to get him, and asked police commissioner James Keeney to overturn the ruling. The police commissioner told Simpson that "clubs like the United Republican Club and the Manhattan Club do no good to anyone. They are a menace to the young men, to the morals of the community and to the poor man and the laborer. The club managers get the working man into their place that they may get him drunk and roll him for every cent he has. That certainly is a detriment to the family."[92] Essentially, the raid on the two black clubs put them out of the boxing business. City lawmakers, however, had to deal with one other black club, William Carroll's newly established Alpha Athletic Club.[93]

It is fitting that Carroll ran a local black baseball team by the same name, the Alphas, because the motives of middle-class black athletic clubs and black-owned baseball teams operated along the same lines. As scholar and Negro League historian Michael Lomax observed, "The Negro Leagues inform us of the ways African Americans strived to compete within the framework of the U.S. economy, and simultaneously they represented the overall pursuit of freedom and self-determination." As he further noted "African Americans made it clear that despite their exclusion from mainstream America, they would develop their own institutions and shape their own sporting patterns."[94] Certainly, as a black businessman in a white dominated profession of boxing, Carroll fit that mold. Controlling the business of boxing in one of the hottest growing markets in the country gave him a lucrative momentary monopoly and an opportunity to shape how black businessmen would be perceived in the area. A month before Carroll opened his club, for example, local black businessmen formed the Colored Businessmen's League, to promote racial uplift through business success. A few years prior, one of the members of the Colored Businessmen's League, J. J. Neimore, urged, "The business and the commercial key is the instrument that will dispel the shades of prejudice and unlock the closed door of wealth and happiness for the boys and girls of the Afro-American race in California."[95] Carroll ran his club clean and orderly, and most importantly, like many black baseball owners, he used white-run facilities to conduct his business. Sure, Carroll had to pay the price to operate in their establishments, and as Lomax shows, like black baseball had to deal with, Carroll lost a cut of the action renting from a white owner, but he proved that he, and by extension other black men, had the necessary stuff to compete in a white-dominated world. And had racism not reared its ugly head, Carroll could have been one of the most important figures in the business of boxing.

When Carroll opened the Alpha in 1901, he purposely modeled his club in juxtaposition to the Manhattan and United Republican Athletic Clubs; instead of marketing to black patrons, he sought to appeal to the white middle class. Carroll rented white middle-class facilities, Turner's Hall and Hazard's Pavilion, to host fights. White audiences considered these arenas clean, unlike the Republican Club, a "veritable death trap" where white and black fans were stuck together with "no such thing as a passageway."[96] As a businessman, Carroll attracted quality fights, because he offered guaranteed purses. In comparison, the other black clubs only offered their fighters gate receipts and mainly promoted meal-ticket bouts. Hoping for good clean fights at the Alpha, a *Los Angeles Herald* writer reasoned, "The Alpha people declare they want to do everything possible to give good clean shows and to 'get in right' they should make a permanent selection of a referee and insist that he judge all contests."[97] To demonstrate his sincerity, Carroll hired the leading white referee in the city, Harry Stuart, as the club's official referee. The Alpha's middle-class strategy paid immediate dividends.

Carroll had successfully provided white men with the necessary outlet for their manly endeavors, and because he ran a "clean" club, whites briefly gave him honorary whiteness. White fighter Jim Kennedy praised Carroll by saying, "The Alpha club is run by some colored men, but they are white in their business dealings, and there was nothing too good for me. . . . I want to say that any fighters who receive offers from the Alpha club need not have any fear about getting a square deal."[98] According to the *Los Angeles Times,* "the success attained by the Alpha Athletic Club, which has been doing business on the square, has aroused the cupidity of men who have been following the local ring with the result that they are trying to cut into the game."[99] Carroll's good character made him mythically white.

Carroll knew that interracial contests made the most money, so for his biggest fight he appropriated the city's La Fiesta celebration—the most popular booster celebration in the city—and hosted an interracial contest between the local black fighter Hank Griffin and San Francisco's Joe Kennedy for the heavyweight championship of the Pacific Coast.[100] In other words, an interracial bout for superiority would highlight the city's biggest tourist event. Admirers of the fight game could not escape the issue of race in this match. The *Herald* observed that "Griffin is a fellow who takes life very seriously—not that he is cross or hard to handle, quite the contrary—but he is unlike many of the colored race in that he seldom smiles. Whatever he attempts is done with his whole heart and soul . . ."[101] In the ring, the fighters presented an unmistakable contrast of manliness. "The two men entered the ring they presented a strange contrast. Griffin came first, and, stripping off sweater and trousers, showed his lanky, sinew frame of coal black hue glistening with perfect health. Kennedy's creamy white skin and bulky proportions seemed to give him a shade the advantage, and, probably on account of his color, the crowd was largely in his favor."[102] They boxed twenty excellent rounds that resulted in an exciting draw. Carroll and the Alpha Club, it would seem, had arrived, but the Kennedy–Griffin fight was the last major prizefight for black-owned clubs in Los Angeles.

In April, white promoter Tom McCarey also opened a new boxing club and, ultimately, the Alpha could not compete with the new club owner's money and his "impeccable reputation." Simply put, white patrons would rather attend white-owned clubs. Plus, McCarey had more money to offer fighters. Thus, he hosted better fights. In June 1901, one observer noted that "in the old days when the [n]egro clubs of Los Angeles were flourishing, a five-dollar note was sufficient incentive for two boys to beat one another to a pulp. Now twenty times that sum is demanded for a short exhibition."[103] By September 1901, Carroll announced that the Alpha Club would no longer host prizefights. The *Los Angeles Times* remarked that Carroll and the Alpha Club "did not seem to have the confidence of the public for some reason."[104] Carroll sold the Alpha's boxing equipment to McCarey, who then donated the equipment to charity.[105]

UNSCRUPULOUS WHITE MANAGERS AND BLACK AUTONOMY

Inside the ring, black fighters battled for money, respect, and fame, but outside the ring they fought for their autonomy from white men. White managers tried to regulate every facet of the fight game, creating a struggle between the black man's quest for independence and the white man's desire for control. Among the white athletic clubs, an unwritten rule existed that all managers had to be white. As sportswriter George Siler noted, "The colored boxer, as a rule, has a white manager. All fight-promoters are white. Therefore, when a colored fighter's manager seeks a match he necessarily is compelled to talk business with a white man."[106] A black fighter who tried to go on his own, or had a black manager, usually relegated himself to meal-ticket fights. "As a general rule," a sports columnist noted, "unless he was equipped with a good white manager, the negro has had little chance to get out of the minor class . . ."[107] White managers like Al Herford (he managed Joe Gans, Young Peter Jackson, Harry Lyons) and Tom O'Rourke (George Dixon and Joe Walcott) controlled clubs locally, and they had national connections black men did not have.

In a business in which white managers had access to the largest fight purses, black fighters stood at their mercy. "The colored fighters seem to be particularly easy marks for a manager," a writer observed. "Half of every dollar these fighters made went to the managers until the contract that bound them expired."[108] Often, the contract "expired" when the fighter was on the downside of his career and the manager had no use for him. A month after George Dixon lost his championship title to Terry McGovern in 1900—Dixon held the title throughout most of the 1890s—O'Rourke kicked Dixon out of his restaurant, an establishment O'Rourke purchased from his cut of the $250,000 Dixon won in his career.

When black fighters understood their power in the fight game, they sought more autonomy in their careers. This awakening did not represent a collective response from black fighters, rather the business between boxer and manager rested at the individual level. In short, if a manager did them wrong, then the black fighter tried to leave for better options. For example, Gans's relationship with the unscrupulous Herford momentarily ruined the champion's reputation and his career. On at least two occasions, Herford forced Gans to throw fights—Terry McGovern 1900 and Jimmy Britt 1904—by threatening to keep Gans from future big-money fights and withholding money if Gans refused to purposely lose. After the Britt fake, clubs around the country claimed they would never bring Gans in again. Tired of his manager's control, in October 1905 Gans fired Herford and bolted for California.[109] He made the right decision. Gans garnered $100,000 over the rest of his career acting as his own manager.[110]

When the black fighter bucked, however, his white manager made sure to make him feel powerless. Because boxers only got paid when they fought, but had to pay their training and travel expenses and, to be sure, enjoyed the sporting lifestyle, they frequently borrowed money from their managers. And their managers were always willing to let their black charges borrow large chunks of money. Why? They wanted to maintain control over their black fighters. If the fighter owed him money, the manager had control over the fighter's career. The great Joe Walcott and his notorious manager, Tom O'Rourke, had a contentious business relationship over money and control. In 1900, Walcott threatened to fire O'Rourke because his manager refused to let Walcott's black friends in his restaurant. But he could not leave his manager, of course, because he owed him too much money. The following year, in San Francisco, after Walcott's fight with the light heavyweight Gus Gardner, O'Rourke quit Walcott, claiming he did not like the way Walcott used him for money. Essentially Walcott, who earned the money with his fists, wanted to keep the majority of the loot in his hands. O'Rourke claimed Walcott owed him $1,300 for a mortgage and personal loans, and after threatening Walcott, his fighter gave him $1,270 of his hard-earned money from the Gardner battle. Before O'Rourke left the city, he told the press, "I was the only man who could handle him and get any results out of him. He owes money to everybody and will owe money to more people before he leaves town."[111] Eventually, Walcott left O'Rourke for good.

After Jack Johnson left Frank Carrillo in 1902—Carrillo reportedly cheated him out of earnings and refused to pay Johnson's train fare to Chicago—Carrillo used his connections in Bakersfield, California, where Johnson was living, to have Johnson charged with vagrancy. To assert his independence, Johnson threatened to boycott his upcoming February 5, 1903 colored championship match with "Denver" Ed Martin if Tom McCarey, whose Century Athletic Club would host the fight, insisted Johnson use Carrillo as his manager. Johnson argued, "If I can't fight Martin under my own management, there won't be any fight."[112] Johnson stayed, Carrillo was out, and Johnson won $1,260 to keep for himself. But Carrillo kept after the black champion for the $297.25 Johnson supposedly owed him and took Johnson to court in October 1903.[113] In court, Johnson and his "new" manager, Zeke Abraham, told the judge that Johnson's contract with Abraham called for Johnson to give all of his earnings to Abraham; and, thus, Johnson did not have money to pay back Carrillo. Abraham told the judge that he fronted Johnson $4,100 and received his money back from Johnson's fight. When the judge questioned why Johnson needed so much money, Abraham responded, "Well he shoots craps with it. You know how that is. Every nigger has to shoot craps."[114] That sealed the deal. Despite the fact Johnson and Abraham played the judge and

Carrillo, the judge naturally believed a black man would waste his money on craps. Carrillo lost his claim to the money.

Johnson publicly promoted and relished his independence as a black man. When he felt his managers got out of line, he fired men like Carrillo, Sam Fitzpatrick, and George Little. During the negotiations for his fight with Jim Jeffries, Johnson attended every meeting and negotiated the contract of the fight, the film rights, and the referee. Acting as his own manager—George Little was his official manager of record—Johnson negotiated more than $300,000 in contracts leading up to the Jeffries fight. As the two sides settled on the referee, Johnson showed his ultimate power in the fight game. At one meeting Sam Berger (Jeffries's manager) and Johnson argued over the referee, with neither side agreeing on a single name. After being fed up by Johnson's stubbornness, Berger asked Johnson, "What's the use of being obstinate Jack? All of the men I have named are honest and competent." Johnson replied, "That's all right I'm a colored man and expected to get the worst of it." Johnson's need to point out his race infuriated Berger. "You do not have to remind people of your color," Berger screamed. "I shouldn't wonder but that you expect to cloud the issue with your talk about color and get the best of the argument." Soon, the two men started to tussle, and promoter Jack Gleason had to break them up. Gleason said they would settle the issue on a later date, which prompted Johnson to hit the table, and yell, "If it comes to that and a man objectionable to me is chosen I will not fight on July 4th."[115] Johnson got his man to referee the fight, promoter Tex Rickard. A month later, Johnson fired his manager, George Little, and told the press, "I need no manager but myself, and am fully satisfied that I am capable to attend my own affairs."[116]

This type of shrewd negotiations irritated white promoters. During Johnson's championship reign, for example, Australian boxing promoter Hugh McIntosh expressed disgust about dealing with the likes of Johnson and Sam Langford, complaining "these blacks have absolutely no sense of business and they have an idea that money flows in Australia like water in America." He further stated, "And they play a peculiar system, these black boys. They always wait until they think they have a promoter in the hole, and then they come along with outrageous demands for more money at the eleventh hour."[117] If whites were not ready for a black man who understood and asserted his financial worth, they certainly were not prepared for a black man who refused to live his life as anything less than a free man.

4

COLORED CHAMPIONSHIP
AND COLOR LINES

On December 7, 1882, nearly eight hundred sporting men packed Harry Hill's notorious saloon in Brooklyn to watch Morris Grant—the colored champion of New York—and Professor Charles Hadley—the colored champion of Connecticut—battle for the colored championship.[1] Born in 1837 in St. James, South Carolina, Grant honed his pugilistic skills while working as a bouncer at one of New York's "popular dives." During his fighting career, Grant had appeared in a number of sparring benefits, an occasional prizefight, and had "beaten all men of his color who had dared to face him either with the gloves off or on," but he could not beat Charles Hadley.[2] His rival, "Professor" Charles Hadley, coveted the colored championship. From 1880 to 1883, he was the best black bruiser in the business. His honorific moniker, "Professor"—he always went by Professor—told others he was a skilled pugilist trained in the manly art of self-defense. To be sure, his insistence on being called Professor also represented a reminder to himself, and others, about how far he had come in life. Born a slave in Nashville, Tennessee, in 1846, at a young age Hadley reportedly escaped slavery and migrated to New York. Once free, he worked as a bootblack and then moved to Louisville in 1862 to jockey for the famed race horseman, Capt. T. G. Moore. In 1868, Hadley moved to Bridgeport, Connecticut, where he started taking boxing lessons. A year later, he had his first bare-knuckle fight against Edward Harrick.[3] Although Hadley had been boxing since 1869, he did not get his big break until he faced Grant for the championship.

When the bell sounded for the Grant–Hadley match, "Hadley rushed at his man, hitting left and right, and driving Grant all over the stage, pounding and thumping him with no intervals until Grant fell all in a heap on the floor." In the second round, Hadley continued his furious fighting and knocked Grant out of the ring. Brave, but badly beaten, the boxer continued to battle. Hadley dropped him three more times. Grant's corner man, Charles Cooley, tried to stop the fight by sitting Grant on his stool, but the crowd wanted more action and yelled at Hadley to "give it to him." The Professor obliged. But before Hadley could finish Grant, Grant fell off his stool to avoid the knockout. Referee Harry Hill declared Hadley the winner and the new colored champion.[4] But the night's festivities were not over. After the fight, Cooley stood in the center of the ring and yelled, "I can lick any 180 pound nigger in the world for $500." An imposing figure, at 5'11" and 195 pounds, Cooley had limited boxing experience, but a tough attitude. More of a street fighter than a pugilist, he had "distinguished himself in many 'skirmishes' about town with men who had some pretensions to fight."[5] But he could not lick a trained fighter like Hadley. The Professor coolly walked over to his adversary and decked him. Cooley got up, and Hadley knocked him down again. During the ruckus somebody handed Cooley a revolver; fortunately, before Cooley could shoot, the police grabbed him and threw him out on the street.[6]

The roots of the Colored Championship started a year prior, from a challenge involving honor, boxing, and black manhood. On January 6, 1882, Professor Hadley sent a letter to the *New York Herald* about a recent slight he had received from "several colored boxers." Hadley wrote, "seeing a challenge from several colored boxers to meet me, I take this method of informing them that I will be at Johnny Saunder's benefit, on Thursday afternoon, January 12, at Harry Hill's Theatre, prepared to spar any of them, [Morris] Grant or [Charles] Cooley preferred." He signed his letter, "Champion Colored Boxer of Connecticut."[7] Hadley's challenge had all the signs of the manly bravado of the sporting culture and prizefighting. He demonstrated the importance of publicly responding to a challenge, named his potential opponent, and coolly let his adversaries know where he wanted to fight. Because Hadley called out Morris Grant, the best black heavyweight in New York, Grant had to show up prepared to fight or risk being shamed as a coward. As expected of him, Grant arrived. He demanded the two men battle for $25. Hadley had to put his money where his mouth was.[8] This was a business meeting. The two "Black Buffers" fought an entertaining four-round draw. Two weeks after the first Grant–Hadley bout, Richard K. Fox of the *National Police Gazette* established the Colored Championship Tournament. The rules were simple;

the boxer who defeated three opponents during the year would receive a gold medal worth $100 dollars and claim the championship. But Fox had another motive behind starting the tournament.

Fox had revenge on his mind and wanted to create a black foe for a white man. The previous year, John L. Sullivan, a heavyweight contender at the time, embarrassed Fox at a sporting saloon when he denied Fox's request to drink with him. Fox never forgave that slight. From the moment Sullivan won the championship in February 1882, Fox used his newspaper to bring down the Boston slugger. He looked for, and promoted, black challengers to defeat Sullivan.[9] What better way was there to disrespect a racist Irish American pugilist then to find a black man to challenge his claim to masculine authority? Thus, from its inception, the colored championship stood as a challenge to white manhood. And the black fighter understood this.

From 1882 to 1908, the black champions—Charles Hadley, George Godfrey, Peter Jackson, Bob Armstrong, Frank Childs, and Jack Johnson—represented the best black bruisers in the business. Although denied true social equality, black pugilists used the colored championship, and the pursuit of that title, to prove their equality with white men. Challenging the white champion signified a front to white supremacy in the ring and American society outside the ropes. Getting the white champion in the ring, however, was a difficult process. White men hid behind the color line.

The color line in boxing indicated who had and did not have racial privileges. In 1882, when Sullivan won the title, he knew enough about race, power, and privilege to proclaim that he would never fight a black man. As Sullivan once told Godfrey, "George, when I get ready to fight rats, dogs, pigs and niggers, I'll give you the first chance."[10] Sullivan's racist stance established the valuable link between whiteness, privilege, and sports, and his prejudice built an insurmountable barrier for black boxers. He used his championship status to achieve what historian Gail Bederman has called "public power."[11] While many sportswriters questioned his stance on the color line, scribes also sympathized with Sullivan's racial rights. As one white writer put it: "Suppose John should go down before black fists—but that cannot be thought of. The American eagle would go off and starve itself to death."[12] In short, the heavyweight championship stood for white supremacy, and if a white fighter lost the title, it would cause a racial upheaval to social order. Every white heavyweight champion followed Sullivan's lead, until 1908, when Tommy Burns sold his privilege for $30,000. After Johnson beat Burns for the championship, in a well-known story, the white press searched for a white hope to defeat Johnson. By 1912, however, without any credible white fighters save the race, white sportswriters subsequently turned black pugilists Joe Jeannette and Sam Langford into black hopes. Although their presence would persist in threatening white masculinity, Jeannette and Langford had so-called "good black" qualities that whites could momentarily live with until a white man could regain the crown.

GEORGE GODFREY, JOHN L. SULLIVAN, AND RACIAL AUTHORITY

Hadley's championship status made the Professor a marked man. Cincinnati's Henry Woodson, Boston's George Godfrey, and Saginaw, Michigan's C.A.C. Smith descended on New York to fight Hadley. Unlike Sullivan, Hadley understood that his role as champion was to face all worthy challengers. For his first title defense, he easily defeated Woodson. Woodson, who won the first round and surprised Hadley with his defensive dexterity, lost stamina by the third round and had to quit the fight to avoid a brutal beating. After the fight, Hadley boldly yelled, "Fetch on some more niggers and I will down them all."[13] Assuming that Hadley actually called his opponents "niggers," it is important to ask, what did he mean by "fetch on some more niggers"? As a noted professor of pugilism, did Hadley make a class distinction between himself and other black fighters? Was he appeasing a white audience? Did a white writer embellish this part? That part is not clear. But his insistence on fighting black men is clear. Hadley had been around boxing long enough to know that white men cowardly hid behind the color line. The last time Hadley challenged a white fighter—Troy's Dick Egan in March 1882—the fighter refused to fight him or any black man.[14] The Professor understood that in the business of boxing, it was easier to arrange fights with black men. He wanted the money, other black men wanted his title, and so he was prepared to "down them all." But his determination to "down them all" would be his downfall. He only held the title for two months. George Godfrey came calling.

The racial symbolism of the Godfrey–Hadley championship fight in February 1883 was pronounced and prophetic, as it foreshadowed the powerlessness the black champion had in the face of white racism. As the two black boxers battled for the championship, John L. Sullivan, in his white power, privilege, and prejudice, performed as the peacekeeper. The racist Sullivan relished the role of referee and the authority the title brought, knowing full well that he would never give either man a chance at his championship. Sullivan declared Godfrey the winner that night, but Godfrey could not have known the depth of Sullivan's racism. He still believed he had a shot at the title. Three years prior, when both he and Godfrey were up-and-coming fighters in Boston, the two men had been in the ring ready to battle, when police stopped the fight for suspicious reasons. Godfrey remembered, "the place was full at $2 a head, and after Sullivan had been rubbed down one of Sullivan's friends went out and brought in a policeman from Howard St. . . . The policeman said to Sullivan 'I know you, you are a South end fellow, and if I were you I would not spar." After his conversation with the policeman, Sullivan surprisingly left the building.[15]

Sullivan would referee black fighters, where he stood as a symbol of authority, but he would never give a black man a chance at true equality. In July 1883, for example, when he heard people making a fuss about C.A.C. Smith as his new challenger, Sullivan told a newspaper, "I won't fight a darky for there is no credit in licking a coon." White sportswriter John B. McCormick took Sullivan to task for his attitude. McCormick believed boxing helped define white power, and he argued Sullivan had to establish the "superiority of the Caucasian race over the negro race." McCormick also remarked, "By the way, if Sullivan's reply to the darky Smith who wants to fight him for the championship is correctly reported John L has queer ideas on the subject of his 'rights and privileges.'"[16] But as a white champion, Sullivan knew exactly what his "rights and privileges" were. He did not have to fight black men.

As champion, Sullivan even took the racial and social authority that derived from his physical prowess to determine who was and was not black. And that meant trouble for Mervine Thompson, an octoroon who was passing as white. Not much is known about Thompson's life prior to his first visit to Boston in June 1883, when, as a Canadian wrestler named Patrick O'Donnell, he tried to pass as a white man and entered in a wrestling tournament, but available documents provide glimpses into his "colored" past.[17] According to the 1870 census, he was born in 1854 in Virginia—it is not known whether slave or free—and Thompson, who claimed he lost his dad and his brothers in the Civil War, lived with a white man, James Webster, in Pavilion, New York, laboring as a farmer.[18] The census enumerator, who had special instruction to "be particularly careful in reporting the class Mulatto . . . because important scientific results depend on the correct determination of this class," marked Thompson as black.[19] Ten years later, however, Thompson's racial status had changed, and the enumerator had marked him as a white man before changing Thompson's designation to mulatto.[20]

Even Sullivan was confused by Thompson's racial ambiguity. In February 1884 after Thompson, "the only man in the country to-day to have a chance to successfully meet Mr. John L. Sullivan," challenged the champion, Sullivan said he had to wait for confirmation before accepting the challenge, because he had heard a rumor that Thompson had "negro blood in his veins."[21] Sullivan only had a rumor to go on, but that was enough for him to delay a battle. If Sullivan broke his stance on the color line, especially to a supposed octoroon, it would destroy both the social capital he owned as the champion and the mystique of whiteness. Despite the fact Sullivan had initial reservations about Thompson's race, most of the sporting public saw him as a white man.

Thompson used fighting to pass, and knew that battling black boxers highlighted his whiteness.[22] Thompson's first fight against a black opponent occurred in March 1884 against C.A.C. Smith. After he beat Smith, the *Boston Globe*'s headline read, "Knocking out a Negro," while the *Cleveland Plain Dealer* reported, "Colored Champion Knocked Out." The *New Orleans Picayune* labeled the match "Thompson, the Cleveland Sullivan, Knocks Out the Colored Champion," and the *San Francisco Bulletin*'s headline read, "A Glove Fight and a Butting Negro," in reference to reports that Smith tried to head-butt Thompson. While some headlines treated Thompson as racially ambiguous, that is to say they did not label his color, others treated him as a white man. The *St. Paul Globe*'s title read, "Smith, the Negro has Grit, but was no match for the White Bruiser." The *Omaha Bee* said "A White Knocks out a Negro at Cleveland," and the *Fort Worth Gazette*'s headline labeled the fight, "A Rough and Tumble Sparring Match in Ohio between a White Man and a Negro."[23] With his thrashing of Smith, Thompson was well on his way to becoming a celebrated white figure—a god that history would not forget—but Sullivan had the championship title, and thus the social capital.

On May 3, 1884, despite a public that had already accepted Thompson as a white man, Sullivan publicly charged Thompson with being black. In an interview with the *Louisville Courier Journal,* the reporter asked Sullivan if he would "lick" Thompson in the street. Sullivan replied, "That's a d——d lie. I have never done anything like that in the seven years that I've been in the profession and I ain't going to begin now. I'll meet that nigger anytime he wants to meet me but on the street I would pass him by, just the same as I would pass the dirt on the street." The idea that Thompson was a "nigger" caught the reporter by surprise, and he followed up by asking if Thompson was a "Nigger." Sullivan answered, "I've never seen him, but one of the boys seen him in Boston when he was wrestling there and they say he's a nigger. He's been charged with it and never denied it. In Boston he went by the name of O'Donnell, but they say his real name's Thompson."[24] Charging somebody with being black without proof was considered libel, but Sullivan, the champion, had the power to act on a mere rumor, and his authoritative assertion had a long-lasting impact on Thompson's life.[25]

This was the type of man Godfrey was up against when he claimed the colored championship in February 1883 and sought to fight Sullivan for the world championship. A man so staunch in his racism, he would go to great lengths to assert and determine someone's masked blackness. Godfrey had no chance of getting into the ring with Sullivan.

Sullivan's racism notwithstanding, Godfrey would much rather fight white men. After all, as he once claimed, "I am satisfied to fight white men. They are easier whipped."[26] But getting a white man to fight him took some doing. White men could always hide behind the color line. To get a white fighter into the ring, Godfrey relied on the idea that publicly challenging his masculinity would push him to fight. In 1887, during Godfrey's negotiations with Jack Ashton, Ashton kept insisting on fighting for $1,000, despite the fact Godfrey wanted to battle for $500, the largest amount he could find backing for. Sensing that Ashton was avoiding the match, Godfrey went to the *Police Gazette* to draw him out. Godfrey argued, "I learn that Jack Ashton won't fight me for less than $1,000 a side and $1,000 gate receipts. I also see that in the same papers he offers to meet Pat Kilrain and other fighters for $1,000 a side alone. Now what is the difference? Why can't he meet me on those terms? He is either afraid to fight me or else hasn't got any money. I have all the money I want and would like to have a go at him."[27] There could not have been a worse insult than for a black man to question the manliness of a white man. Although it took another two years to get Ashton into the ring—and a year after Godfrey lost his colored championship—when Godfrey and Ashton battled in 1889, the Black Bostonian knocked him out in the fourteenth round to win $1,200.[28]

After the Ashton victory, although no longer the champion, Godfrey continued to see his fight purses against white sluggers soar. In 1890, he faced the talented Patsy Cardiff and the credible "Denver" Ed Smith, and he won $1,500 and $1,800, respectively. The following year he battled his old nemesis Jack Kilrain in San Francisco for $8,500. Although Godfrey lost a hard-fought forty-four-round battle, he earned $1,000 for his troubles. Because he fought gamely, he still could command a fair price for his skills, and in 1892 he bested Joe Lannon for $2,200, and he lost to the Jewish American star Joe Choynski in a $5,000 match. In 1894, the Irish champion Peter Maher knocked him out, and Godfrey took home the losers' share of a $1,200 contest.[29] For white men, the aged Godfrey was still a credible contestant, but not as dangerous a proposition as other black fighters, so many felt they could lift their color line to battle him.

As the colored champion, Godfrey only defended his title three times against black men. He battled McHenry Johnson twice—once in 1884 for

$250 and another time in 1888 for $750—and lost to Peter Jackson, the "Black Prince," in 1888 in a $1,400 contest. Jackson was too big, fast, and skilled for Godfrey. He had his man by twenty-five pounds and used his weight advantage and fistic prowess to pummel Godfrey for nineteen rounds. After he won the championship, Jackson had no desires to defend his title. He only engaged in exhibitions against black men and did not give them a shot at his championship. Jackson wanted the world heavyweight championship. He wanted to fight white men.

THE BLACK PRINCE AND WHITE PRIVILEGE

For four years, Jackson tried to get Sullivan into the ring, but the white champion did not budge. Jackson even had members of the white press supporting his cause. A writer for the *New York Sun* argued, "there must be no bigotry in champions' methods. They cannot be choosers anymore than can beggars. There can therefore be no professional tolerance of Mr. SULLIVAN'S refusal to contest the fistic palm with the Australian black man, Jackson, who has just wiped the Pacific Slope with JOSEPHUS McAULIFFE." According to the *Sun* writer, not only had Tom Cribb famously fought the black American Tom Molineaux in 1810 for the heavyweight championship, but he also added, "the whole history of warfare shows that it admits of no color line. White men have not only fought face to face with negroes, as in the case of the British against the Zulus at Isandlwana, but they have fought shoulder to shoulder with them, as at the recent battle of Suaka [*sic*], where the black troops were particularly mentioned for bravery." The writer continued with his diatribe, reminding readers, "the Constitution forbids any discrimination against the dark skin."[30] Sullivan did not care about the Constitution; he cared about his white privilege.

Despite his black skin, Jackson's disposition made whites momentarily content with his potential championship. Speaking about a potential fight between Jackson and Sullivan, the *Inter Ocean* gleaned, "There can be now no question that Sullivan is the finest specimen of brute strength in man at present time in America, unless the exception be made in favor of Peter Jackson, whom, forsooth, the champion refuses to meet, because he is a colored man." But unlike Sullivan, Jackson was "a temperate, sober, unassuming fighter and not a drunken bully who frequently disgraces and degrades the nobles fight of nature."[31] In other words, he was a "good black," a black man with a white soul, many said. Whites believed they did not have to worry about Jackson challenging white superiority, because he knew his place. White writers frequently regarded Jackson with having black skin, but a white soul.[32] Trevor

Wignall, a white boxing writer from the 1920s, reflected, "Even to-day he is frequently called the whitest black man who ever lived." On another occasion Wignall concluded, Jackson "was black only in hue; otherwise he was as white as snow."[33] But a white soul was not a white skin, and character only counted for so much. Sentiments could not trump Sullivan's feelings of racial privilege. The only way he would fight Jackson, Sullivan concluded, was if he could "fight the nigger with nothing but a baseball bat."[34] Jackson did not have any rights that Sullivan needed to respect.

Sullivan's overt racism toward Jackson, however, irritated the respectable sensibilities of the black press. In comparing Jackson to Sullivan, the *Indianapolis Freeman* remarked, "Peter Jackson, unlike our country's blowhard and 'ham' actor, John L. Sullivan, is a gentleman and a fighter." The editor also argued, "MR. JOHN L. SULLIVAN, the 'bean eating' gladiator, of Boston, objects to standing up before a Negro. All right, nobody objects but coming from a man instead of an animal, how silly and purile [*sic*] such an objection would seem."[35] They saw Jackson as a middle-class black hero, and the black press hoped that one day their class would trump their race. If Jackson could get over on whites, then so could the black middle class. Sullivan's ardent racism, however, reinforced to the black middle class the unbendable power of the color line.

In hopes of enticing Sullivan into the ring, Jackson kept fighting the best white fighters.[36] In May 1891, Jackson fought one of the most critical contests of his career when he contested San Francisco native "Gentleman" Jim Corbett for $10,000. Although, for three years, Corbett had drawn the color line against Jackson, Corbett momentarily sidestepped his personal Jim Crow system, because he believed that a victory over Jackson would net him a match against Sullivan. He was right. Corbett's sixty-one-round no-contest with Jackson—the club stopped the fight because neither man had enough energy to finish off his opponent—convinced white fans that Corbett was worthy of a title shot. In September 1892, Corbett outclassed Sullivan to win the championship.

Jackson wasted very little time in challenging the new champion. Jackson believed that Corbett had forfeited his racial privileges when he fought him the first time, and thus he could not cite the color line. Jackson told a London reporter, "If Sullivan had worsted Corbett I would have nothing to say, for I know that Sullivan declines to meet colored men. But it is not so with Corbett . . . I am willing to fight anywhere except in towns where the color line is drawn."[37] For his part, during a shouting match with Australian heavyweight Joe Goddard, Corbett claimed he was not hiding, and he told

Goddard, "I'll fight Jackson, as soon as he gets ready, for any amount he wants."[38] In July 1893 Jackson's manager, Parson Davies, signed articles of agreement with Corbett for a match to take place after Corbett's battle with white contender Charles Mitchell. The articles also stipulated the fight had to be above the Mason-Dixon line.[39] The following January, Corbett knocked out Mitchell, opening the gate for the Jackson bout.

Whiteness had its privileges. A few months after Corbett defeated Mitchell, Corbett reminded Jackson about the limits of a black man's racial rights in the ring. In an interview, Corbett stated, "in view of what has passed in pugilism, Peter Jackson, on account of his color, ought to feel highly flattered that I ever recognized him as a fighter."[40] But Corbett was not done yet. The champion claimed he would fight Jackson, but insisted on battling in Jacksonville, Florida. He knew Jackson feared the possibility of southern racial violence and would not fight in the South. If Jackson changed his mind and agreed to fight in the South, Jim Crow would constantly embarrass the proud black man. In the end, on account of his racial pride, Jackson refused to fight. He told a reporter, "It is pretty plain that all this is merely an advertising dodge of Corbett's. I am tired of being a party to it, and I quit right here."[41] Corbett, however, used Jackson's prideful refusal as an opportunity to label Jackson as an uppity black man. "The truth of the matter," Corbett said, "is that this man hates Americans because he is not allowed to pose and strut about and be looked up to and worshipped as he is on the other side of the water." After more character-damaging words, Corbett concluded, "Peter is a coward."[42] Waiting for Corbett to fight, however, effectively ended Jackson's career. The distraught Jackson did not fight until 1898 when he needed the money. In the interim, his muscles grew soft, dissipating from heavy drinking. He died in 1901 of tuberculosis.

BOB ARMSTRONG, FRANK CHILDS, AND WHITE FEAR

During Parson Davies's tenure as Jackson's manager, Davies learned that he could make money by marketing a muscular black man as a white champion's foe. At the peak of Jackson's career, Jackson was one of the most marketable fighters on three continents. Everywhere he went fans—white and black—mobbed him. During the 1890s, only three other fighters—Jim Corbett, Bob Fitzsimmons, and George Dixon—could match Jackson's appeal. Davies believed that a credible black fighter in Jackson's mold could re-create that star power. In 1895, Davies found a new man to do the trick and crowned Iowa's Bob Armstrong the colored champion.

Like other black champions, Armstrong had a tough upbringing. Born the son of ex-slaves in Rogersville, Tennessee, in 1873 his family abandoned a Tennessee plantation and a life as sharecroppers and migrated to Washington, Iowa, where his dad, Roger, found work on a farm. In Washington, Armstrong attended school until the fourth grade when he got "'too big' to go to school." He found work helping with the trotting horses, and he labored at the racetracks in Des Moines and Minneapolis until he realized he could not make a living working the tracks. "Finding that 'swiping horses' wasn't a profitable occupation," Armstrong claimed he "took one of those side door sleepers [empty box cars] and proceeded to Des Moines. That's where my career as a fighter started." Desperate for money, he had his first prizefight in 1894, when a white man, Bill Crockett, walked into a bar and challenged any man to a fight. The $1.50 Armstrong earned after he whipped his white opponent convinced Armstrong to change his career path.[43]

Armstrong's size, 6'3" and 200 pounds of ripped muscles, deservedly caught the media's attention. He reminded whites of Peter Jackson. After his knockout victory over black Chicagoan Will Mayo in 1897, the *Chicago Tribune* glowingly wrote, "The big colored man is a copy in some respects of Peter Jackson; has a low guard, a piston rod movement of the arms, and is especially

The *Los Angeles Herald* mocks the color and size of Bob Armstrong as a typically skinny Sambo character. At the time, Armstrong was known for his muscularly defined body. (1898, *Los Angeles Herald*)

quick at whipping in the right at close quarters."[44] Ex-fighter Dan Creedon added, "If I ever told the truth in my life it wouldn't surprise me a bit to see this Armstrong come to be champion heavyweight of the world."[45] In an article entitled, "Parson Davies's Colored Hercules," the *San Francisco Call* told readers Armstrong "is a wonderful human structure, built on the same lines as Peter Jackson, whom he resembles greatly in features. He is not so clever as Peter, but he is shifty and is apt in learning."[46] Unfortunately, too much press, and excessive fawning over his physical prowess, hurt Armstrong's potential profits. White fighters got scared.

The real revenue was in fighting credible white men, but the more press a black pugilist received, the more his chances of reaping financial rewards diminished because he became a threat to a white manhood. Top white fighters who believed they were on the cusp of fighting for a championship would not risk their luster against a credible black foe. As a Philadelphia promoter acknowledged, when top white fighters "found out they were to meet Armstrong they immediately drew the color line."[47] In 1897, at the height of Armstrong's fame, Davies complained, "As to Bob Armstrong, my colored heavyweight, he cannot get a match on account of the color line being drawn. Big Jim Jeffries of California, and Ruhlin, the 'Dutch' giant of Akron, O., have drawn the line of color. Jeffries has fought colored men, but they were not as big or good as Armstrong. You can readily see why these pugilists draw the safety line."[48] In fact, Jeffries—an up and coming heavyweight during Armstrong's short reign as colored champion—did not fight Armstrong until after Armstrong lost his championship.

The color line forced Armstrong to face tough black competition if he wanted to make a living fighting, and black men were always ready to take on the challenge, especially Frank Childs. On January 29, 1898, Davies matched Armstrong with his sparring partner, Childs. Childs, whom the *San Francisco Chronicle* once described as "strong as an ox and his muscular development around the chest and arms is something out of the common," had been a popular boxer in New Mexico and in California before making his way to Chicago in 1893.[49] But Childs struggled to find meaningful work in the ring and had to settle for work as Armstrong's sparring partner. As the supposed "sure loser" in his championship bout with Armstrong, in January 1898, Childs only earned $20. To everyone's surprise, "The local pugilist shattered the newspaper fame and pugilistic aspirations of 'Parson' Davies' world challenger." The next month, Childs and Armstrong had a rematch in Cincinnati. At that time, the city was using boxing, much like it used baseball, to booster its reputation, and the Childs–Armstrong match was centerpiece to those plans. Before the match, a local writer described Armstrong, admiring, "His enormous height is apparent only on contrast, so perfectly is he proportioned. He is on the greyhound order, but superbly muscled."[50] He was five inches taller than Childs, but his left jab, the only punch he seemed to have the night of their rematch, could not get in. Childs spent six rounds ducking under the jab, getting inside, throwing lefts to the breadbasket, and then coming upstairs with a well-placed right to the jaw. In the sixth round, desperate to improve his chances, Armstrong rushed his man, but Childs caught him with a perfect punch. Armstrong "staggered and wabbled [sic] sideways to the ropes. He was like a crippled rooster in the pit. He went flying around the ring, first leaning to one side and then on the other." When he stood up, Childs caught him with a left and wobbled him again. His manager "humanely threw up the sponge." With that defeat, Armstrong's hopes at the heavyweight title "collapsed" like "a toy balloon punctured with the point of a needle."[51]

As the new colored champion, Childs's victory should have produced profits, but race restricted his revenue. White men feared him too. According to a Chicago writer, Childs "never had a chance—that the fact that he is black and poor without the fight of talk or a clever manager had kept him down fighting for what little he could pick up around the city." The paper also noted, "Childs is a powerfully built, very black, good-humored negro, standing about 5 feet 9 ½ [inches], weighing 165 pounds. . . . He is a comedian and a clown in the ring and seldom seems to exert himself in battle." The reporter continued, "All his clowning, however, is but a mask for a punch that is as hard as a cannon-shot, as quick as a flash of lighting. If he would settle down to business, train hard and fight with care, the man could whip the best of them at his weight, barring Joe Choynski."[52] Childs went undefeated in the ring from 1895 to 1902, and held the colored championship for four years, but he never received the financial windfall he deserved.

JACK JOHNSON ERASES THE COLOR LINE

There was something about the skinny kid from Galveston, Texas, that captured boxing writers' imagination. In 1900, for example, after seeing Johnson beat the black fighter Josh Mills (Ohio) in Memphis, a local reporter described the action: "Hammer and tongs are naught. Sledge hammers and pile-drivers and catapults are nearer to the mark." In that bout, Johnson, a 10–3 favorite, knocked his man down in every round, and twice in the sixth round. From the opening gong, Mills, while clever and aggressive, had no answers for Johnson's defense and counterpunches. Johnson was, even at that green stage of his career, a skilled defensive fighter that most heavyweights could only hope to be. Johnson, the reporter sized up, "is a threat against any negro heavyweight in this country." A month later, after Johnson defeated "Klondike" John Haines in Memphis, the same writer announced, "Johnson is likely to become the best colored heavy-weight in the country," and added, "For a negro he has an intelligent face."[53] The writer, however, also cautioned that Johnson would have to be more aggressive in the ring, a common critique of Johnson throughout his career. "Johnson lacks but one thing that is useful in his business, and that is a knockout blow. He will have to develop one before he achieves distinction in the ring. If his hands were as fast as his feet he would be a dangerous contender for the championship honors." To be sure, Johnson's counterpunches and precise uppercuts were worse than a one-punch knockout for his opponents. The barrage of punches, combined with his impregnable defense, suffocated and smothered his opponents. In his Memphis fight with "Klondike," Johnson closed his opponents' eye early in the fight and continued to wallop Haines in the eye, forcing the young black fighter to quit.

Johnson finally received his coveted chance at the colored championship in 1902. Coming into his match against Frank Childs in Los Angeles, most local experts did not give Johnson a chance. "Built on the plan of an ebony Hercules, possessing a bull neck and tremendous biceps," Childs had not lost a fight in seven years. The *Los Angeles Express* reasoned that "when a man who has not made any more of a national reputation than Johnson, be he ever so good a fighter, goes against the colored champion of the world, it is to be expected that he will be on the short end of the betting."[54] But Johnson was ready for this fight. This one was personal. When Johnson first started in the business, and had traveled to Chicago in the late 1890s, Childs hired Johnson as a sparring partner. "Frank didn't have a dollar to pay me, but he bestowed on me the title of 'head trainer,' which had a nice ring to it! Since we didn't have enough money to rent two rooms, I slept in the bed with Frank." One night, however, when Childs's wife arrived in town, Childs put Johnson out in the snow. Johnson remembered, "I didn't have enough in my pocket to pay for a five-cent bed. I spent the rest of the night wandering the streets, in the rain, sometime stopping in a doorway for a bit of shelter until I heard a policeman's footsteps. Then I would start walking again." Johnson never forgot that moment. When he faced Childs for the championship in Los Angeles, he was "merciless." "I gave it to him good for a full thirteen rounds, hitting him like a hammer hits an anvil," he said. Johnson won.[55]

No colored champion understood his economic worth more than Johnson. He first asserted his economic power and privileges when he negotiated his second title defense against Sam McVey. Their first contest in February 1903—a victory for Johnson—received a lot of fanfare, and the public clamored for a rematch. "In the Johnson-McVey fight," the *Los Angeles Express* reasoned, "the public will be given the greatest card in the pugilistic world today, with the possible exception of a fight between Jeffries and a white man who is in his class. But such a man is not to be found at this time, so the Johnson-McVey contest follows as the next highest on the card."[56] Johnson recalled that after the first McVey fight, "several critics went so far as to say that the two of us had been equal and that only chance could have made the scales tip in favor of one or the other. . . . This opinion put forth by certain journalists encouraged Sam and his partisans. From the minute they heard it, they were eager to sign for a rematch with me." Knowing this, Johnson "waited only for the necessary funds to be raised to offer me a sufficiently large purse."[57] Although the local promoter, "Uncle Tom" McCarey, believed he had a sure deal with Johnson, Johnson turned to clubs in San Francisco to create a bidding war until McCarey guaranteed to pay for both fighters' expenses and guaranteed $4,000 for the fighters to split. Johnson got what he wanted.[58]

Like his predecessors, Johnson wanted to use the colored championship as a springboard to take on the white champion. During his reign as champion, Johnson battled some of the best black fighters in the history of the sport, but he also believed it was his right to fight Jeffries for the championship. By 1903, a number of writers on the West Coast supported Johnson's challenge. The *Los Angeles Times* claimed, "The public, through the daily newspapers, demands a fight for the championship on behalf of Jack Johnson. Jeffries must heed the call."[59] A local writer predicted, "A match between [Johnson] and Jeffries would attract the attention of the entire world."[60] San Francisco promoters also tried to persuade Jeffries to fight Johnson. In December 1903, San Francisco's leading fight promoter, "Sunny Jim" Coffroth, traveled to New York to convince Jeffries to cross the color line. Coffroth told Jeffries that Johnson was the only man San Francisco sports wanted to see him battle; however, the champ did not budge.[61] Two months later, Jeffries told a reporter, "You can't make it 'too strong.' I don't think the public wants me to defend my title against any one but a white man. Don't think I am afraid of a negro. I'm not. They can be licked just as easily as anybody else. I simply have promised myself that I would fight only white men, and I won't break my word."[62] Although Jeffries had battled black fighters in the past—Hank Griffin, Peter Jackson, and Bob Armstrong—Jeffries stayed true to his word. He retired in 1905, after he dispensed all suitable white men.

The two white champions that followed Jeffries, Marvin Hart and Tommy Burns, failed to carry the mantle of white greatness. Hart, a lackluster heavyweight and a Kentucky native, who earned a controversial decision over Johnson in March 1905 before he won the championship, told fans in Louisville, "Johnson can keep on challenging till he is white in the face. That is all the good it will do him. I never wanted to fight a black man, but was forced into a meeting with him and then defeated him soundly. Johnson will not get any other chance."[63] Luckily for Johnson, Hart talked better than he fought. His reign as a champion was short-lived. He lost his title to Burns the following year. Burns, a Canadian, coveted the money more than the championship. In a well-known story, Johnson chased the elusive championship until 1908, when Burns finally dropped the color line. Johnson easily demolished Burns.[64] Like his white predecessors, Johnson had no plans to fight black men. He only wanted white foes.

WHITE PRESS, BLACK HOPES

Between 1908 and 1912, Johnson's ability to defeat all credible white opponents put the white press in a bind. No white man could beat him. When white hope Frank Moran lost in 1911 to a second-rate white fighter named Joe Savage, the *New York Times* dejectedly wrote, "The army of the 'white hopes' suffered another drop in its membership roll last night when Frank Moran of Pittsburg drew his discharge papers and qualified as a bona fide member of the Order of Exploded Phenoms."[65] To pile on the problem, white heavyweights could not defeat any of the top black challengers, Sam Langford, Joe Jeannette, and Sam McVey. R. H. Cain of the *Philadelphia Record* pointedly stated, "This agitation over the heavyweight championship among the white heavies may develop some really good man, for the reward for effort in that line is well paid nowadays, but there will always be shivers running down the backs of these ambitious heavy-weights as long as Sam Langford is running loose."[66] Knowing this reality, some writers argued that white hopes "should not go any further than the white race."[67] In 1911, *Boxing*, a weekly magazine in London, nervously reported, "We [white people] don't seem to have advanced much further in our investigations as to the identity of the white man who is to wrest the crown of supremacy from the colored race." The writer declared, "We want a real good man, too and we want him badly. With Sam McVey making almost an even break of it with Langford, the four top places must be conceded to the representatives of the colored race.... Either could almost certainly have disposed, with ease, of the very best white man in the world, and the conclusion is not a very gratifying one."[68] A *New York Globe* writer weighed in on the situation and complained, "It will not be long before the white hope class will be as hopeless as it was the evening that Jim Jeffries took the count at Reno. Over the big stretch of the world there does not appear a white man who is capable of giving Jack Johnson even a little bit of a run for his title."[69]

For the black press, the whole ordeal of the white hope was laughable. Lester Walton wrote, "Finding a 'white hope,' one who will be able to provide Champion 'Jack' Johnson at least several rounds of lively entertainment, seems to be a hopeless task these days." Walton continued, "Each week ushers in a new 'white hope' who, after he has given an exhibition of his fistic prowess, is ushered out of the back door in a woeful state, both mentally and physically, and with all the aspiration he once possessed relative to some day being Johnson's antagonist shattered and as badly damaged as the ambitious one's physiognomy."[70] Another black writer joked, "It is a hard pill for some of these weak kneed sore headed white sports to swallow, but what can they do? There is no one in sight to beat Johnson and besides, we have several other dangerous blacks who can beat any of the present white hopes."[71] In their mockery of the white hope, one headline for the *Philadelphia Tribune* read, "White Hopes Not Safe Until Langford in Jail," while another headline mocked, "Other Black Boxers Better Than Pale Skins." In the latter article, the writer concluded, "And another thing sticks out prominently when we are told to hope for the early return of supremacy of the white race. There are exactly three large clouds on the horizon that must be taped before such a situation can be brought about. These clouds are labeled Jeannette, Langford, and McVey . . . but alas and alack, there isn't a white person in sight who stands the ghost of a chance with them."[72] Without a quality white hope on the horizon, what options did whites have?

The white press saw the same racial reality. In a 1912 article entitled "Jack Johnson's Successor Will Probably Not Be a White Fight," *Cleveland Plain Dealer* writer J. P. Garvey argued that McVey, Langford, and Jeannette were the best fighters, and "the white hopes are not experienced enough to beat either of these stellar negroes."[73] In hopes of wresting the title away from Johnson, whites demanded that Johnson fight one of these fighters. When Johnson drew the color line, so to speak, the press called him a coward for assuming the same rights and privileges white champions had assumed. But Johnson dictated the terms, he had all the power, and Johnson, the son of ex-slaves, would decide who he would fight and for how much money. He made it clear that if promoters wanted him to fight a black man, they would have to offer the same price they gave him to fight a white man, $30,000.

What did the white press see in Jeannette and Langford that softened the press on the race issue? Like Peter Jackson before him, Jeannette had respectable qualities that whites could live with. "Although some people look down upon Negroes, no white man ever conducted himself better in any branch of the sport than Joe Jeannette," reasoned one white writer. Jeannette had "the good will of the white people" and was a credit to his race.[74] *The New York Sun* noted that Jeannette's features "are more of the Hindu or North American Indian type than the full blooded Negro. His skin is a rich nut brown and when he is in perfect condition it flows with health, which, together with his wonderful muscular structure makes him a sight worth more than a second glance." Their description of the light-skinned pugilist prompted the black writer Lester Walton to argue, "that Johnson is a Negro without any question of a doubt has always been a source of gratification to me; for had he been even of a dark brown in hue long ago some white writers would have sought to prove that he was other than of Africa extraction."[75]

For his part, Jeannette played the role of black hope well. On several occasions Jeannette called Johnson a coward, a "moving picture fighter," and noted "this hop, skip, and jump affairs will not do. He is afraid to meet me because he knows he cannot whip me over a long route."[76] Besides calling out Johnson, Jeannette frequently attached himself to the next great white hope, like Frank Moran, and trained them to battle Johnson. If one of his fighters lost, he found himself another white hope to train.[77] Jeannette was not an "Uncle Tom," but his constant persistence to train white hopes fit the personality type that whites wanted to see in blacks. The sight of a big black man sacrificing his championship aspirations for a white fighter reminded whites of the old loyal Negro.

This concept of a loyal Negro also rang true with Sam Langford, the "Boston Tarbaby," who, although vicious in the ring, had a nickname that conjured up images of the old plantation days of the docile Negro. And Langford played the part. At one point, for example, Langford suggested, "I may be colored, but I've got a white heart."[78] The press took note. As one Los Angeles writer noted, "Sam Langford has often been called 'demon' the 'cave man,' the 'giant killer.' Judging from these terrible names one might believe to meet Samuel would be taking one's life in one's hands. But two-minutes' conversation with him would dispel the fears of the most timid. Sam is nothing but a real, live, jolly, good-natured man and a real one at that. . . ." "As for being a demon or anything else of that kind," the writer continued, "that is simply press agent talk. He would not harm a child, he loved children too well."[79]

Langford and his white manager, Joe Woodman, smartly used Langford's first southern venture, a trip to Memphis in January 1910 to fight the "Dixie

Kid" Aaron Brown, to also make the case about the anti-Johnson black man. They wanted to show that he had the power to defeat Johnson and the docility to be the proper black champion. In the Memphis ring, Langford proved he had the stuff. The white press could not help but to fawn over his body: "When Langford strips, one is surprised at the breadth of his shoulders and his depth through the chest. About the shoulders he's probably just as big as Jim Jeffries today."[80] Jeffries was nearly five inches taller than Langford. In the ring, Langford proved all business. Against "Dixie Kid" he was so dominant and dangerous, the "Dixie Kid" fell down several times in the fight to avoid punches. In the third round, the former welterweight champion was so defeated he tried to stay down for good, but referee Dave Berry kicked him and forced him to his feet. He only lasted two more rounds. But proving his worth in the ring was only half the battle. They had to show white southerners that Langford knew his place. Woodman told the *Memphis Commercial Appeal* that Langford and Johnson were two different types of blacks. Under the byline that read, "Negroes but Different," Woodman convinced the press that Langford saved his money while Johnson would die a pauper. The paper also noted that Langford bought a house for his black wife in Cambridge, Massachusetts, whereas Johnson was an urban vagabond never willing to settle in his proper place.[81] Remarks like that played perfectly in the South. The local writers took notice. One writer observed, "Langford is really the idol of the negro race. He is looked up to in ability fully as much as Johnson, and he is liked better by his race, for he has shown none of the disagreeable traits of the Galveston negro. He is reputed quiet and unassuming, with never a thought of ever being on equal with the white men."[82] If the white hope Jeffries failed, they had their man.

For the white press, the issues of race, sex, and marriage were never far from the conversation in context of Johnson and the black hopes. As champion, Johnson laid public claim to his manly authority and openly flaunted the white women in his life. He dressed them lavishly and dared anyone to say anything about his love life.[83] If it was true that only another black man could beat Johnson, then that black man had better know his place. Langford knew his place. In 1910, after rumors in Memphis circulated that Langford tried to stay at a white hotel, Woodman claimed, "Langford knows his place. He didn't try to stop at a white hotel, and even had he wanted to, I wouldn't have allowed him to queer us by trying to get a room in a big hotel here . . . I was fixed up at the Arlington and he went down to Beale."[84] On the subject of race, thrift, and marriage, a writer for the *Picayune* noted, "There has been more scandal connected with Jack Johnson since he became prominent in

Canadian-born Sam Langford in a fight pose. (1910–1915, Library of Congress)

pugilism than there was with the names of all the other negro boxers put together." "Take the case of Jeannette and Langford," the writer observed, "they are both married men who follow fighting for the sake of earning enough to keep their families as comfortable as they can." The writer finished by noting that Johnson's "private life has been such that it has often been wondered that any well-regulated community would stand for him, and he has done more to turn people against black fighters than all the men of his race put together."[85]

The quest to make Langford into a black hope, however, did not sit well with the black press. Walton of the *New York Age* noted, "After searching every nook and corner of the earth for a 'white hope' to give Champion Jack Johnson a serious argument at fisticuffs, and all to no good purpose, those most active in this world-wide search have hit upon another plan of attack—to try and recapture the championship title through a black hope."[86] Even though Langford reportedly lived clean and harbored their middle-class values, blacks did not trust Langford as champion. In short, they feared he would be a race traitor. After hearing a rumor that Langford would dope Johnson if they fought, and then let a white man beat him, a writer for the *Defender* remarked, "To think such a villainous plot should be hatched against our noble Jack, and for one of his own race to participate in it, gives us much pain." The paper further suggested that Langford had a lot to learn about being a race man, and that "if he will but walk in the noble footsteps of the first colored champion of the world, he will teach these petty whites that the time for buying and selling a Negro has long since passed." In 1914, after Johnson said he would fight Langford, the *Chicago Defender* claimed blacks were afraid of Langford and would "have no particular love for him." The writer also added that rumors suggesting Langford would let a white fighter beat him "make even their [blacks] regard for him grow less."[87] But black contempt toward Langford only lasted until Jess Willard defeated Johnson in April 1915. Soon after Willard became the champion, the *Defender* promoted Langford as a championship challenger. When whites did not need Langford, however, he went back to being the same savage whites had portrayed him as. Unfortunately for Langford, Willard drew the color line. Even if Willard had not drawn the line himself, the white press would never let him tangle with Langford. In reality, he too presented too many racial problems for white America.

5

SAMBOS, SAVAGES, AND THE SHAKINESS OF WHITENESS

Whites called him "the original nigger in the woodpile," "smoke," "cave man," "Tham," "Sambo," and most commonly, the "Boston Tarbaby," but with one look at Sam Langford's body, one had to acknowledge his physical perfection. "Built like a wedge, with strong, wide, shoulders. His body narrows down from shoulders to feet, and he is the very picture of strength well muscled and hard. He has long, rangy arms, and is capable of very powerful blows," one writer fawned.[1] In the ring Langford's brawny black body turned into a fighting machine. Langford, who was born in Nova Scotia, was so vicious that one southern white writer joked, "Local 'mammies' will probably use Langford's name as a sort of 'bugaboo' to scare their pickaninnies into the straight and narrow path."[2] Regardless of his opponent's race—whites often complained that black fighters lacked aggression when they faced each other—Langford attacked his rivals with violent, yet controlled, aggression. While white fighters often showed trepidation before they tangled with Langford, black fighters readily battled. They rarely had a choice. He fought the best black boxers in the business: Jack Blackburn, Dave Holly, Young Peter Jackson, the "Dixie Kid" Aaron Brown, Joe Jeannette, Joe Gans, Sam McVey, Joe Walcott, and Jack Johnson. Although Langford was black—very black—in the context of manliness and physicality, white fans appreciated his skillful fistic attacks and his magnificent body. He displayed what white men thought whites had inherited: violent, yet controlled, aggression.

There was something both primal and powerful that pulled white men to prizefights. "The old Saxon lust for blood, which must have an outlet in a strong race, was satisfied in this fight," one writer observed in 1905.[3] The

toughness, discipline, courage, physicality, and manly aggression white boxers displayed were thought to be inherent racial qualities that proved white
authority over the rest of the world. "This contest of men with padded gloves
on their hands is sport that belongs unequally to the English-speaking race,"
Jack London once observed. "No genius or philosopher devised it and per-
suaded the race to adopt it as the racial sport of sports. It is as deep as our
consciousness and is woven into the fibers of our being. It grew as our very
language grew. It is an instinctive passion of race."[4] Contrary to their racial
arrogance, however, white men did not have a monopoly on pugilism or
physicality.

Black boxers' ring superiority challenged any notion whites assumed about
white physical authority. This was especially true of a man like Langford,
who had a knack for the knockout. In 1910, his pugilistic presence became
such a problem in Pittsburgh that the chief of police prohibited Langford
from fighting a white man, Montana Jack, in the city, because, as the chief
claimed, the "one-sided show" would produce race prejudices. In fact, between 1902 and 1912, Langford only lost to one white fighter—a reported bad
decision by the referee—and often had to fight white fighters in higher weight
classes because white men his own size refused to meet him on equal terms.[5]
Hoping to coax white fighters into battle with Langford, white dailies often
mocked their white brethren, like Stanley Ketchel, as cowards for avoiding
contests with Langford. White manhood had to be proved. Most white fighters remained unmoved but, still, there were some white men brave enough
to try to tackle the tumultuous task, including heavyweights Jim Barry and
Jim Flynn, who each outweighed Langford by more than twenty pounds.
Langford demolished them too. One fight against Flynn was so racially re-
pugnant, Los Angeles writer Harry Carr headlined his article "Cold, Gory
Horror, Pitiful, Revolting," to describe the destruction. The racial imagery
Carr created was literally one of a white man versus a black gorilla. "Flynn,
was put into the ring with the negro, who, in physique, is a shaven gorilla."
Carr asserted, "It wasn't hot, passionate, blood-letting. It was cold, deliberate slaughter." "Langford, the cave man, would put his left hand against the
white man's bleeding face and push him away to arm's length, his little red pig
eyes running critically over the maimed white body, a connoisseur selecting
a vital spot: then his fist would drive in with a crash." Before Langford ended
the fight, he "looked over the white boy's shoulder down at the sporting reporters," and he told the reporters, "'I'm going to git him in a minute." And
Langford did just that. "A black arm shot to the white man's blood smeared

The *San Francisco Chronicle* sketches Sam Langford as the bogeyman, inferring that white fighters are terrified of the black Langford. (1910, *San Francisco Chronicle*)

jaw," and knocked Flynn cold out. "Without disrespect to Langford," Carr insisted, "It was like a white boy fighting a jungle man."[6]

Seeing the muscular black body in the ring was an important revelation for whites, because previously it had been thought to a white populace anxious about its racial position that black muscles were only suitable for manual labor. To put it another way, as scholar Ronald L. Jackson asserts, "Since the emergence of race as a social construct, Black bodies have become surfaces of racial representation. To say it bluntly, race is about bodies that have been assigned social meanings."[7] The black boxer's half-naked body revealed his musculature, and his actions in the ring against white opponents demonstrated the new capabilities of his body, that, when pitted against white pugilists, challenged whites' conception of the interconnection of manliness, civilization, and white superiority. Commenting on the importance of white muscles as a symbol of racial superiority, scholar Richard Dyer explained, "The body often figures very effectively as a point of final explanation of social difference. By this argument, whites—and men—are where they are socially by virtue of biological, that is, bodily superiority. The sight of the body can be a kind of proof."[8] But with two muscular men stripped down in the ring, with no perceived advantages, boxing exposed the ideologies of white manhood and racial superiority. White bodies were not supposed to seem so fragile. As Dyer argued, "A naked body is a vulnerable body. . . . The bare body has no protection from the elements—but also in a social sense." "The exposed white male body is liable to pose the legitimacy of white male power: why should people who look like that—so unimpressive . . . have so much power," Dyer concluded.[9] If the ring represented an arena for racial superiority, and a contest of manhood, what would whites say about a black man like Langford, who showed no regard for supposed white authority? Rather than acknowledge black muscular and physical superiority, whites socially and legally prevented the black body from becoming a legitimate challenge to white manhood.

While fighters drew the color line, and cities and states banned interracial competition. White sportswriters did their part to by caricaturizing black boxers in a myriad of despicable ways to assuage white anxieties, and thus allowed for their continuation of their white voyeurism to see and to believe that the black body somehow represented denigration. These racial descriptions included portraying black fighters as docile Sambos, uncivilized savages, or comparing black musculature to animals. For instance, writer Harry Carr once told his readers, "Langford is simply a cave man. His is not an athlete: he is a chapter out of the mysterious and prehistoric past."[10] In juxtaposition to their descriptions of black bodies, white writers propped up white bodies as embodiments of racial superiority. Champions like Sullivan, Corbett, and Jeffries demonstrated the innate determination, aggression, and physicality white men had within them to succeed. Importantly, these descriptions of black and white bodies occurred just as anthropologists started to legitimize social Darwinian thought, and as confirmed experts in their own field, sportswriters' words read like legitimate explorations into civilized whiteness and uncivilized black manhood.[11] As black men kept winning, these derogatory racial descriptions took on supreme importance because the disparaging descriptions offered protectionism to the fallacy of physical manhood as it related to racial power.

This became even more imperative when Jack Johnson won the heavyweight championship in 1908. His vicious victory over Tommy Burns emphatically embodied blacks' persistent physical challenges to racial assumptions about white superiority. Collectively, to save the race, whites placed their hope in ex–heavyweight champion Jim Jeffries, the greatest white man of them all, and trusted he would win the championship back from Johnson, and thus reestablish white physical domination. The hype surrounding their battle constituted a racial combustion chamber of white cheers and fears about white civilization.

WHITE BODIES ON SHAKY GROUND

During the 1880s, the white middle class began admiring the muscular white male body as a symbol of white might and manhood. In this developing construction, boxers, with their hardened muscles and disciplined bodies, took on a new role in society, and their bodies became canvases of desire that reflected white male social and political power.[12] To describe the boxers' body, writers commonly used words like "hard as a rock," "specimen of manhood," or compared pugilists to gods. In 1884, when the press thought Mervine Thompson was a white man, without ever seeing Thompson, one Los Angeles writer told his readers, Thompson's "muscular development is perfect and he is a most striking specimen of strength and physical manhood."[13] During an interview with Thompson, white sportswriter John B. McCormick of Cleveland had Thompson "go into a back room and stripped to the waist," so the writer could "better judge of the physical development." McCormick acknowledged, "He is one of the finest specimens of a perfect physical man that I have ever had the good fortune to see." He also observed, Thompson's "flesh is as hard and firm as a rock," and "he has the finest fighting neck and head I ever saw on a man's shoulders." McCormick closed his article fantasizing, "When Sullivan and Thompson strip there will be seen the two finest gladiators the world ever saw, and the wonder will be, 'Which is the finest?'"[14] The two gladiators never battled, because Sullivan exposed Thompson as a black man. Sullivan remained the epitome of white manhood throughout the 1880s.

Fans clamored at the sight of the white fighter disrobing and displaying his ripped body before battle. In other words, white men loved to see other white men strip. In this early infatuation for massive male muscles, Sullivan best represented "this cult of 'elemental virility.'"[15] According to Michael Kimmel, Sullivan was "a walking embodiment of the remasculinization of America . . ."[16] In 1883, during an exhibition in Boston, for example, "The shouts which greeted the champion on his entering the ring were deafening. Many present had never seen him, as the sporting term says, 'stripped' and when they did they all acknowledged that a finer specimen of manhood never stepped inside a ring."[17] His power was so mesmerizing, and the pull of his perfect body so magnetic, that everywhere the champion went, whites showered him with praise and celebrated his magnificent manly physique. In Chicago, eight thousand people packed Battery D Arena to watch Sullivan in one of his famous sparring exhibitions, in which he demonstrated his physical skills in a tame, yet aggressive manner. The objective was to captivate the white audiences that flooded the arenas hoping to get a glimpse of white power. Sullivan delivered the goods. "When the magnificent proportions of the Boston pet loomed up in the crowd the audience cheered hastily . . . He was stripped to the waste [sic], and his giant proportions excited wonder and admiration."[18] When Sullivan stayed in shape, and did not binge on alcohol, the words "specimen of manhood" and "John L. Sullivan" became synonymous.

Despite his prowess in the ring, the question about Sullivan always remained, "Could he respectfully represent the race?" Sullivan was a notorious heavy drinker, and during the reign of his championship his massive body dissipated. No longer a mountain of a man, by the late 1880s, Sullivan was a flabby fool. According to Elliott Gorn, "Sullivan's difficulties kept piling up. His drinking was becoming serious, even life-threatening. His wife Annie, moreover, initiated divorce proceedings, and her charges of brutality and adultery against Sullivan became a public scandal. To make matters worse, the champion's avoidance of the regular prize ring caused many of his followers to desert him."[19] Sullivan's physical and moral shortcomings showed cracks in the shield of whiteness.

Time after time, however, with every new media critique about the champ, and white challenger presented to take his crown, Sullivan, like a true man, got his body ready for battle and beat his beleaguered opponent, until he could no longer do it. He remained an undefeated champion for ten years and convinced whites, and himself, that the white body could overcome anything. Months before his 1892 fight with "Gentleman Jim" Corbett, for example, after having binged on beers for years before training, Sullivan looked to prove his physical perfection and had himself checked out by a doctor. His doctor assured the champ, "In all my life I have never seen such a magnificent specimen of muscular development, and, indeed, I do not think that another such man is living today. You are in perfect health, Mr. Sullivan."[20] After ten years of drinking, however, Sullivan could not regain his once-powerful form, and in 1892 Corbett, the skilled fighter, the clean fighter, easily defeated him for the heavyweight championship.

White heavyweight champions who followed Sullivan understood that their role in upholding racial manhood meant they had to display the power and prowess of whiteness. As an example of their capable white bodies, and their understanding of the economic market for whiteness, they used the vaudeville stage to display their manly bodies for admiring audiences. To be sure, these shows were about racial power. In 1893, a year after Corbett defeated Sullivan for the championship, Corbett traveled to Chicago to perform in his hit vaudeville play, *Gentleman Jack,* and take advantage of the large crowds who came to the city to witness wonders of civilization displayed at the World's Fair. In the play, Corbett, the new embodiment of middle-class manhood—he was both an athlete and a gentleman—wowed crowds as he played a banker, college student, and boxer. After successful runs outside the fair, organizers placed Corbett inside the World's Fair to market his talents to correlate with the racial theme of the fair showcasing white supremacy. According to scholar Valerie Babb, the fair "sought to represent America as an emergent world power and a civilized nation." Babb added, "symbols and images engendered by or present at the exposition did not mirror the nation's diversity, however, but rather advocated a white nation in which racial difference was contained or erased."[21] Like the fair, Corbett's show symbolized white civilization. As one advertisement read, "Visitors to the World's Fair will see many of the noblest works of man, but Nature has only one exhibit in the city of her noblest work—the perfect physical man, James J. Corbett."[22] Instead of performing in the White City alongside other representations of white civilization, however, Corbett played at the Midway as the only white attraction. "Where the White City celebrated the white man's civilization as outstandingly manly," Gail Bederman notes, "the Midway depicted savagery and barbarism as lacking manliness entirely."[23] At the Midway, a greater racial contrast did not exist than seeing the heavyweight champion challenge Dahomians from the jungles of Africa or "Orientals" to fights. Of course, onlookers knew Corbett's challenges to the uncivilized guests represented a ruse; no savage stood a chance with a beacon of whiteness.

As Corbett sparred surrounded by supposed savages, his stance as a white civilized champion and carrier of white manhood confirmed what scientist had recently stated: black bodies posed no threats to white civilization. According to scientists, the 1890 census proved black inferiority, because the black population had declined relative to the previous census. In 1896, for example, Frederick L. Hoffman published his influential text *Race Traits and Tendencies of the American Negro* and argued that the "Negro race" was on route to extinction. Although he used his date to come to faulty conclusions, other writers would continue to cite his work to prove their own theories about the dying race.[24] Historian George Frederickson notes the census "coincided with the full triumph of Darwinism in American thought, and thus the statistical evidence that blacks were failing to hold their own readily fitted into a thesis of 'the survival of the fittest' in an inevitable 'struggle for existence' among human races." "As a result," Frederickson claims, "the 1890s saw an unparalleled outburst of racist speculation on the impending disappearance of the American Negro. From the most reputable sources came confident predictions of black extinction through natural process."[25] In reality, however, whites who paid attention to the prize ring could not be too confident about a diminishing black race.

Although most whites tried to avoid the topic, the black boxer's body and success in the ring challenged scientific assertions of a dissipating race. In other words, the belief that the racialized body equated to white civilization and black inferiority rested on shaky ground. As early as 1890, for instance, one white writer openly questioned, "Is the colored race to step in and steal the laurels from us white folk in this way? If so, perhaps those to whom only brute force can appeal as an argument may begin to respect the negro as a man and brother."[26] Whites also realized that black fighters like Peter Jackson had superior bodies to white men. In 1894, for example, the *San Francisco Examiner* printed a picture entitled "Three Types of Manly Form," in which strongman Eugene Sandow and Peter Jackson flanked a statue of Apollo. Omitted from this picture, of course, was the heavyweight champion Jim Corbett, who, like Sullivan, could not compare to Jackson's marvelous muscles. And in the ring, black men outperformed white men. In 1895, a paper confirmed, "The African race has shown much aptitude for the manly art of fisticuffs . . . and they have conquered more Caucasians than have conquered them."[27] In 1901, after Jack Johnson beat the white fighter Jim Scanlan in Galveston, the Phoenix Club in Memphis cancelled Scanlan's next appearance in the city because white fans were upset at him that he fought a black man. "It seems to go against the sporting grain of boxing enthusiasts in this part of the country to look at a white apostle of pugilism after having engaged in a contest with his black brother. . . . There seems to be no doubt that Scanlan will be ostracized by the local stuffed mitt cult for throwing down bars to the color line."[28] Having heard the news of Scanlan being ostracized in the South, a friend wrote to the *Memphis Commercial Appeal* explaining that most white men had fought black fighters, "Yet Jim Scanlon has never met but one colored man and now his friends are giving him the knife. These twentieth century sports are fickle."[29] Indeed, white men were fickle regarding mixed bouts. To solve these racial challenges, white fighters could draw the color line. But most white fighters and white fans would not hear of this. White manhood had to be proven.

Whites yearned to see big, strong, muscular white bodies perform, and at the turn of the century, no white man better represented the race than the 220-pound Jim Jeffries. His muscular body was the very definition of white masculinity and white authority. In 1895, when San Francisco fans viewed his body for the first time they fantasized that he was "muscled like Sandow, with a frame like a youthful Hercules," and "the physical form that the Greeks defined."[30] On another occasion, a Los Angeles writer described Jeffries, noting, "His shoulders are like the arms of a roomy davenport, yet he is not fat. There is no suggestion of padding in the big frame—just a tremendous man, fairly covered with flesh and blessed with good health."[31] In 1899, Jeffries cemented his manly status when he defeated champion Bob Fitzsimmons and became "the best man with nature's weapons living in the world."[32] The remark about "nature's weapons" told readers about the necessary innate manliness and virility white men possessed.[33] While the government had been bulking up the navy to demonstrate American might and modernity, Americans could not forget what made them great: their superior use of "nature's weapons." The link between Jeffries's primal manliness, modernity, and America's white racial authority became abundantly clear when the champ and Admiral George Dewey met in San Francisco in October 1899. Jeffries, who arranged the meeting, told the Admiral "you are the biggest man I ever met," which made the Admiral gush, "you are twice as big a man as I am. Why, you look strong enough to carry the Olympia away with you."[34] When the two men met, Dewey was the leading hero of the Spanish-American War, a purveyor of the white man's burden, a symbol of manliness, and "the highest type of American civilization."[35] Together, Jeffries and Dewey represented the pillars of white American might and strength.

White managers understood the racial mania surrounding Jeffries's physical prowess and were always looking to unearth the next big white hope to pit against the champion. Because of the infatuation with the white body, fights between two white men for the heavyweight championship commanded the most attention. The bigger the better, and white fighters like Gus Ruhlin, Jack Monroe, Sandy Ferguson, Fred Russell, and Toothpick Kelly—all mountains of men—were touted as possible opponents for Jeffries. But while white managers searched for behemoths like Toothpick Kelly to best Jeffries, the heavyweight division was also flooded with some of the greatest black talent in the history of the division. Men like Bob Armstrong, Frank Childs, Hank Griffin, Jack Johnson, Ed Martin, and Sam McVey posed a serious challenge to white manhood. Before Toothpick Kelly fought Sam McVey in 1903, one Los Angeles writer asked "Is 'Toothpick' Kelly the man who is to put Champion James J. Jeffries out of business," while another writer noted Kelly was the biggest white heavyweight and built, "straight as an arrow and is splendidly proportioned. It is claimed that his punching talents are on a par with his size."[36] In the fourth round of his fight with McVey, however, the "Oxnard Wonder" shot two jabs to the stomach, which dropped Kelly's hands, and then he knocked him out with a shot on the jaw. There went another white hope. The press quickly changed their tune about Kelly. The *Los Angeles Express* headline called him a "Dough Boy" and their writer complained, "'Toothpick' is a big, strapping fellow with plenty of muscle and weight; but that is all."[37] White marvels like Kelly that hoped to fight Jeffries, but did not have a clear path to the top, had to work their way up the heavyweight ladder, which often meant fighting the best black fighters and potentially exposing the myth of whiteness.

White heavyweight Fred Russell's fights against black men best demonstrate the burdens of race white fighters faced when they could not uphold their end of the racial bargain. By racial rights, white fighters were supposed to defeat black men, but Russell became a virtual whipping boy for black men.[38] Before his fights with black men, Russell's muscular body signified the embodiment of white manhood. Prior to a match with Griffin in Los Angeles, for instance, the *Los Angeles Times* described Russell as "tall as the Eiffel Tower and nearly as broad as a hasty campaign assertion. His general appearance leads the hasty observer to the conclusion that his diet is shingle nails and unground quartz."[39] And the *Los Angeles Herald* compared him to

Jeffries: "He looked like a bigger edition of the champion [Jeffries] himself. South of the neck Russell is a fine looking man." *The Los Angeles Express* predicted that there had been so much talk about his "terrible hitting powers, phenomenal height and reach that many probably will attend just to see so strange a specimen of physical manhood."[40]

In truth, Russell was all brawn and body, but could not box. He fought all the top black fighters—Frank Childs, Hank Griffin, Jack Johnson, Ed Martin, and Sam McVey—and all but Griffin, who lost because of a referee's mistake, mangled him. Even in his fight with Griffin, in September 1902, Griffin dominated that action. In the first round Griffin bloodied his face, and by the third round, "a straight left to Russell's chin followed by another to the head, cutting Russell's eye, caused the white man to stagger. The blood trickled down Russell's face and the spectators predicted that he would be blinded." But reporters also predicted that if Russell could not beat his black opponent, he would, like a coward, intentionally foul him. And he did just that in the thirteenth round. He fouled Griffin, which sent him to the floor, but instead of giving Griffin an opportunity to get up, the referee allowed Russell to hit him while he was down, and he knocked his opponent out.[41] But in November, he had to face McVey. Although Russell was the betting favorite, in the first round "McVey surprised him in an unguarded moment and landed so suddenly and so hard on the point of the giant's jaw that the big man measured his length on the floor and lay insensible for half a minute."[42]

While Russell's white body impressed white observers before fights, his failing body disappointed white fans in defeat. After his failure against Jack Johnson, in December 1902, the *Los Angeles Express* called Russell a "ring coward," and the *Los Angeles Herald* noted the "white man" was not "game enough to take a beating." Even more to the point at cutting Russell's manhood, a *Los Angeles Times* sportswriter claimed Russell "wears long chrysanthemum hair, and always goes mincing into the ring like a coy little girl." The writer further added that Russell "has large, wondering blue eyes which seem to be saying, 'Oh I am such a itay [sic] bite a fing [sic] to be all alone with all these men.' . . . You expect him to say every minute 'Now Gerald if you try to kiss me I'll scream.'"[43] Although Johnson licked Russell, Johnson did not yet register as the "bad Nigger" as whites would later portray him. Instead, whites treated Johnson like a good Negro, a black man who would not question white authority. According to the *Herald,* Johnson "appeared to be a well behaved, orderly negro, thoroughly interested in his business, which is boxing, and has made a great number of friends."[44] Physically gifted, yes, but whites need not worry about a "well behaved, orderly negro." Russell, on the other hand, could no longer represent white manhood, for if he did, whites were in trouble.

WHITE PROTECTIONISM AND THE IMAGE OF BLACK BOXERS

With black men dominating in the ring and with their bodies clearly more muscular than white fighters, in order to help their readers understand the visual and physical racial challenges black fighters presented to white manhood, a number of white sportswriters compared black fighters to horses. This allowed whites to fetishize over the black body while denying black men humanity and equality.[45] For instance, a writer described Hank Griffin's body, calling him "a picture in bronze. The muscles stand out in his brown body like small mountains. The veins are like whip cords. He looks like a Kentucky race horse ready for the Futuristic."[46] On another occasion, the paper called Griffin "a superb big animal, with the long aquiline features as often seen in mulattoes . . ."[47] The *Los Angeles Times* described "Denver" Ed Martin: "He is built like a dragon about the hips, slender and flat in the loins. Then he broadens out in beautiful lines to a chest and arms and shoulders that might go into statue." And the *Times* commented that Johnson's "thick muscular arms and legs are like a horse in their sleek but massive symmetry."[48] These black men were physical marvels, but they were not racial equals.

Beyond focusing on black musculature to dehumanize black fighters, sportswriters wrote about features like skin and hair to create an image of black savagery.[49] In the early twentieth century, heavyweight Sam McVey became a favorite target of the white press. Though Johnson was clearly the best black fighter of his era, earlier in the fighters' careers, white fans were more enamored with McVey than Johnson. Johnson was a highly skilled heavyweight in the early 1900s, but he was a slight 180 pounds and too defensive for whites' taste. As a writer noted, "Jack Johnson bears the reputation of being the most cautious man who ever put a leg through the ropes. He protects the money first, last and all the time and never cuts loose when there is a chance to win without it."[50] Johnson lacked that innate manly aggression white fans celebrated, but McVey exhibited the power and aggression whites touted. The *Los Angeles Herald*'s Harry Stewart said no fighter "possessed of a better physique than McVey—six feet in height, weight 210 pounds and hard as nails, with no bad habits and his twenty-first birthday yet to greet him."[51] With a powerful punch—a punch that was measured more powerful than Jeffries's—McVey reminded fans of a black Jim Jeffries.[52]

One of the great heavyweights of his generation, Sam McVey poses for the camera. (1910, Library of Congress)

While McVey's prizefighting skills challenged white perceptions of white physical superiority, his features allowed whites to minimize his threat. One writer explained, "His skin would make a nut-brown taste feel like a false alarm. His hair is kinky and his face is blacker than his body. His face would make a black hole in the darkest kind of night and he doesn't show the whites of his eyes when he is beaten in the nose." Another journalist contended that "any man who could stand up twenty rounds before McVey's face, however, and not run howling through the round for help deserves a great reputation for bravery. McVey has a countenance that would scare back the rising moon."[53] When a *Los Angeles Herald* writer learned that McVey traveled from Oxnard to Los Angeles so that he could adjust to the weather a week before his fight, the writer racialized this smart decision: "McVey need not worry his dear little head about such a small thing as climate. If you shipped that dark gent to the North Pole he would soon have all the big white bears coming south for their health. Climate hurt him? They only way that such a thing could ever happen would be to steer Samuel up against a piece of

Kansas climate with a man's size tornado on the tail end of it. And as for my humble opinion, I would back McVey to put an average tornado away in ragtime. Yes, indeed."[54] And six years later, sportswriter Tip Wright for the *Tacoma Times* used pseudo-anthropological musings about McVey to cast the fighter at the lower end of social Darwinian evolution. Wright told his readers, "Imagine a great big, overgrown chunk of black humanity, of the type that sometimes gives credence to Darwin's theory that we are creatures of evolution, with a small, cone-like bean, powerful torso and ape-like arms, possessed with little intelligence and as ignorant as a freshly landed Slav immigrant . . ."[55] That was McVey in white men's eyes: a fighting machine, but black and ugly as ever. Soon they stopped calling in the "Oxnard Wonder" and started calling him Sambo.

In the context of race and the ring, to help assuage white fears about black male physicality, sportswriters often caricaturized black fighters as Sambos: passive, dim-witted, happy-go-lucky throwbacks to the old days of slavery.[56] According to the scholar Joseph Boskin, "The ultimate objective for whites was to effect mastery: to render the black male powerless as a potential warrior, as a sexual competitor, as an economic adversary."[57] Also on this note, historian Leon Litwack has argued, "To flatter their egos, as well as to assuage their doubts and apprehensions, whites during slavery had invented the figure of Sambo. . . . If whites embraced this image during slavery, they became downright ardent in their reverence for it after emancipation. They needed Sambo more than ever before."[58] McVey and Langford, both named Sam, were regularly denoted as Sambo. They also happened to be the two most aggressive black fighters.

Despite black domination, white writers told their readers that black fighters lacked the necessary manly courage of white men; grittiness and toughness belonged to white men. In 1889, for example, one writer remarked, "The question has often been asked: Has the negro the grit and the staying qualities of the white pugilist? Can he stand the punishment and face the music as well and is he equal in skill?" While this particular writer claimed he knew a few black fighters who "possessed all these qualities," and made "surprising records," most white writers would not, and could not, acknowledge black grit. Instead, writers continued to push the threadbare lie that black fighters had a yellow streak. For whites, labeling black men as having a yellow streak was a suggestion that black men, like boys, cowered at the first sight of adversity.[59] In 1904, for example, a writer noted, "The negro fighter, no matter how clever, is generally regarded as being the possessor of a big 'yellow streak,' and if given considerable punishment, would quit."[60] But anyone who paid attention to prizefighting would prophesize otherwise.

But the assertion about black docility could easily be disproved by black action in the ring. Even that same writer from 1904, who claimed black fighters had a touch of the yellow streak, had to admit that "the past few years has demonstrated that there are many black fighters who are capable of taking great amount of punishment, and in this respect they compare favorably with the white pugs."[61] Specifically, blacks had won a championship in every division except for the heavyweight division. By 1907, some white writers willingly acknowledged the unthinkable; black superiority. That year, after Joe Gans successfully defended his title in January, one writer confirmed, "Once again the physical and mental superiority of the black over the white as a fighting man has been demonstrated. I add mental to the physical, because it takes thought as well as strength and quickness to win in the prize ring."[62] What explained black domination?

To account for the unthinkable, white writers developed a myriad of reasons to explain black superiority in the ring. All of their answers rested on whites' belief that blacks lacked civilization. In 1908, for example, in his article, "What Makes the Negro Such a Fighter," writer Harry Burke argued, "Since the game began the Anglo-Saxons, or those transported into their atmosphere and environment, have been champions, be it at war on the field with gun and power or in the roped arena with five-ounce gloves." But, Burke explained, black fighters like Dixon, Gans, Walcott, Johnson, and Langford challenged whites' monopoly in the fighting spirit. To explain his assessment, Burke used scientific racism and suggested that black fighters dominated the ring because black men naturally had hard heads. "It is useless to pound a negro on the head. Any white fighter will tell you so. The body is his vulnerable spot." In opposition to the black fighter, the "white man's chin is his vulnerable spot," Burked claimed. To support his opinions, Burke quoted Dr. Stephen Walker, who expertly concluded, "It would be hard to explain to the lay mind, but the fact is that the negro's jaw is stronger than the white man's, and the shock to his does not carry the message to the base of the brain as quickly and decisively as it does to that of a white man." With their hard jaws, blacks had dominated every division in boxing except the heavyweight class, but as Burke warned, "the dusky brethren" were "camping on [Tommy] Burns' trail and Tommy is worried."[63] Years later, Los Angeles sportswriter De Witt Van Court urged, "It is also a well-known fact that the best and easiest way to defeat a colored boxer is never to waste time hitting them in the head, but to confine punches to the body." Van Court argued "It is a scientific fact that a negro's skull is twice the thickness of a white man's, and punches aimed or landed on their heads are usually wasted, unless they are lucky enough to land a good and solid punch squarely on the point of the chin."[64] For white fighters, this was always easier said than done.

Indeed, by 1908, black fighters Langford, McVey, and Johnson all clamored to get a shot at heavyweight champion Tommy Burns. Lacking great white behemoths to fight, Burns could not hide from all of these black men. The public demanded action and insisted that Burns prove and protect pillars of whiteness. In the end, Burns sold his championship status for $30,000 and signed to fight Johnson.

To buoy his confidence for his bout with Johnson, Burns used scientific racism to discredit Johnson's manhood. He argued that black men had hard heads, but soft stomachs, and he asserted he would attack Johnson in the abdomen. Burns also argued that once he began his onslaught on Johnson, Johnson would turn yellow. "Take it from me," Burns urged, "that if ever I make a man quit when I get him in the ring it will be that nigger. Remember what I say, because you know as well as any one else that he has a yellow streak in his makeup a hundred feet wide, and all that is needed is to sting him a time or two and it's pay day."[65] Burns was wrong. The physically superior Johnson toyed with his diminutive white opponent on his way to shattering the myth about black inferiority.[66]

THE FIGHT OF THE CENTURY

When Johnson defeated Burns on December 26, 1908, white Americans knew they had to act. His victory put blacks in a position of racial authority, or at least that is what black men believed. As one black writer bragged, "now that the victory at last has been achieved the unwilling civilized world must admit the physical prowess of the black race."[67] Ever since Sullivan won the championship in 1882, whites had been convinced that a white heavyweight champion was a symbol of white power and authority.[68] Heavyweight champions Sullivan, Corbett, Fitzsimmons, Jeffries, and Marvin Hart supported this racial assertion and refused to let black men fight for the championship, but Burns broke the unwritten pact, and his loss to Johnson unleashed a new movement: a search for a white hope to restore honor to the race. Led by writer Jack London, whites begged Jeffries—he retired an undefeated champion in 1905—to win back the championship. "But one thing now remains," London pleaded the day after Johnson defeated Burns, "Jim Jeffries must now emerge from his alfalfa farm and remove that golden smile from Jack Johnson's face. Jeff, it's up to you. The White Man must be rescued."[69] As Johnson continued to dust off white foes in 1909, the pressure on Jeffries built up until the weight of the moment finally forced the former champion

Halloween In Fistiana

On the day before Halloween, the *Memphis Scimitar* cartoon suggests that nothing scares the white man, Jim Jeffries, especially not Jack Johnson. (1909, *Memphis Scimitar*)

out of retirement to save the white race. "Jeff thinks that every white man is dependent upon him to redeem the honor of the white race; he thinks the whole white man's burden has fallen upon his shoulder," a southern writer exclaimed.[70] After he signed his contract in December 1909, Jeffries told the press, "I decided to meet Johnson to regain the title of champion heavyweight of the world, to win back for the white race the title which the other fellow allowed to be wrestled from him."[71] Jeffries had to win the battle. After all, he was, "the white man. Mothered of a race which has dominated the world."[72]

The Jeffries–Johnson match was more than just a championship battle; the contest represented a racial contest about proving primal power. In order to win, Jeffries had to display he was the "abysmal brute," a word that on its surface seemed derogatory, but in reality represented a compliment about white determination and virility. Coined by London—he first referred to Bat Nelson as an abysmal brute after Nelson knocked out Jimmy Britt—the abysmal brute had the primal instinct to reach deep inside his soul to recoup the necessary vitality within the race to win a fight. According to London, "This protoplasmic vigor may be our brute heritage, but whatever it is it is a good thing to have whether one is a prize-fighter or not." Only true representations of manhood, however, had the "abysmal brute" in them. "In the fibers of the one resides a primitive vigor and capacity for exertion that the other lacks."[73] Importantly, London assured whites that Jeffries had the necessary ruggedness and physicality to do the job. "He is a big bear, heavy and rugged, and he is physically a man that one may well say occurs no oftener than once in a generation."[74] As Jeffries prepared for his fight, he tapped into this wellspring of primal authority deep down inside.

Leading up to the fight, Jeffries's training camp represented a primitive venture that reassured white men that they still had the virility their ancestors once held. Before he headed to training camp, Jeffries, the avid hunter and mountain man, spent some time in the Los Angeles mountains to get himself right for the fight. He "returned from the mountains lean, lank, and active," and his body, according to one writer who saw Jeffries in the bathroom, "was a magnificent specimen of physical perfection to look upon."[75] For his official training camp, Jeffries stripped down to the bare essentials and trained in the mountains of Rowardennan, California. Buying into this white racial fantasy of primal man, the press called him the "Big Bear," the "California Grizzly," and showed their readers endless pictures of Jeffries's hairy bare-chested body, flexing his muscles, wrestling, and exercising in the river as a natural man. From being out in the sun so long, his body showed signs of rugged primitiveness: "Jeffries tanned to the healthy brownness of a prospector, looks almost the Indian . . ."[76] In an article entitled "Big Fellow's Love of the Open Will Prove Savior," one New York doctor argued that being an outdoorsman preserved Jeffries as a perfect specimen. "Jeffries has lived much in the open," the doctor observed. "He farms, fishes, rows a boat and loafs around. This is the ideal for a man of his temperament."[77] One member in Jeffries's camp, wrestler Farmer Burns, claimed swimming in the icy cold waters proved Jeff's toughness: "When you find a man who can take a plunge in water as cold as that and then, after swimming around a quarter of an hour, comes out without being chilled, you can bet your last dime that he has the vitality," Burns said.[78] Jeffries had gone primal and was ready for the fight.

In the great paradox of prizefighting, however, while the white press turned black pugilists into Sambos, the black fighter's words, training, and built body told white readers otherwise. For the most important battle in boxing history, the papers had to address Johnson's training habits, which also meant writers had to acknowledge his manly body. The press showed pictures of Johnson working with the medicine ball, cutting wood, sparring, and running, and newspapers printed pictures of his built black body posing with his muscles flexed, which revealed a far more superior body than his opponent's. Even worse, doctors confirmed whites' worst nightmare: Johnson was a specimen of manhood who rivaled, if not surpassed, Jeffries. In January, the leading physical culture expert, Dr. Dudley Sargent of Harvard, concluded that Johnson had some of the finest measurements ever. In April, Dr. C. W. Piper, who examined both fighters, observed "If Jeffries is a Hercules, then Johnson surely is a black Achilles—the Roland the black race represents for combat with the Oliver of the whites. If the Caucasian is physically perfect it must be admitted in fairness that the black is equally so." Dr. Piper continued, "Jack Johnson, in brief, is primordial man, big boned, steel muscled and impressive—capable, it would seem, to grapple with a cave tiger of the first era, or with his war club to stalk the mighty prehistoric buffalo. Here, indeed, is a man, even though his skin be black."[79] How could whites refute an expert?

To pronounce his own physical perfection, Johnson used the press to claim his manly superiority. The champion argued, "The pugilist world has never had a fighter more capable of defending a championship than I am. It is a shame Jeffries isn't the champion of old, for I believe his defeat at my hands would be just as much a cinch under such conditions as it is now." He continued, "I am not egotistical but I honestly believe Jeffries will not be able to land a blow on me."[80] Tackling the issue of his supposed yellow streak, Johnson reminded whites that he had manly grit. "Remember what I am going to tell you now," Johnson told a reporter, "Men with the yellow streak in them do not work themselves up until they reach a world's championship. They stumble and fall and the 'yellow' splashes all over them long before they get within reaching distance of a title." With all of his racial passion and pride, Johnson proclaimed, "I would rather be carried dead from the ring than by any sign, move or action to show that I am not the 'yellow' creature that I have been branded." "I am making a strong talk now," Johnson concluded, "but one which I intend to stand by."[81] Because Johnson's body proved a threat to white power, and his manly words suggested he would die to prove his manhood, the white press had to remind their readers of Johnson's blackness.

Despite the proof of Johnson's physical perfection, white writers tried to counter that reality by depicting Johnson as a lazy darky, a chicken-eating colored boy. While Johnson shipped in his own bottled water, brought in his own chef (black hotel owner Frank Sutton), and sent for a doctor (the black doctor F. C. Caffey from Montgomery), white reporters readily mocked Johnson's diet and seemed more focused on his fascination with watermelon and chicken rather than his affinity for training. One cartoon sketch printed in the *San Francisco Examiner* depicted Johnson jogging twelve miles on the beach juxtaposed next to a sketch of a grinning Johnson waiting for his dinner at his chicken coop he had built on his training quarters. The *San Francisco Examiner*'s W. W. Naughton wrote an article solely dedicated to Johnson and chicken. "The news that Jack Johnson covers from eight to twelve miles a day on the road is commonplace. The news that the same Jack Johnson devours from eight to twelve chickens a day is crisp and startling. And is true." Appealing to the racial sensibilities of his white readers, Naughton said, "As a hobbledehoy in his native Texas, Jack used to close his ears to the rattle of dice and the yells of the crap-shooters. He saved up his pennies and as soon as he could command the price gorged himself on his favorite dish." Naughton continued, "He grins when you ask him why he didn't respect the traditions of his race and secure his chicken the 'natchel way.'" Johnson reportedly replied, "No stolen chicken ever passed the portals of my face."[82] Across the bay, the *Oakland Tribune*'s Eddie Smith quipped, "When the champion fighter of the world mentioned watermelon you can believe me he smacked his chaps in lavish anticipation of what he would do to the first melon he gets during the 1910 season, and if you were to ask me right now the best way to get on the right side of the gentleman of color I would say produce a watermelon."[83] Unlike Jeffries, who enjoyed fishing, Johnson, writer C. E. Van Loan observed, "does not care anything about fishing or hunting. The only time he manifests any interest in a speckled mountain trout is when he finds one on his plate. A chicken is the only game which he cares to slaughter."[84] How could a chicken-eating coon beat the epitome of the white race?

To further deny Johnson his manhood, the white press turned the champion into an uncivilized Sambo. In white writers' summation, Johnson, the happy-go-lucky black, was devoid of thought. "Johnson, essentially African, feels no deeper than the moment, sees no farther than his nose—which is flat and of the present. No dark fancies to come to daunt him. Without imagination to lead him onward, he makes no excursions into the blind, unmeasured, unsearched caverns of futurity," a writer claimed.[85] In comparing the two gladiators, Eddie Smith told his readers, "A careful study of the men

The *San Francisco Chronicle* racially mocks Jack Johnson and insinuates he has a natural love for chicken. (1910, *San Francisco Chronicle*)

yesterday leads me to believe Jeff is the more worried of the two." "Johnson," Smith contended, was "true to his traditions of his race, loved music, has a hearty laugh and finds amusements in things that would be passed over by the white mass as trifles beneath his notice." Jeffries, however, was "playful at times but it is the playfulness of a sullen bear. He plays a few moments and then sulks about his yard as a captive bear would about his cage."[86] And Jack London observed, "In shirt sleeves, [Johnson's] shoulder muscles and biceps bulge knottily. Like Jeffries, he too is every inch a big man. But they are vastly different types of men. Under all his large garniture of fighting strength, Johnson is happy-go-lucky in temperament, as light and carefree as a child. He is easily amused, he lives more in the moment, and joy and sorrow are swift passing moods with him. He is not capable of seriously adjusting his actions to remote ends."[87]

For his part, however, Jeffries wanted to hear nothing of the race talk. He knew whites had been blinded by their obsession with race. "When you get into the ring with a man you are exactly on the same footing with him in every way, whether he's black, white, yellow, or brown. That's the way I stand on this black and white proposition."[88] In the ring, according to Jeffries, democracy, discipline, and determination would prevail. But it was too late for racial reasoning. As Max Balthasar of the *Sacramento Star* said of Jeffries, "the white race pins its hope of wrestling the world's heavy-weight championship from the Ethiopian."[89]

Situating Johnson as a man-child created a racial dilemma for whites. If Johnson, the childlike Sambo, beat Jeffries, what would that mean for the interconnection of physical superiority and white authority? Johnson dominated the fight from the first bell with a steady diet of left jabs and right uppercuts. By round six Johnson had eliminated whites' hopes. He hit Jeffries's eye with a sharp left uppercut that nearly closed the eye. In the fifteenth and final round the final fireworks began. A flurry of punches from Johnson sent Jeffries down to the canvas for the first time in his career. During training camp Jeffries had assured whites that he could come back for this fight because he had never been down. "Why, I have never even been dazed in the ring—never," he told the press. "Did you ever figure that way? The boys that don't come back are the lads that have been flattened—boys that have been so badly beaten that they have never quite recovered."[90] Jeffries, and white fans, had entered into uncharted territory. Jeffries got up, but Johnson quickly swarmed him again with a series of punches and knocked the challenger down for the second time. Jeffries's corner began to scream to referee Tex Rickard to stop the fight, because they did not want Jeffries to be knocked out. Rickard did not oblige. When Jeffries rose up, Johnson commenced to hit him with more vicious punches, and for the third time Jeffries went down. Rickard had seen enough, and declared Johnson the winner.[91] Jack Johnson had proven the fight experts wrong and had retained his heavyweight title.

Johnson's victory made whites momentarily reassess the relationship between physicality and superiority. Instead of putting stock in the white male body, white writers reasoned that brains, and not brawn, made white men superior. The idea of the "primitive masculine" had seemingly died. Sportswriter Rex Beach claimed Johnson "demonstrated further that his race has acquired full stature as men: whether they will ever breed brains to match his muscles is yet to be proven."[92] Another editorial urged, "Never you mind, white man. You have something still which lifts you above the black: the Bible, Shakespeare, Milton, Goethe, Fulton, Stephenson, Edison, and Darwin."[93] In his

Jack Johnson with his golden smile. (1909–1915, Library of Congress)

racial reasoning, psychologist and criminologist W. C. Morrow claimed that Jeffries's superior racial intellectual abilities hindered him in the ring. Morrow asked, "What makes a great prize fighter? Brains? No. Culture? Heaven forbid! That Jeffries has a larger brain than Johnson goes without question. With a higher brain development he had, as a matter of course, a more efficient nervous organization." Morrow added, "If we imagine the two men in their normal state, each with the strength and training that we know them to have had, Johnson could not possibly have stood before the white man through three rounds." In the end, it was the "temperament of Jeffries, and behind it brains and nervous organization, all of them superior to anything of the sort possessed by Johnson, that proved the white man's ruin. The white man was destroyed by his superiority—his superiority in everything, but the one vital thing, and understanding of the black man from the Congo."[94] The criminologist labeled Johnson a savage, not a civilized citizen, and in doing so he tried to protect the construction of white manhood.

In what now has become a common conversation about black athletic superiority, in 1912 Australian promoter Hugh McIntosh, who worked with Johnson, Langford, and McVey, became the first person to relate black success to slavery. "The American negro, for example, is bound, at his best, to be physically equal, if not superior, to the class from which the white boxer

Puck imagines reversed roles in *Uncle Tom's Cabin* if Johnson beats Jeffries. (1910, Library of Congress)

is drawn." "In recent times," McIntosh noted, "his ancestors have had to survive the horrors of the Middle Passage; to work fourteen hours a day in the cotton fields, and be speedy and resourceful enough to escape, over rough country, from well-mounted slave-owners and their highly trained bloodhounds." This horrific history, McIntosh concluded, meant that blacks "needed amazing vitality to resist the awful living and insanitary conditions, poor food, dreadful climates, and ill-usage generally which were their lot."

In the ring, this meant that "every willing slam which the African black has received from his white master through the ages has done a little to make Johnson, McVea, and the rest the affluent folk they are." In this understanding, the slave whip prepared black men for pugilistic punishment. "In the ring, when the negro is getting a thrashing, he feels neither rage nor shame; he is only getting what his forefathers had been getting over since civilization first prized the race out of its primeval forest."[95] But in truth, white fighters struggled to beat black men. Whites needed something more than the same-old newspapers racism; they need lawmakers to save the race.

6

FOLLOWING THE COLOR LINE

Progressive Reform
and the Fear of the Black Fighter

On March 13, 1902, when Louisville lawmakers passed legislation regulating prizefighting, the city joined a host of cities across the nation implementing policies to reform boxing. Claiming that he wanted to "restrict local boxing matches to a certain extent for the benefit of the public to prevent brutality and to prevent accidents," Harry Brennan, chairman of the Board of Public Safety, eliminated heavyweight bouts from his city.[1] With other cities mobilizing against prizefighting, Louisville ranked as a potential location to assume the mythical mantle of "Mecca of Boxing," and local progressives feared that a heavyweight championship match would seal the city's fate as the center of the fighting world. In the context of progressive reform and prizefighting, Louisville's decision to reform boxing, rather than abolish the sport, made sense. Cities that reformed boxing did not want a reputation as open towns. But these cities also understood that a significant number of white citizens enjoyed seeing boxing matches as a way to recoup, build, or maintain manhood. In most instances, regulation was about pacifying reformers on the one hand and appeasing men concerned about physicality and manhood on the other hand.

Brennan, however, did not explain his other decision that day, a development so severe that it deserved reasoning. Along with eliminating heavyweights from performing in Louisville, the Board banned black boxers from fighting and working as corner men in the city. Only a handful of credible black fighters—Steve Crosby, Brutus Clay, and Jim Watts—regularly performed in Louisville, and of those men, only Watts, a second-tier fighter, received national acclaim.

To be sure, black fighters challenged white political and social author-ity, especially the presence of Jim Watts. Louisville's Board of Public Safety realized they could not tame Watts, better known as the "Pendennis Pet," and if whites could not check the "Pendennis Pet" into docility, how would other blacks react in a city where servile employment was the expectation for black men? Born and raised in Louisville, Watts had worked as a waiter before becoming a professional fighter. While employed at the Pendennis Club, an elite organization for the wealthiest whites in the city, club mem-bers heard that Watts could handle himself, so they put him to the test, and members backed him to fight other local boxers.[2] Between 1887 and 1897, Watts carved up the competition, black and white, and never lost a fight in the city on his way to becoming the self-proclaimed colored middleweight champion of the South.[3] In 1897, Watts headed to New York to take on the best fighters and earn more money from the wealthier clubs. Although he lost to Joe Walcott, Watts returned with a new swagger that captured whites' atten-tion. With his newfound riches, he returned "wearing white shoes, striped trousers, a red vest, and a sky-blue coat. He had a large diamond in his shirt front, and was at once the most prominent negro resident in Louisville." In other words, boxing helped him rise above servile work, and he adorned flashy clothes to signal his freedom. What if other negroes acted like Watts? Equally as worrisome for whites, Watts came back with improved boxing skills. According to a local expert, "All the negroes were afraid to meet him, and he had trouble in matching himself with a good white man."[4] To tame the "Pendennis Pet," clubs kept trying to find fighters to beat him, especially white men, but very few were up to the task. In May 1897, in his first fight back from the East, local Louisville promoters thought they found the right man in Joe Peterson, the "Terrible Swede." They were wrong. Watts viciously beat Chicago's Peterson and knocked him down five times before the police stopped the fight. To make matters worse, in front of five hundred people, the man they called the "Pendennis Pet" laughed as he beat his white opponent. "'The Terrible Swede' tried to be terrible in that he rushed at Watts repeat-edly, but as repeatedly found Watts elsewhere, smiling and smirking and delivering left hand punches with sang-froid and considerable force. It was a case of punch, clinch and get away, with the Swede's face as red as a lobster and Watts smiling like he found money." On the fight card that night, the other black fighter, Steve Crosby, beat an Italian fighter too. "Africa came out first best last night over at least two representatives of other countries."[5] The following January, promoters put another white fighter in front of him, and Watts knocked down Lucas Siefker several times before the police stopped that fight. In March 1898, whites finally found a white fighter to defeat Watts when Australian Jim Ryan stopped him in the twentieth round. Ryan would be the only white man to beat Watts in Louisville.[6] By 1902, when the Board of Public Safety banned blacks from boxing in the city, Watts had fought in more than one hundred career fights, with the majority of the battles coming in his hometown.

Louisville's decision to ban black boxers stripped Watts of his trade and his ability to earn a living on his own terms. With no local fight prospects, Watts momentarily quit the ring and claimed he was heading to Kalamazoo, Michigan, to work as a waiter. When asked if his decision to move had anything to do with the new law, Watts said, "I have recommendations from men at the Pendennis Club, where I worked before entering the ring, and I am going to Kalamazoo and work at my trade. There is more in waiting than there is in the prize ring."[7] But, in reality, it was too hard for a man to transition from a fighter to a waiter. One job required him to physically prove his manhood, while the other forced his docility around whites. In 1904, Jim Watts moved his family to Sandusky, Ohio, and opened up a sparring academy.[8] In Ohio, he found momentary financial success, but like so many second-tier fighters of his generation, he quickly fell out of the spotlight. When Watts resurfaced in 1913—that is to say, a newspaper cared enough about him to discuss his life—he was living in Indianapolis selling coal. He claimed he had squandered more than $200,000 in career earnings, had been in four hundred fights, but also noted he ate three meals a day. According to a local black writer, however, Watts looked "slow and groggy as if a fighter waiting for his knockout blow."[9] In the end, unable to ply his trade in his hometown, his career suffered from the cruel fate of the color line.

The brief story about Watts and Louisville is the story of progressive reform, race, and manhood. Though Louisville was one of a few cities to outright ban black boxers—Memphis briefly banned black boxers in 1910—during the Progressive Era, a number of cities and states outside the Deep South eventually barred mixed bouts. Between 1900 and 1908, St. Louis, Milwaukee, Baltimore, Louisville, Los Angeles, Pittsburgh, and Chicago drew the color line.[10] After Jack Johnson won the heavyweight championship in 1908, the search for white hopes, combined with the hope to reenergize white males, pushed a few states to change their laws to legalize fighting, and even those states, Tennessee and New York, banned interracial matches.

In the context of prizefighting, progressivism, and prejudices, lawmakers wanted to protect white superiority. Each black victory in the ring against white opponents—and there were plenty by black men—stripped away at the notion of white male social and political authority, a confidence that partly hinged on whites' racial belief in physical superiority. Whiteness had no value if it could not be proven. Moreover, the move to bar mixed bouts was also a progressive movement against local black communities and the fear of so-called black criminality. As one California paper asked before the Johnson–Jeffries bout in 1910, "If the negro wipes up the earth with Jeffries will this country belong to the coons? Will we be forced to repeal the 13th, 14th, and other amendments to the constitution for self protection?"[11] If whites could not control black men inside the ring, whites worried, they could not control blacks outside the squared circle.

BALTIMORE: A WHITE MAN'S CITY

The Joe Gans–Charles Sieger bout on November 14, 1902, for Gans's lightweight championship was a vicious, one-sided affair that challenged local reformers' vision of a white man's city. "It is doubtful," the *Baltimore Sun* reflected, "if any fighter ever took more punishment and remained on his feet in the history of the prize ring than the New York boy received." For fifteen rounds, despite taking an insurmountable amount of punishment, Sieger, the overmatched "Italian Game Chicken" who had "features like an Algonquin Indian and the courage of a martyr," refused to quit.[12] The bloodied and battered Sieger hit the canvas six times that night, prompting reformers to lead a fight against prizefighting.

But it was not just the beating that pushed reformers to move; it was the unmistakable racial imagery that captured progressives' attention. A significant portion of the fans could not shake the fact that "Sieger was severely mauled for 15 rounds by his negro antagonist." For one man, described as a "gentleman from one of the Southern States" in the press, the "exhausted and bloody condition of the white man" burned an image of racial brutality and betrayal that he could not shake. This type of beating was not supposed to happen to a white man. Upset by the racial role reversal, the southern gentleman left the fight and told fans sitting near him, "he did not care to see a negro beat a white man, especially when the white man was so clearly the physical inferior of his colored opponent."[13] The highlights of the fight described in the daily press the next day also fueled the flames of white unrest. "Time and again," the *Sun* wrote, "the colored boy crossed over that deadly right and landed it full on the point of the jaw . . ." In the tenth round, a straight right to Sieger's jaw "put the white boy on 'queer street,'" and in the eleventh round, the "white boy fell like a log," from a barrage of Gans's punches.[14] But

Gans was not just a "colored boy," he was a man, the lightweight champion, and a hero in Black Baltimore.

Whites feared that the combination of Gans's championship status, his standing in the black community, and prowess in the ring would have a damaging effect on their ability to control black citizens. One concerned citizen wrote, "What is more disgusting than to see a negro and a white man (poor, degraded wretch) stand up and fight?" This writer also worried that other blacks would wrongly interpret the meaning of mixed bouts, and he argued that interracial fights "certainly has an effect on the boisterous and rough element of negroes." A police officer who attended the fight, Deputy Marshall Manning, also claimed, "The sight of the negro defeating a white man in the prize ring had a most unwholesome effect upon the rough colored element and tended to make that element unruly and disorderly."[15] And the city marshal, Thomas Farnan, recommended to reformers "that permits be refused for boxing contests between white and colored men," because he believed, "no matter how the contests resulted, they caused race feelings." He further warned, "no one knows just exactly what might occur at a boxing contest, when the audience is frequently excited, because of the success or defeat of the contestant each individual favors."[16] In a city that was nearly fifteen percent black, with one of the largest black populations in the nation, something had to be done about mixed bouts.[17]

The push to ban interracial bouts was an extension of the 1899 "good government" movement that linked modern reform with racist protectionism.[18] During Baltimore's 1899 election, Democrats argued that under Republican rule, blacks had received too many political appointments and the so-called black rowdy element had become a physical threat to whites. Race riots the previous year in Wilmington, North Carolina—sometimes known as the Wilmington Racial Massacre of 1898—inspired white Baltimorean politicians to rid themselves of their negro problem. During the height of the Baltimore campaign, a Wilmington newspaper reported, "A distinguished gentleman was in Wilmington on the eve and during the revolution in November. He told us that Baltimore would soon or late have some such experiences as Wilmington was passing through." The reporter continued, "He thought it inevitable as like causes would produce like results. The race issue in that city has become critical. The race prejudice is getting to the front. . . . It says, however, that there is 'an ugly negro element in certain sections of the city.'"[19] The following year, in Baltimore during the 1899 election, political rallies were filled with signs that read, "This is a White Man's City," "The White Man's Burden," and "No Coons for Me," with the latter sign having a picture of a rough-looking black man, a clear suggestion to whites that black men had to be stopped.[20] At one rally, a speaker linked Good Government with white power, suggesting, "There is another aspect of the question of good government that is too serious and too palpable to be obscured. I refer to the danger of negro domination that is indissolubly connected with a continuation of the Maister [Republican Mayor] contingent of the republican party in possession of the city government."[21] And in his speech to Baltimore's Democratic voters, Governor Fred Brown applauded a ward delegation for carrying a banner that read "This is a White Man's City," and he proceeded to tell voters, "It only remains for the white people of the city to see that they are properly registered on Monday next, and that their ballots are cast in favor of good government . . ."[22] Backed by Democrats geared toward maintaining white superiority, Theodore Hayes handily won the mayoral election, and right on cue, Democratic leaders in Baltimore worked to strip away black rights. A reformist government that ruled to maintain white power could not have prizefight promoters in the city who undermined the racial remaking of Baltimore.

To be sure, some progressives also looked at the Gans–Sieger match as an opportunity to completely get rid of boxing. News of the bloody fight brought reformers out in full force, including a number of clergymen who sent Mayor Hayes letters urging him to ban boxing. Reverend Junius W. Millard, pastor of Eutaw Place Baptist Church, complained, "These so-called boxing contests have been nothing else than prizefights, pure and simple, and their effect has been to brutalize those who have witnessed them and to outrage the sense of public decency on the part of those who oppose them."[23] Ten days later, a delegation of leaders with the Methodist Episcopal Church adopted a resolution calling for the abolishment of boxing. But reformers had a battle on their hands. A sizeable number of Baltimoreans believed the city, especially boys, benefited from boxing. Without boxing, some argued, the youth, and thus white manhood, would suffer.[24] But make no mistake about it: Just as the Good Government campaign that brought Mayor Hayes into office linked government reform with ending negro domination, the campaign to clean up Baltimore by banning boxing was intertwined with a need to stop so-called black power.

As the move to reform boxing grew, Mayor Hayes had two major issues in front of him: How could he reform boxing while appeasing both white reformers and the supporters of boxing, and how would he deal with the race issue? On the first concern, promoters tried to meet Mayor Hayes halfway, and they pleaded with him to reduce fights from twenty rounds to ten-round contests instead of abolishing the sport. Limiting the number of rounds, they argued, would make the sport seem less brutal and would prevent championship matches. Promoters also tried to exert pressure on Mayor Hayes to merely reform mixed bouts, as opposed to banning them outright. Promoters knew that top-notch black fighters, like Gans and Joe Walcott, made the clubs more money when either of the black champions faced white opponents. Unwilling to lose those potential matches, promoters asked the mayor to allow interracial contests featuring top black fighters. Surprisingly, Mayor Hayes initially put forth a reform plan that would ban mixed bouts in preliminary contests, but would allow interracial fights for championship battles. It is possible that Mayor Hayes hoped that a white fighter would defeat Gans or Walcott in Baltimore as a symbol of white might, but before he moved to reform mixed bouts the mayor had to be convinced that blacks would not become unruly if Gans fought and won. According to one report, "The Mayor was strenuous on the inadvisability of matching the races, as he thought it tended to create disorder among certain elements in the community," but the mayor "asked for a description of the character of Joe Gans, and was told that Gans is probably the fairest boxer in the ring, and that he is noted for quiet deportment." In other words, Gans was a "good black," not a threat like the so-called rowdy element, and he would not embarrass his white opponents or rile up black fans.[25]

The talk of racial reform in the ring disappointed Gans, who had hoped to fight the rest of his career in Baltimore. In his public defense, Gans cast himself as a model citizen and a humble black man who just wanted an opportunity to work near his family and friends. A dejected Gans told the *Sun*, "I have lived in Baltimore all my life, my relatives and friends are here, and, in spite of what may have been said to the contrary, I have found the audiences here generally fair in their treatment of me." He continued, "I am a taxpayer here; and am, and have always been, a law-abiding citizen. I regard my means of gaining a livelihood as legitimate and honorable as any man's." Speaking about the pride he had when he won the championship in May—and definitely making sure he was not gloating as to not upset white men—Gans humbly noted, "One thing which made the winning of the championship sweet to me was the thought that I could show my fellow-townsmen that I was all that my admired credited me with being. I was also proud to bring to this city an honor it had never previously possessed." Gans also believed the mayor wanted him to lose to a white man in Baltimore: "In regard to the Mayor's compromise to allow contests between white men and colored champions only," Gans argued, "I take it to mean he will permit white men to meet me until my laurels are snatched from me, and then I will be given no chance to regain them. I ask, is that sportsmanlike? Is it fair play [?] . . . What opportunity does that give to poor colored lads who, like me, are trying to climb the pugilistic ladder?"[26] Gans closed his remarks by pleading with Mayor Hayes to reconsider his potential ban.

But Baltimore could not be a "white man's city" with a black champion who beat up white men, so instead of legally reforming the sport, Mayor Hayes stopped issuing permits altogether. In his decree, he cited, "I am of the opinion that boxing will do the community no good; that it is fraught with dangerous possibilities, and that the tendency is not uplifting," and he expressed a "doubt of the ability to have boxing conducted without brutality, gambling or a menace to good order . . ."[27] Boxing did not come back to Baltimore until July 1903 when a new mayor, Robert McLane, who also won his job under the banner of "a White Man's City," issued his first boxing permit because he believed boxing's manly values were good for white Baltimoreans.[28] Although promoters banned mixed bouts, between 1904 and 1907, they allowed Gans to fight three white men. He beat them all. To blunt Gans's victories, white promoters more frequently hosted battle royals meant to demean the black combatants. It is no coincidence that the elimination of mixed bouts and the increase in battle royals occurred simultaneously as the city stripped black rights away.

LOS ANGELES AND TOM MCCAREY'S NIGGER CLUB

In January 1901, grumblings from Ohio Governor Gary Nash about banning Cincinnati's scheduled heavyweight championship match between Jim Jeffries and Gus Ruhlin shook Los Angeles boosters. If reports were true, and Nash banned boxing, Los Angeles fight promoters and boosters would finally have a chance to land Jeffries, their hometown hero. John Brink, the former head of the white middle-class Los Angeles Athletic Club, reasoned, "I look at it this way—if Jeff and Ruhlin can't come together in Cincinnati the public will want them to get together somewhere else. Why not Southern California?" Brink and several leading businessmen reached out to Jeffries, who said. "I would rather go there than any place I know of. A fellow always has a yearning to show his friends what he can do."[29] For boosters, however, the allure of Jeffries fighting in his hometown went beyond making money and grabbing headlines; this was about race and place. Since the 1870s, Los Angeles boosters had been selling the city as a "white spot," a safe haven for white migrants, as the mythical last line of defense against political, economic, and racial challenges to white manhood. This concept, historian Mark Wild suggests, reflected white Angelenos' anxieties about politics, labor, and race.[30] In 1877 for example, city officials changed the name of Calle de los Negros (Anglicized as "Nigger Alley") to Los Angeles Street, a move historian Mark Wild suggests "marked the first steps toward constructing the vision of a 'white' Los Angeles that would resonate so strongly with [their] descendants."[31]

With his bulging muscles, Midwest background, and manly aggression, Jeffries fit nicely into boosters' plans. The future champ was born in an Ohio log cabin on a 160-acre homestead in 1875, where his father, A. C. Jeffries, had toiled in the fields as a "natural man," before the family migrated to Los Angeles in 1881.[32] Their journey was like many other white midwesterners who were enticed by booster ads promoting racial paradise. According to historian Natalia Molina, "The city was developed as a place for whites . . ." and "by luring mainly white Midwesterners and by racially segregating neighborhoods as they began to be settled by immigrants and migrants, the city fathers sent a clear message: social membership in the city would be reserved for whites only."[33] In Los Angeles, Jim's father purchased one hundred acres of land (ninety-seven acres of fruit trees) several miles from downtown, and he built an exquisite two-storied fourteen-room home where he raised Jim to be a farmer and a preacher.[34] The muscular champion was tailor-made for a city that sold itself as a "white spot." But despite boosters' persistence to get the Jeffries–Ruhlin fight, the two battled in San Francisco. In fact, the local fighter never fought a championship match in his hometown.

With cities in the East and Midwest reforming prizefighting, Los Angeles, which did not restrict fighting—California allowed for municipal control of boxing—had become a popular destination for boxers. In March 1901, after Biddy Bishop, a leading boxing manager on the West Coast, sent a letter to the *Los Angeles Times* asking about potential fights, the paper bragged, "Los Angeles has been picked out by fighters and their managers as the Mecca for ring contests." Less than a month later, the *Times* reported, "the prizefighting proposition in this city is assuming momentous proportions. The managers of the 'pugs' generally are looking toward Los Angeles as a prospective Mecca."[35] By 1902, led by the promoter Tom McCarey, who opened his Century Athletic Club the previous year, Los Angeles had started to rival San Francisco as the "Mecca of Boxing." That year, a local writer observed, "As the pugilistic profession around the country awakes to the fact that Los Angeles is now one of the best towns for the sport in the country, there is a steady increase in the number of fighters who are asking for a chance to come here. A year ago, when the sport was not on its present footing, it was hard to persuade good men to make the trip without a guarantee, but things have changed."[36] Although McCarey helped put boxing in Los Angeles on the map, his boxing business blunted boosters' vision of a white Los Angeles.

Understanding the interconnection of race, manliness, boxing, and business, McCarey knew that in a city marketed as a white spot, race sold. To build his business, he brought in the best black talent. The list of notable black fighters that battled in Los Angeles included Hank Griffin, "Denver" Ed Martin, Frank Childs, Sam McVey, Jack Johnson, Young Peter Jackson, Joe Walcott, Billy Woods, and the "Dixie Kid" Aaron Brown. In the first two years of running his business, McCarey rarely put on a main event featuring two white fighters, and he never hosted a fight card that only featured white men—instead, he preferred all-black fights or mixed bouts. Los Angelenos took notice. After McCarey's first all-black card on June 20, 1902, which consisted of three fights highlighted by a Johnson–Griffin match, the *Los Angeles Express* noted, "Never before has an all-black competition been given by the club. In every previous fistic carnival given by the local club there have been at least one or two white contestants." The *Los Angeles Times* called the show a "dark night," and the *Herald* told readers, "several months ago Manager Tom McCarey announced an intention of arranging for the Century Club a 'dark night' of fistic sport, which would combine with some class a great deal of downright, outright scrapping, and would be of a nature to satisfy the desires of the most ardent followers of ring sports." The *Herald* writer ended his observation noting, "by degrees [McCarey] has been working to it until at last a card in which six ebony-hued gladiators will contest is the final outcome."[37] In the main event that night, Johnson and Griffin fought a fast-paced twenty-round draw. Surprisingly, in the fight, Johnson, the counterpuncher, came out aggressive and almost put Griffin out, but with a bloodied nose, in the fourth round Griffin picked up the pace. For the next fifteen rounds, he was the aggressor. He paid for his tactics, however, as Johnson easily countered his punches. In the end, the referee declared the match a draw, because Griffin remained aggressive the whole fight.[38] A month after McCarey's first all-black card, Young Peter Jackson beat the white fighter Mike Donavan in a twenty-round bout.

McCarey, who once proclaimed, "I do not think much of the color line proposition," was one of the few promoters in the nation who openly supported mixed bouts.[39] Some suggest his affinity for black fights and mixed bouts was what earned the nickname "Uncle Tom," and the public, at first, enjoyed these mixed bouts. As the *Herald* stated, "Two negroes seldom make as satisfactory a mill as a black and a white man, owing to their race sympathy

. . ."[40] The only problem; blacks dominated their whites foes. Between June 1901 and June 1903, in main events black fighters went 15–1–2 against their white opponents.

The inability of white fighters to live up to their supposed racial capabilities always upset white fans. After a match between Jack Jeffries (Jim's brother) and Jack Johnson in 1902—the interracial contest was part of the city's biggest booster event, La Fiesta—the *Los Angeles Times* said that "by rights," Jeffries should have won, because he was "a fine-looking young fellow, with a figure like a Greek god, muscles all glistening over to his seconds." In front of four thousand fans, however, Johnson hit Jeffries with a right hand to the stomach, "which must have made Jeffries ribs battle," and then followed that with a right to the jaw that sent Jeffries to the mat with a hard "thud." The referee counted Jeffries out.[41] After Johnson's victory, the *Los Angeles Times* reassured whites that Johnson was a "good-natured black animal," and not a threat to white manhood.[42]

Between McCarey's "dark nights" and his interracial contests, whites had grown increasingly worried about boxing in the city. To fully understand this growing white anxiety about black bodies in the ring, however, one must take into account the city's increasing black population. In the midst of black domination in the ring, Los Angeles experienced a significant racial demographic change that heightened white anxieties about black fistic success.[43]

The connection between black migration, black muscles, and black victories cannot be separated. Local black leaders also boosted Los Angeles. The land boom and better job opportunities, along with false perceptions that the city was nearly free from racism, enticed black migrants to move to Los Angeles.[44] As historian Lonnie G. Bunch III suggests, "The chance for home ownership and the potential for more individual freedom had an even greater appeal to those whose choices were circumscribed by race."[45] During the 1890s, the black population nearly doubled, and in 1900 Los Angeles had the largest black community in California. A decade later, the city held the largest black population west of the Mississippi.[46] At the peak of black migration, from February 1903 through March 1903, more than two thousand blacks arrived in the city.[47] During that short period, McCarey hosted two colored championship fights, a welterweight championship bout between Joe Walcott and the local black fighter Billy Woods, and three interracial contests. The same day (February 27, 1903) that the *Los Angeles Times* told their readers about the Johnson–McVey battle, claiming, "They don't arrange these coon fights right. The afternoon before the fight they ought to run the fighters through a steam carpet-cleaning machine, and set a pair of men pounding them a while with meat cleavers. A little thing like twenty rounds of punching can't worry a coon like McVey much. He could stand up for twenty rounds lashed to a post and let the other man take an ax," the paper also printed a headline reading, "Nearly a Thousand Negro Colonists," for an article about a huge influx of black southern migrants.[48]

Less than a month later, on March 20, in an article entitled "Negroes are Coming," the *Herald* warned readers, "Southern California is about to become the Mecca for thousands of negroes." An executive for the Southern Pacific Railroad said, "Colored people of the south think that Southern California is a land flowing with milk and honey." Noting the "Negroes are Coming," however, might as well have been an article about black boxers. In March, *Herald* readers also read the headlines, "Joe Walcott Will Come," and "Mississippi in Town." "Mississippi," born John Willis, was "a stocky built little fellow with thin legs and a torso something like a miniature of Jack Johnson's," who came to the city to fight the white fighter Kid McFadden on March 18. On March 19, the papers told of the conquests of the black fighters. The Mississippi–McFadden fight lasted eight rounds, with Mississippi dominating the majority of the fight. Commenting on Mississippi, a local white writer said, "Mississippi is nothing but bone and muscle, and knows how to handle his fists to good advantage." During the eight rounds, he repeatedly hit McFadden with quick straight rights that McFadden had no answers for. In the eighth round, he knocked him down twice before McFadden's trainers threw in the sponge. It took several minutes before they carried him out of the ring, and the white fighter claimed he would never fight again.[49] In the main event of the evening, the local black fighter Hank Griffin beat his white opponent Soldier Tom Wilson "in a jig time."[50] The next day, in an article entitled "The Negroes are Coming," the *Herald* warned their readers about the seemingly unstoppable black migration.

With an unstoppable influx of black migrants, combined with unbeatable black fighters, McCarey's strategy of relying on interracial fights generated a lot of white backlash. The first printed complaint that McCarey ran a "nigger club" came a week after his 1903 La Fiesta fight card in which McCarey promoted three interracial contests. The main event of that May 5 card featured a battle of racial supremacy between Sam McVey and Kid Carter. In fact, McCarey relied on Carter, who had a reputation for beating black men— he knocked out Joe Walcott two years prior—to deal with the racial threat black fighters posed. Carter was "a rushing whirlwind fighter of the kind few colored men like to meet, for he seems only maddened by punishment, and blows apparently only sting him into renewed effort." "Beating the gentry of the dingy skins has always been one of the Kid's strongest cards" the *Herald* bragged.[51] McVey, however, quickly ended all notions of white superiority in the ring, when the "black terror" "lifted fierce uppercuts and repeatedly drove in short jolts to the body with either hand, and they all hurt."[52] The *Herald's* writer could not help but notice the racial significance of the La Fiesta card. "Tuesday night certainly was a great occasion for the black men, for all three of them won their bouts from the light-colored gentry. There are many places in the country where a colored man cannot get a square deal in the ring, but in Los Angeles they all look alike when they climb through the ropes."[53] When given an equal opportunity to compete, black men dominated white men.

On June 9, 1903, McCarey's interracial fights finally pushed the limits of white tolerance in Los Angeles. The fights between Jack Woods (black) and "Young" Balmer (white) and Billy Woods (black) and Neil Foley (white) whipped the crowd into a racial frenzy. In the Jack Woods–Balmer contest, Woods gave his opponent a severe beating, and knocked out his two front teeth. After the loss, Balmer stood on the ropes and complained to the crowd, "a white man never gets a square deal against a 'nigger' here." White fans agreed and threw money at Balmer. In the next fight, the excitable crowd witnessed Billy Woods completely outclass Foley, until the referee disqualified Woods for fouling. Afterward, the *Times* argued, "As a matter of fact, there have not been any white fighters in this city for months who could earn a decision over the darkies, as results will show."[54] Therein lay the problem: McCarey kept sending in white fighters to get whipped by black men.

Prior to the match, Woods was a local phenomenon in good standing with white fans. In an era in which muscularity meant manliness and superiority, Woods's perfect body caught the attention of white men. One article noted, "Men always like to look on the form of a perfect specimen of their kind and to those who understand physical development the accompanying photograph of Woods' torso will be worth looking at. His back is about as near perfect as it could be." While another article assured, "Woods is not yet 21, has not a vice in the world and is the possessor of a magnificent body which he has so far preserved in perfect shape. He does not drink; nor does he smoke, and his clean habits may be the way of winning him a fortune tonight." Woods was a "clean limber young fellow about the color of a new English saddle; muscular in physique (such a model as might have been chosen by a Greek sculptor); with the speed of lighting and the strength of Hercules—Billy Woods."[55] Whites even attributed Woods's aggression in the ring to his Irish American roots and not his blackness. According to McCarey,

Woods' father was "a big six-foot two fighting Irishman," and McCarey suggested he would bet "much on that breed any time."[56] If Woods were white, he would have been the perfect white man. But he was black, and that was a problem.

For white Los Angelenos, Woods's victory highlighted the problem of the black body as a challenge to white authority. Leading up to the contest, the *Herald* ran a cartoon sketch of Woods training that caricaturized the light-skinned fighter as a dark Sambo. The fight with Foley, according to the *Los Angeles Times,* brought out the innate animal instincts of the negro. Foley did not stand a fair chance. The paper explained, "The white man is a boxer, but the negro is a savage, ferocious, hardened, fierce, little brute—trained to fight to hurt men." The writer continued, "No words can describe the terrible fury of his fighting. It is like the sudden loosing of a caged, hungry wild beast torn away from some mountain fastness. He did not seem to strike, but to tear his man to the ground like a hound." To witness the fight was a "sickening thing," because "Foley was so slender and so pale and he looked so afraid as he stood against the lithe, crouched black body."[57] After beating Foley in four rounds, "A negro crassed [*sic*] with lust for blood, lost all control of himself, and leaped on his white antagonist with the fury of a wild beast, throttling him around the throat with one of his great black arms." Four thousand fans started to scream like "enraged animals" and then started to run into the ring like "maddened cattle," and one young man yelled, "Kill the nigger."[58] Afterward, the *Herald* noted the racial pulse of the city: "While there are plenty of men who will say that a white man who will box with a colored man 'ought to be licked on general principles,' still, the fact has been brought home to McCarey with telling force that Los Angeles audiences do not like to see a white man defeated by a man of color."[59] With white manhood at risk, the city council decided to save Los Angeles by forcing McCarey to ban interracial fights.

For progressives, eliminating interracial boxing matches was also part of a larger city cleanup movement making Los Angeles the ideal "white spot." Over the past year, reformers had passed the initiative, referendum, and recall and banned gambling and prostitution.[60] These middle-class whites who opposed mixed bouts focused on building the good community. Commenting on the idea of the good community, historian Robert Fogelson wrote, "The late nineteenth- and early twentieth-century metropolis, as the newcomers in Los Angeles perceived it, was the receptacle for all European evils and the source of all American sins." For these migrants, the city "contradicted their long-cherished notions about the proper environment and compelled them to retreat to outskirts uncontaminated by urban vices and conducive to rural virtues."[61] These newcomers "believed that likeminded persons, joined in voluntary associations and settled in residential suburbs, could prevent 'the blight of demoralizing metropolitanism' from spreading over Los Angeles." When discussing the city's decision to ban mixed bouts, the *Times* observed, "The City Fathers do not believe that exhibitions which arouse the animal instincts to such a pitch are a good thing for the city."[62] The city council discussed "the disgusting, nauseating features of the slugging match between the black fighter Woods and the misguided representative of white humanity . . ."[63] The Council also suggested that if McCarey did not take care of this racial problem, then they would abolish boxing.

To protect his business, McCarey promised he would only promote fights between "men of the same color," and he assured fans that he had found a suitable white pugilist. One of the white fighters he banked on was Aurelio Herrera, a terrific lightweight Mexican American fighter from Bakersfield, California. Though clearly seen as nonwhite, Spanish-speaking Mexicans in Los Angeles could represent the city's whitewashed past when whites needed a cleaner image of their racial reality.

Although reformers and city boosters believed boxing morally corrupted the city, they tolerated the sport as long as McCarey banned interracial fights. He relegated his club to the downtown business district but, in October 1903, referee Harry Stuart and local businessmen decided to break McCarey's monopoly and erect their own club. The proposed club, with eight-thousand-person capacity and west of downtown on Third Street, irritated white residents. This would bring more black fighters into racially restricted white spaces.[64] Immediately, reformers in the local Crown Hill Improvement Association "declared that the minds of little children would be poisoned, that women would be afraid to pass through the tunnel for fear of meeting the class of characters that hang about prize fight headquarters and that property values would depreciate if the plan of the promoters was carried out."[65] Their grassroots campaign prevented the completion of the new pavilion, and their victory sparked other reformers to join a movement to rid Los Angeles of boxing. Their test case was the upcoming Jack Johnson–Sam McVey battle, a rematch for the colored championship on October 28, 1903.

With the biggest fight in city history a week away, a fight many argued would lead to the victor fighting Jim Jeffries in Los Angeles and surely make Los Angeles the most important fight city in the world, the city council moved to ban boxing. One article suggested, "There is no reason to doubt that the prevalence of thugs and crooks of all sort with which this city is constantly cursed is due in no small degree to the reputation Los Angeles has gained as a 'wide-open town' for fistic encounters." Three days before the fight, the city attorney drafted a bill to ban boxing, including an emergency clause to stop the upcoming contest.[66] But too many businesses stood to lose money if the city banned the fight, so Mayor Snyder allowed the affair to proceed.[67] As of November 1903, however, boxing was temporarily banned in Los Angeles. That ruling did not last long, however, because white men needed their fix. In May 1904, a local judge overruled the law because the state of California permitted boxing.[68] Buoyed by the judge's decision, McCarey started to re-build his business and, once again, he leveraged top black talent.

McCarey's continuous insistence on using black fighters demonstrated a great paradox with white thought and black bodies in the ring: In short, whites simultaneously desired and detested black bodies. McCarey's first choice for a fight, a match between middleweights Billy Woods and Young Peter Jackson, made whites cringe, and the hue and cry that McCarey wanted another "nigger club" started again, but, months later, when McCarey signed Johnson and "Denver" Ed Martin for a championship bout, white fans cel-ebrated.[69] The *Los Angeles Times* could not help but notice the great white paradox: "McCarey in putting on this battle of the black heavyweights is deferring to a frequently expressed wish of the boxing public, which seems to be one of the most fickle quantities that can possibly be conceived." "Not long since," the writer continued, "the hammer brigade shouted their heads off about too many coon fights in this city, but now most of the same fellows wish to see this big pair in action again."[70]

The following year, however, when McCarey built his new arena in the downtown district—church leaders signed a long-term lease with Hazard's Pavilion ensuring McCarey could no longer hosts matches there—McCarey temporarily banned black boxers from working in Los Angeles. In 1906, a writer argued, "McCarey has put up the bars against colored men in his club, not that the ebony-hued fighters are in disrepute with the local manager, but McCarey does not consider them a card calculated to please his audi-ence." In 1907 when discussing a potential interracial match between Jimmy Tremble (white) and Kid Lewis (black), the *Herald* claimed the match was "improbable" because "the question of negro and white fighters meeting each other in the local arena is one that always receives a negative answer from the audience."[71] But by the end of 1907, McCarey was at it again. He brought Sam Langford and Jim Berry together for the city's first mixed bout in four years. Like Baltimore promoters had done when they brought back boxing, McCarey started to use battle royals to attract white fans and blunt the blows the black boxers brought to white egos. As one report observed, "The battle royal that will be the second number on the card fills a long felt want. The fans have been asking for this for a long time."[72] This was a racial bargain, because mixed bouts had to come with battle royals.

FROM HOPE TO DESPAIR: JACK JOHNSON AND THE NATIONAL PROBLEM OF RACE AND MANHOOD

As noted by numerous scholars, the search for a "great white hope"—and the anxieties in white manly confidence Johnson's championship created—also broadened the popularity of the sport as white men looked to boxing to reclaim their physical and racial superiority.[73] In this developing racial order, states that had previously banned boxing, like Tennessee and New York, eventually passed laws giving life back to the sport in hopes of raising a new crop of white men prepared to maintain the mantle of whiteness. But the national search for a white hope and the simultaneous celebration of white bodies did not defeat the problem Johnson and other black pugilists presented; only progressive lawmakers could do that.

After Johnson won the championship, Tennessee lawmakers re-legalized boxing and permitted eight-round matches in licensed clubs. In Memphis, the leading fight scene in the state, clubs took advantage of this new law and started hosting weekly fights. Promoters rounded up the best local black and white talent, and held interracial events that featured all-white bouts and all-black bouts, but they never hosted mixed bouts, which had been banned since the 1890s. The southern black fighters included meal-ticket men like "Kid Congo," "Hock Bones," and Louisville's "Kid Phillips." In October 1909, observing the increase in black fighters, the *Commercial Appeal* noted, "The darker brethren have so far seemed to nearer satisfy the appetite of the fans for real fighting . . ."[74] In other words, in this southern city, these smaller black fighters, with minstrel-like mocking monikers, did not challenge white superiority. In fact, whites enjoyed seeing men like "Kid Congo," and "Hock Bones," slug each other in fast-paced eight-round bouts. Before one "Hock Bones" bout, one report noted, "Hock is in perfect condition, and threatens to knock Coleman's head off." Reportedly, Hock Bones told the white writer, "I'se going to try to kill the nigger. He told everybody there was no fighters in Memphis. When I gets through with him he won't want to fight here again."[75] This was white voyeurism. They could mock these no-named black meal-ticket men.

But soon, the Phoenix Club started bringing in popular black fighters with national reputations, including Jeff Clark "the Joplin Ghost," the "Dixie Kid," "Battling" Jim Johnson, and Sam Langford.[76] Their migration and domination created a problem. The successful performance of "Dixie Kid" in fall of 1909, in combination with the national white anxiety created by Jack Johnson—Johnson beat Stanley Ketchel while "Dixie Kid" was in Memphis—opened the door for a potential interracial match featuring "Dixie Kid" and an unnamed white fighter. In the middle of a Good Government mayoral political campaign led by eventual winner Edward Crump that linked reform and racism with a quest for white power, why would promoters try to host a mixed bout?[77] Was this about proving white authority in the age of Jack Johnson, or simply a move to make money preying on white fans' need to see white primal authority? As quickly as that interracial door opened, however, the Phoenix Club closed that potential racial problem. The "Phoenix Club management, although admitting that the match proposed with the white man would be a feature bout from purely a pugilistic standpoint, makes the announcement that bouts in the Phoenix arena in the future will be 'all white' or 'all yellow' or 'all black' or 'black versus yellow,' gingerbread, chocolate, copper-colored or taints in any shade."[78]

Instead of hosting mixed bouts, Memphis clubs increasingly relied on all-black fight cards. By November 29, 1909, the Phoenix Club put on their first all-black fight card, which was headline by a fight between the "Dixie Kid" and a Philly fighter named Bert Whirlwind, "a coon," according to one local writer. It was an easy knockout for Dixie, who left the "Philadelphia coon" with his head dangling over the edge of the ropes after a knockout. Despite the exciting matches, the white fans noticed that white fighters were missing. "An all-black card was offered by the Phoenix for the first time. Manager Carroll says he is finding it hard to get white boys on in prelims, but fact is the white end of the audience would be tickled to see some white fights."[79] The clubs, however, did not listen to the white complaints.

The increase in black fighters in Memphis upset white fighters, fans, the press, and the newly elected Mayor Crump. In January, after Langford beat "Dixie Kid," promoter Tommy White, who ran the Memphis Athletic Club, announced he would no longer allow black men to fight in main event contests. "Darkest Africa will be presented in secondary pugilist considerations offered . . . but the ambitious Jacksons, Sam Langfords, George Dixons or Joe Jeannettes of the future will be forced to tune the little fiddle while white boxers fill the limelight in feature bouts," reasoned the *Commercial Appeal*.[80]

"Mack," the city's leading sportswriter, who wrote for the *Memphis Scripter*, admitted, "Peculiar as it may seem, the biggest houses at the Phoenix have been drawn by negro fights," and claimed "the patronage was always about three whites to one coon," and that "white bouts have never drawn" comparable crowds in Memphis. The writer argued for "more white prelims," and "Mack" also predicted "more white bouts" in place of black bouts "would make a hit with the fight crowd."[81] Just days later, city lawmakers led by Mayor Crump discussed passing a law that stated only white men could fight in main events. According to reports, "'Too much color' has been conspicuous in past bouts is the whispered rumor, the report being current that Mayor Crump may soon ask promoters to confine their feature bouts to whites," because "so much limelight for the African colony is said to be distasteful to the members of the new commission."[82] Mayor Crump denied these charges. By the end of January 1910, however, the *Commercial Appeal* observed that the clubs had been listening to the racially charged complaints, and the "Memphis A.C. members, comprising bankers, millionaires and others, have gradually placed more white and less black in the color scheme for the preliminary sport." The paper further noted, "there may be a dark dab or so in tonight's proceedings, but the Caucasian race will predominate, and there are many good members of it waiting around for matches that will be given preference."[83] Make no mistake about it: Demoting black men was a deliberate move to deter any notion of black superiority in Memphis. Pushing white fighters to the top billing in main events highlighted white masculinity by commercializing their manliness and virility as first-rate fighters as their bodies were juxtaposed against the second-rate black fighters like the diminutive Kid Congo or Hock Bones on the undercard. This seemed to work for a few months.

Johnson's victory over Jeffries on July 4, 1910, however, forced Mayor Crump to further evaluate the problem Johnson and black fighters posed to white Memphians. Before the Johnson–Jeffries fight, whites in Memphis were convinced they had a sure thing in Jeffries. City officials, from the mayor to the police department, all openly pulled for Jeffries. Police Chief W. C. Davis claimed, "I am disgusted with that sort of sport, especially where a white man fights a negro. I hope, however, that Jeffries will win." Captain John M. Couch added, "I think Jeff will win, but have little sympathy with a white man who will fight a negro. However, this fight was forced on Jeffries to wrench the championship of the world from the black." Detective Will Smiddy held out for a murder, exclaiming "I hope Jeff will kill that nigger, and I believe he can do it if he wants to."[84] But things did not go as planned. To assuage local white fears, one editorial warned, "Let no fool negro get biggity because of the result of the fight at Reno yesterday."[85]

After Johnson's victory, Mayor Crump used white public anxiety to eliminate potential challenges to white male authority and maintain a depressed black working caste. He wanted pickers, not pugilists, and he banned black boxers from fighting in Memphis. Days after the fight, Mayor Crump stated, "Labor is needed on the cotton plantations badly. Negroes may make an honest living there."[86] While most states in the South allowed black men to fight other black men—Memphis would bring back black fighters—they all banned interracial contests. States in the North soon followed the South's lead.

As Johnson's manliness and championship status became too much to bear, other states, including New York, which had legalized fighting in 1911 in hopes of making money from white hopes, banned Johnson from fighting in their state as a move to preserve white power. In 1913, New York took their discrimination against Johnson one step further, and banned all mixed bouts for the "preservation of peace."[87] The state's move to bar the likes of Joe Jeannette and Sam Langford—Johnson had fled America—rested on preserving white manhood and making money from white hopes. When the state legalized fighting in 1911, they gave the boxing commission all of the power to dictate who fought in their state, and the law also awarded the state boxing commission 5 percent off all gate receipts. While the most lucrative fights were interracial battles that pitted black fighters against white ones, those fights could only take place if the white fighters had credibility. The boxing commission quickly learned that when a white boxer lost to a black fighter, the white man lost his prestige and thus earning power for the club and the state. One sportswriter reasoned he "discovered why it was that the New York state boxing commission refused to let Sam Langford, Joe Jeannette and other battlers of color swap punches with some of the 'white hope' persons who infest this locality." In 1913, the boxing commission made $38,871 from the net receipts of $775,506, and "a large portion of this money came through the staging of alleged fights between 'white hopes.'" But if Langford or Jeannette fought a white hope, the writer reasoned, "there wouldn't be any 'white hopes' left to pit against each other in a very short period and the commission's rakeoff would hardly supply the members with cigar money."[88]

Unfortunately, the color line suppressed black fighters' wages by forcing them to fight the same black foes. When New York banned mixed bouts, Langford lost a $10,000 opportunity to fight the White Hope "Gunboat" Smith. Instead of fighting "Gunboat" Smith, Langford fought Joe Jeannette for the ninth time and considerably less money. Langford's lawyer asked, "Why should he be deprived of earning his livelihood as a boxer in the State of New York, where boxing is legal?"[89] He received no answer from the state.

In 1914, Langford also lost money when Wisconsin banned black fighters in order to stop a fight between Langford and Sam McVey. McVey, who had grown accustomed to the big-money fights abroad, linked the color line and loss of his wages to his civil rights. On McVey's behalf, his manager George Lawrence argued "the boxing commission of Milwaukee has gone to a greater extreme, where it positively prohibits two colored men from boxing at a club, which is an illegal act and means that the boxing commission has overruled the Fifteenth Amendment of the United States Constitution."[90] Lawrence also sought an injunction to overturn New York's ban on mixed bouts. He did not win.

Like Langford and McVey, New York's decision to eliminate "mixed bouts" also hurt Jeannette's pockets. During the previous two years, Jeannette had defeated white hopes Al Kubiack, Tony Ross, "Porky" Flynn, Joseph Smith, and Jeff Madden. Realizing the financial losses the color line cost Jeannette, a sportswriter remarked, "Since the Boxing Commission placed a ban on mixed bouts, Joe Jeannette, the formidable Hoboken negro, has been practically out of employment."[91] To momentarily supplement his income, Jeannette ventured down South to fight other black men.[92] In Memphis in 1913—apparently Mayor Crump lifted his ban against black boxers—Jeannette battled Jeff Clarke, but the local referee declared the match a fake, and withheld the fight purse despite the fact Jeannette dominated the match. On the undercard of that fight, white fans were treated to a battle royal featuring five black youth fighters. "All Black" and "Blacker Than" were the last two standing.[93] Using the battle royal as a preliminary contest for a fight featuring a skilled black heavyweight like Jeannette—a potential replacement for Johnson's title— helped blunt any potential anxieties whites might have had about Jeannette's presence. For Jeannette, however, the discrimination was just another reason to quit the ring. When discussing his 1916 retirement, Jeannette said, "The color line left my field somewhat limited. Langford and McVey were the only opponents I could hope to meet and these I have met so often that the public could scarcely take seriously that kind of competition."[94] In 1914, for example, Jeannette fought "Battling" Jim Johnson in three separate ten-round bouts that resulted in three no-decisions. After their third contest, one paper asked, "do you suppose that two boxers like battling Jim Johnson and Joe Jeannette could get away with seven ten-round draw fights in those good old days? . . . There would have been some result between this pair of dusky warriors, or they would have been thrown out of the ring." Another sportswriter added, "The firm of Joe Jeannette and Battling Jim Johnson has been dissolved. The two black mastodons fought . . . at the Stadium club in New York the other night, and the bout was so unsatisfactory that a majority of the spectators left before the ninth round started." The author closed his remarks noting that the "corporation of Battling Jim Johnson and Sam Langford is now in the field."[95]

The restrictive laws ended black domination. In January 1915, two years after lawmakers had run Johnson out of America, and three months before Jess Willard defeated Johnson in Havana, Cuba, a *New York Tribune* writer noticed a racial change in the boxing ring. "The day of the negro boxer is swiftly passing," he observed, "and unless a new crop is developed in the next few years a high grade negro pugilist will be as rare as a good white heavyweight is to-day." He argued that the great black fighters, Johnson, Jeannette, Langford, and McVey were getting old and concluded "the number of bouts between negroes, in fact, the recurrent bouts, they might be called, are due in no small measure to the feeling against so-called 'mixed bouts" throughout the country. They must fight amongst themselves or quit the ring."[96] Was this a racial hope, or a racial reality? As the black journalist Lucien H. White concluded, the *Tribune's* remarks "embodied the hopes and desires of the white man." White argued that New York's decision to ban mixed bouts "saved white pugilists from the ignominy of being defeated by a Negro." And he claimed, "The action of the New York Commission found an echoing response in other states, and in one or the other, means were found to put a stop to mixed bouts in most of the states which give legal protection to pugilistic exhibitions." What happened if a black man failed to get a chance to fight? White concluded, "He must necessarily turn his hand to some other pursuit, for the law of life is inexorable and a man must eat to live. To eat he must work."[97] After Willard defeated Johnson and immediately drew the color line, Joe Jeannette momentarily gave up all hope of fighting for a living. Jeannette said, "Willard has drawn the color line . . . I should have liked to make one more fight, but feel it would be unfair to the public to ask for a match with any of the present crop of hopes. With no one to box my fighting days are over, so I intend to devote all my time to business."[98] In 1919, Baltimore's Young Jackson complained, Johnson was "the bird that killed the black fighter. His actions in and out of the ring drove the colored fighter to work. Put him back so far in the minds of ring followers that it will be a long, long time—if ever—that they will again be given the matches they once had little trouble in getting." He closed his diatribe: "Yes, sir, we have nobody to blame but Jack Johnson."[99] If he could not work in the ring, then he had to go back to a life of drudgery.

EPILOGUE

Beau Jack moved beyond the battle royal, but just barely. Born Sidney Walker in 1921 in Augusta, Georgia, Jack, whose parents left him with relatives at a young age, grew up poor and had to drop out of school in the second grade so he could help support his family. Eventually he found work at Augusta National, the famed golf course, where he worked as a bootblack for the wealthy white guests. One night, the guests were looking for southern entertainment, so the head bootblack, Bowman Milligan, rounded up a group of young black boys to participate in a battle royal. They blindfolded the poor black boys and made them fight for the rich white men. Smaller than the other fighters, Jack hid as best as he could until his moment came and then unleashed a reckless barrage of powerful blows. Despite the dreadful act of forcing young kids into these bloody battles, Jack seemed unfazed; he loved fighting and the feeling of money in his hands. In 1940, Bowman took Jack north to start a professional career, and after only a few fights the white men from the club wanted in on the action. After all, they claimed, they loved their bootblack and he loved them back. His whirlwind style he developed during those despicable days stayed with him throughout his career. White people loved watching him fight with reckless abandon; it connected them to the battle royal days, and this white voyeurism resulted in Jack smashing the Madison Square Garden record as the most profitable fighter on his way to winning the lightweight championship. In his heyday, from 1941 to 1945, his fights grossed 1.5 million dollars. But nobody looked out for Beau Jack.[1]

To white people, Beau Jack never moved beyond the battle royal. Whites liked thinking of him as the poor happy-go-lucky illiterate bootblack who had no aspirations but to serve their desires. They made sure he stayed that way, both in reality and in their imagination. "He makes a good interview," his manager said, "on account of his southern drawl." The white press did their part and told tales of his battle royal days and his continued docility and supposed simplemindedness. They could not have another Jack Johnson, so they purposely propped up Beau Jack, an aggressive fighter, as a docile and loyal man-child outside the ring. At a time when black Americans started to assert their rights, writers used Beau Jack as the antidote for their white egos. He was content. Even at the height of his career, white writers celebrated that Jack could still be found shining shoes at Augusta. And to make this docility a sure reality, his handlers kept him illiterate and dependable. Nobody taught him how to read or write, and in fact, they fired the cook who tried to teach him to write his name. His handlers even kept him on a $1 per week allowance, then $2, and then finally $5 a week. How could this be? How could a man who sold out Madison Square Garden only receive a $5 per week? In his uneducated dependence, Jack gave power of attorney to one of his handlers, who then proceeded to make the two of them a joint account. He earned the money, and his handler deposited the checks. But who cared? After all, they said, he had no need for money. "With him," his manager contended, "money is secondary. 'Money,' he says, 'is for givin away.'"[2]

The black press, however, hated the story. They hated what Beau Jack stood for. Why did Beau Jack let white men control him? Why did Beau Jack go back to the South to shine shoes? Why did Beau Jack always smile around these white men and let them call him boy? He must be an Uncle Tom, they charged. And the black press had no time for an Uncle Tom. Besides, they had other heroes in the ring to follow. Men like Joe Louis, Ray Robinson, Jimmy Bivins, and Ike Williams, men who asserted their manhood. To be sure, the black press congratulated Jack when he won the lightweight championship, twice, and they were happy when he won 1944 fighter of the year, but they wanted him to be a man and take control of his own life. Eventually, Jack realized that his so-called white friends kept him dependent, but by the time he realized it, it was too late. Everything was gone.

In 1949, as people began to wonder what exactly happened to his money, Beau Jack sat down with *Ebony* to tell his story. As the illiterate boxer explained, the problem with boxing, and also his economic status, was the direct result of the promoter and the "cutthroat manager who regards his fighter as a beast of burden or an article to be bought, bartered or sold."[3] Jack might have been illiterate, but he was not dumb. These words from a black man, born poor in the South, had implications of race and labor. At a time when black fighters had started to dominate the ring rankings, and the business of boxing had started to heavily rely on black and brown bodies, Beau Jack was speaking as an exploited black worker. Though he never gained financial freedom, this interview was his emancipation. He was the product of the South and a racist system that operated to keep him undereducated and, to make matter worse, he worked in an exploitive business that operated to keep him broke. After his last fight in 1955, Jack lived the rest of his life working as a bootblack in Miami. One of the most talented fighters of his generation had one of the most heartbreaking stories. But Beau Jack was not alone in this cruel game. Most black fighters struggled to keep what they earned.

Since Jess Willard defeated Jack Johnson in 1915 through to Floyd "Money" Mayweather's retirement in 2015, black fighters have continued to face the same kinds of challenges and obstacles to financial security. To be sure, white boxers are not as prevalent in the sport. The color line is finally gone, and the profits have increased, but the same forces that push black men into the ring—poverty and a quest to assert their manhood in a society that tries to deny black masculinity—remain. When the fighter receives his earnings, he buys the things he always wanted, the items that make him stand out in sporting society and give him an air of financial autonomy: cars, clothes, and jewelry. He tells himself that he will not end up broke like the other black fighters. He also wants to be recognized for his manhood beyond the ring and the sporting culture. To this end, he tries to take care of his family financially; he invests his money in businesses or property, and makes sure to tell the press about his latest business venture. After all, most fighters have the same economic and familial aspirations the black middle class has. Even Beau Jack invested in three farms and a rib joint, and talked about the need to support his kids and ensure they received the education he never did. Some kept their promises, but in the end, the same forces that worked against the black fighter in the days of Dixon, Gans, and Walcott continued to drag him down: unscrupulous businessmen and the black fighter's desire to live the life of a good fellow has been a strong two-punch combination. To understand how these forces continue to work to drag most black men down, it is important to briefly explore how key boxers over the last one hundred years, like Beau Jack, sought to move beyond the battle royal.

By the 1920s, black fighters had lost most of their so-called gains in the business of boxing. America, and the boxing business, was still reeling from Jack Johnson's national nightmare. Promoters and state officials did their best to bar mixed bouts, and top-notch white fighters would not tangle with the top brown talent. Although two black fighters won championships, Tiger

Flowers and Battling Siki, they were the only black men to get title shots. The top heavyweights—Kid Norfolk, George Godfrey, Bill Tate, and Harry Wills— had to settle for meal-ticket fights against each other. The white heavyweight champion, Jack Dempsey, the man who came to represent the Roaring '20s with his rags to riches story, rugged good lucks, and aggression in the ring, drew the color line and ducked Wills, the best of the lot. Years later, Dempsey told a writer, "One reason that I never fought Harry Wills was the he was a Negro." According to Dempsey, fight promoter Tex Rickard, who famously promoted the Johnson–Jeffries bout, refused to make the match because of the criticism he took for the Johnson–Jeffries affair. "When Johnson won," Dempsey noted, "Tex was accused of humiliating the white race."[4] But, while Dempsey drew the color line against Wills, the "Black Panther," as fans called him, showed black fighters a path to financial success.

Born and raised in New Orleans, Wills started his twenty-year boxing career fighting on the city's docks and won his first official fight in 1911 against Nat Dewey. In the early 1920s, he and his wife settled in Harlem, where Wills, the most famous black fighter of the decade, epitomized the New Negro with his clean suits, sleek cars, business acumen, and black pride. Despite the racism he faced in the ring, Wills succeeded in society by investing among his own people. In 1922, he bought his first property in Harlem, and then kept buying property in the well-known black neighborhood of Sugar Hill. In his retirement, Wills owned more than a quarter million dollars' worth of property, and collected $2,000 a month from his holdings. Wills was class personified and represented the man the black press wanted black fighters to imitate. As the black sportswriter Dan Burley said, "He is a model of what an intelligent prize fighter can do to keep his ring earnings for security in later life and a welcome contrast from the poverty-stricken, punch-drunk stumblebums that haunt gyms for a handout in the years after their heyday."[5] But very few black boxers followed his lead. They were more comfortable asserting their manhood in the sporting culture.

If Wills represented the pathway to success, Kid Chocolate, the Cuban-born fighter, represented the gateway to the disastrous sporting lifestyle. He changed the game. The featherweight champion (1930) was the first black fighter of the post–Jack Johnson era who refused to straddle the line between respectability and the sporting lifestyle. He gave no pretenses of wanting to properly invest his ring earnings, unless, of course, it was in himself or the hordes of hangers-on who followed the fighter. He was a good fellow, plain and simple. "Like the colored champions who were to follow him, Chocolate was more than generous with fur coats, dresses, steak dinners, flowers, and rent free apartments for the belles who won his eye. The army of hangers-on that followed him wherever he went, helped him get rid of the rest," remembered Burley.[6] As blacks in urban areas struggled in the Great Depression, Kid Chocolate showed them a flash of hope. A black man could win the championship, treat himself like a champion, and not have to worry about white people getting mad. At one point, he reportedly had a Bentley imported from England, ordered the exterior silver-plated, and had running water installed in the back. The colored sport was back. Before Joe Louis won his heavyweight championship and represented the hopes of black America as a so-called symbol of racial democracy, future fighters dreamed of being like Kid Chocolate. Ezzard Charles, the heavyweight champion from 1949 to 1951, who was raised in poverty in Cincinnati, recalled seeing Kid Chocolate stroll through the Cincinnati ghetto in one of his expensive cars as kids clamored to be near him. When one kid asked the champ how many suits he had, Kid Chocolate bragged, "Man, I got suits for every day in the year. I got 365." Upon hearing that, the ten-year-old Charles made up his mind. "I'm gonna be a fighter and have clothes like that."[7] As heavyweight champion, Charles owned four houses, invested in several properties, and owned seventy-five suits and twenty-four pairs of dress shoes. But, unfortunately, like Kid Chocolate, Charles went bust. As Charles suggested in 1962, "One reason why I was taken so clean, is that I was a guy who believed in people. If a guy said he was my friend—I though he was my friend. . . . I used to carry what I called an emergency or operating expense fund of $200 to $250 in my pockets every day. Some guys always seemed to need money. It would cost me at least $30 to go to the corner and talk about events."[8]

Henry Armstrong felt the same inspiration from Kid Chocolate. While living in the ghetto of St. Louis, he read in a newspaper that Kid Chocolate made $75,000 in one fight, and Armstrong promptly quit his job on the spot. He told the naysayers, "If he's going back to Cuba with a Lincoln, I'm going back with a Cadillac."[9] Armstrong, who bought his Cadillac, and then some, swore he would never end up like Chocolate—they all claimed the same. But the best black fighter since the days of Joe Gans got a quick lesson in being black in the business of boxing. Born Henry Jackson in 1912 on a Mississippi plantation owned by his white grandfather, who had once owned slaves on that same plantation, Armstrong moved to St. Louis with his family at a young age as they escaped the ravages of a nasty boll weevil outbreak. But soon after moving to St. Louis, his mother died and his dad had to care for his sixteen children on a black butcher's salary. Armstrong, who had dreams of becoming a doctor, had to find work to support his family. He turned to boxing. At first, he struggled to find meaningful fights. White promoters in St. Louis would not host mixed bouts and forced most black boxers to fight in battle royals. Armstrong had too much racial pride for those battles: "What they were usually doing at that time, and I wouldn't subject myself to it, they wanted the colored kids to get in there and fight in what they call a Battle Royal, where they put a black towel around your eyes and put five, six, seven guys in a ring and let them fight against each other blind and laugh at you. I wouldn't go for that. I was really too proud."[10] He left the city and headed west. Eventually Armstrong got his big break and soon became the first boxer to hold three championships simultaneously (featherweight, lightweight, welterweight), and became the second most popular fighter in black America behind Joe Louis. Unlike Kid Chocolate, Armstrong straddled the line between sporting manhood and middle-class respectability. He invested his money in businesses, including a film about himself, *Keep Punching*—the movie is a moral message to black youth about working hard and about avoiding the sporting lifestyle—and he also gave speeches to black churches and to troubled black youth. But when he was forced to retire in 1941 because he could not defend himself in the ring, he had nothing to show for it. Armstrong had lost nearly a million dollars.

While Armstrong is partly to blame for his economic downfall—he lived the sporting lifestyle and spent lavishly—managers, promoters, and state-sanctioning governing bodies colluded to make sure fighters had little power. They kept him dependent. While working as a preacher after his retirement, Armstrong reflected on the powerlessness of fighters: "If I had my career to live over again, I would see in the boxing world that every fighter would get his own check instead of giving it all to the manager. . . . If I had to live over again, I would sure make that change because I would have had so much more and I would have been able to guide myself better because I would have known what I had and the manager couldn't pad the bills on you, which they did tremendously." The problem with boxing, as Armstrong argued, was the manager received the money first from the promoter or arena that hosted the match. This made the fighter dependent on the manager for his money, and if the fighter lacked math skills, or borrowed too much, which so many did, it meant that managers would easily and readily rip him off.

When Armstrong made his comeback in 1942, it seemed he had learned a lesson about tangling with white managers when he hooked up with George Moore, the preeminent black manager in the business. Since the 1920s, Moore had been the leading black manager and the most significant for advancing the cause for black fighters. It was Moore, in fact, who helped black fighters gain more lucrative fights when he defeated New York's law against mixed bouts. In Los Angeles in the late 1930s, Moore helped Armstrong fight the American Legion's ban on mixed bouts when Armstrong refused to fight for the club until they dropped their unjust rule. Throughout his career, the black press sang the praises of Moore and, of course, they did not miss this opportunity to celebrate the Moore–Armstrong relationship. Joe Bostic of the *People's Voice* praised, "Moore isn't just a manager, he's a crusading institution. He's made it possible for Negro fighters to make real money via mixed fights in Oregon, California, and New York. More important, he's proved that a Negro can be a successful manager, if he knows his business—especially the angles."[11] With Moore as his manager, in 1942 Armstrong purchased a $25,000 income property in Los Angeles that supposedly netted him $400 a month, and he made substantial money during his comeback.[12]

Although Moore never robbed Armstrong, a black manager has never guaranteed that a black fighter would avoid the perils of exploitation. Just ask Mike Tyson. Tyson, who blew hundreds of millions of winnings during his career because he lived the sporting lifestyle, also lost hundreds of millions to his black manager, Don King, who stole the money. In 2004, a broke Tyson, who owed creditors millions, sued King for 100 million dollars.[13] King was a crook and to this day is synonymous with the crooked business of boxing. Not even a reportedly clean character like Moore could avoid criticism. In 1944, Dan Parker of the *Los Angeles Mirror*, a white writer, charged Moore with exploiting Armstrong and maintained that the ex-champion should not have been allowed in a ring. Armstrong had bad eyes and damaged scar tissue around his eyes from years of fighting too soon before his wounds healed, because his previous manager had kept him active, trying to get extra money. In reality, Moore should have let him stay retired.[14] But Armstrong kept punching. It was inevitable, therefore, that Armstrong would experience eye problems that led to more damaging hits in his comeback.

Like the days of Joe Walcott and Joe Gans, unfortunately, if the black boxer bucked the system, managers froze him out of boxing. Ike Williams learned that hard lesson. Most who followed Williams's career thought he would be one of the lucky ones, the one to truly escape poverty. In 1950, *Sport* magazine had touted Williams the "businessman of boxing." He owned a lovely home and had invested more than $80,000 in property. But for Williams, who grew up poor in Trenton, New Jersey, and turned professional at sixteen to support his single mother, the twin evils of the brutal business of boxing and living the life of a good fellow did him in.[15] Williams loved to gamble on golf, and after his skills in the ring started to fade, he started to drink heavily.

These habits were fine as long as he was winning, but the winning stopped, and the large paydays ceased.

Worse yet, Williams did not get a chance to spend or invest most of his money, because his manager stole his winnings. In 1945, after he won the lightweight championship by knocking out Juan Zurita in Mexico City, he fired his manager, Connie McCarthey—who bought Williams's contract from Joe Woodman, the ex-manager of Sam Langford—because McCarthey was always drunk and inept. Williams told him he would make his own way, but when he headed back East, the new champ could not find work in the ring. Boxing managers in the East had just formed the Boxing Guild, a trust, and stuck together to keep Williams from fighting. According to Williams, Jimmy White, the head of the Boxing Guild, said, "We're going to stop Ike Williams from fighting. Anybody that fights him, we're going to black ball them."[16] The only one who would help the world champion was Blinky Palermo, a manager from Philadelphia who was connected to Frank Carbo and the Mob. Palermo paid Williams $27,000 for his contract and gave him a Cadillac. As his manager helped get Williams his fights, and he retained his title until 1951, Palermo also asked him to take dives and stole his money. "He just robbed the hell out of me from my money. He had robbed me of quite a bit of money," Williams recalled. In two cases, Williams did not even receive a penny from his $33,000 purses.[17] Like so many other fighters, Williams suffered because the system was rigged to give managers and promoters the power.

In a business with powerful white managers, white promoters, and white syndicates, if a fighter tried to assert his independence and demand a fair shake, he lost revenue and respect from the mostly white boxing writers. There is no clearer example of this than the career of "Sugar Ray" Robinson. Born Walker Smith in Detroit—he took the name Ray Robinson from another amateur fighter in Harlem—Sugar Ray grew up in poverty in a Harlem ghetto. While his mom took in laundry to support her three children, Robinson did odd jobs, like fetch wood from the Hudson River or dance on the side of the streets for coins, to make whatever he could so the family would not go hungry. But after a local church leader caught Robinson playing a game of craps, the elder forced him into the church-sponsored youth center so the young boy could learn some discipline and stay out of trouble. In this sanctuary, the skinny, underfed kid fell in love with boxing, a sport he was introduced to while living in Detroit, where he trained next to future champion Joe Louis. After a few years in the business, everyone knew Sugar Ray was the best welterweight in boxing, but until 1946 he could not get a championship fight. Champions avoided tangling with the tough kid from

Harlem, and managers and promoters hated dealing with him because of his fierce independence and his insistence on understanding the business of boxing. Worse yet, less-talented white fighters made more money than Robinson. This runaround made Sugar Ray bitter. While Robinson had an official manager, he always insisted on being in negotiations and fighting for a fair price, and after he won the championship in 1946, his demands and insistence on autonomy increased. Although people loved to see him fight, in truth, a number of white writers and boxing managers hated Robinson for his independence. Writers used their power in the media to paint him as "boxing's bad boy" and constantly described him as a malcontent. His public image took such a hit that the champion wrote a letter in *Ebony* to clear his name and assert his right to his autonomy. In "Why I'm the Bad Boy of Boxing," Robinson meticulously refuted the accusations white writers and managers made about his business strategy and also told readers about the need for boxers to be better businessmen. The article is an important document on the quest for independence from a black man who grew up in America's ghettos, and who as an adult tried to survive in a business that thrived on black bodies. "Most fighters end up broke," he said. "The managers and promoters usually get theirs in front. Fighters have got to learn to fight for their interests outside the ring as well as inside it. A fighter these days must express himself, must speak up when he thinks he's being shoved around. . . . They must be businessmen as well as athletes." Robinson insisted on maintaining his independence, because the hard times he had lived through while growing up taught him how to fend for himself. Nobody would take that away. "I have had to struggle hard for what I have. Nobody gave me anything. As a boy in Detroit and New York I roamed the streets most of the time without a penny, and had my fill of life in the slums." Money and his independence meant the most to him: "Next to solid financial security, I love freedom and independence." He also asserted that fighters, especially black fighters, should learn how to account for every dollar they earned: "It's a good habit, and one I wish more Negro fighters would acquire."[18] Robinson believed that if his friend Beau Jack had done his own bookkeeping, he would not have gone broke. But Beau Jack, like most black boxers, lacked the necessary education and business leverage to keep his own books.

Robinson, who like Joe Louis was an idol in the black community, straddled the line of respectability—the black press celebrated him for his multiple businesses in Harlem, and he even won a father of the year award—and the sporting life, but took that sporting lifestyle to a whole new level. The clothes, the cars, and the clubs were manageable, in fact expected of a boxer, but he turned being a good fellow into a full-time job. Robinson was the first athlete to have a posse—a term today that is more derogatory than laudatory—and paid each member for his services. He also paid for their women, their food, and their drink. Included in this entourage were his barber, a stylist, the golf pro, the chauffer, the guy to get the drinks, and guys who were just there for the experience. Wherever he went, they went. It was a recipe for financial disaster, and by 1955—he retired for a few years to become a full-time dancer and entertainer—Robinson was broke. He had not paid his property taxes or his mortgage, and the bank took his Harlem property. The impressive portfolio, which consisted of a block of businesses in Harlem, included a liquor store, apartments, a bar, a barbershop, a beauty shop, his own office, and an office for the Salvation Army.[19] Then Uncle Sam came for his tax money too. For the rest of his career, just like the great Joe Louis, Robinson chased glory, titles, and the money to pay off Uncle Sam.

With every new story about the old problem of black fighters going broke, a sense of shame and sadness simmered within the black community. Since the days of Peter Jackson, the boxer came to represent the hopes of the black community. The grit and determination they showed in getting to the top, the might and power they displayed in the ring, the admiration from black fans, and the fighter's fancy clothes and cars, captured the imagination of the black community. With Louis, Armstrong, and Robinson, the greatest fighters of all time, losing it all during their careers, the downfall for fighters seemed inevitable. If the fighter could not make it out and avoid the perils of the sporting life and exploitive white and black businessmen, then who could? To this day, very few black fighters have tried to avoid the life of a good fellow. Men like "Old" George Godfrey, Joe Jeannette, Harry Wills, Archie Moore, Floyd Patterson, George Foreman in the second phase of his career, and Lennox Lewis did fine economically after their ring careers and publicly set examples as respectable black men whom the black press celebrated. However, for the majority, and most famously Mike Tyson, thieving managers like Don King and living the life of a good fellow beat them in the end.

Only one fighter has successfully straddled the line by living the life of a sporting man and controlled the business of boxing. First calling himself "Pretty Boy" in 1996, and then "Money" in 2007, Floyd Mayweather escaped poverty and an unequal school system in Grand Rapids, Michigan, and successfully turned the image of the colored sport into a promotional bonanza. Like Jack Johnson and Ray Robinson, he wore expensive jewelry, bought the finest cars, gambled large sums of money, draped multiple women on his arms, flashed wads of cash, and spoke in the language of a young free black man who was carefree and could not care less what the public thought. He epitomized the free spirit of the so-called hip-hop "bling bling" generation: young, black, rich, and famous. In fact, many people grew to dislike him because of his arrogant blackness—to be sure, Mayweather did jail time for domestic violence, but most boxing fans, and even some casual fans, largely ignored those transgressions—and paid large sums of money to see him lose. He never did. Like "Sugar Ray" Robinson, he took control of his fight future. In 2007, the notorious gambler—he is known to bet five figures on a sporting outcome—made his most successful bet; he gambled on himself and bought his contract from fight promoter Bob Arum. The $750,000 buyout gave Mayweather the power to dictate his own terms and reap the large profits from his fights. From 2007 to 2015, he fought in ten consecutive fights that each grossed him more than twenty-five million dollars. All told, he made more than half a billion dollars boxing. While people speculate that he will go broke, because that has been the fate of most fighters (and to be clear, he is a young black man with a lot of money and historically, the American public, especially the white America public, have rooted against these men) it seems nearly impossible Mayweather will lose it all. He has made too much money.[20] But this is not improvement, or a way forward for black fighters. Floyd's financial success is not attainable for other boxers. Something must change.

For fighters who do not have the money or power to control their fate like Floyd, in 2000 Congress finally passed some sort of relief, the Ali Act. It is fitting that the law is named after Muhammad Ali, one of the most recognizable people in the history of America, a black man who was once hated by the white establishment because he asserted his black autonomy in a white-controlled world. In fact, between 1966 and 1967, when the American government was after Ali for his refusal to be drafted into the military, Ali, along with Jim Brown and the Nation of Islam, invested in a boxing promotion company to ensure he got his money off the top. Despite the fact that state-sanctioning bodies tried to fight Ali and restrict his fighting opportunities, his promotional company, Main Bout, Inc., financially succeeded until Ali could no longer fight. Even without his championship, however, Ali remained the champion of the world in spirit and esteem, and a thorn in the side of the establishment, because he spoke truth to power. Eventually, when he could no longer speak clearly—the combination of the beatings he took in the ring and Parkinson's disease seriously limited his speech—white America celebrated Ali for his independence.

The Ali Act is an attempt to clean up the business of boxing. The law tries to ensure that unscrupulous managers do not steal from their fighters, and that promoters do not exploit a man's needs and desire to fight and earn a living by throwing him into a fight while he is injured or underprepared to battle.[21] Although the legislation seemingly has nothing to do with race, it is hard to imagine that a law named after a fiercely independent black man, a law that regulates a sport where in the public's imagination the majority of fighters who have gone bust are black men, and those who continue to fight today and risk their lives to earn a living with their fists are brown and black men trying to avoid hard times, has nothing to do with race. But no law can protect a fighter from his or her desire to find freedom in their finances and materialism, and no law can truly hold back an unscrupulous promoter and manager. Moreover, the Ali Act cannot fight the broader racist elements of an American society that is resistant to change and continues to push men into the ring to prove their manhood.

NOTES

INTRODUCTION

1. "Professor Godfrey," *San Francisco Chronicle*, July 30, 1888.

2. Jim Hornby, *Black Islanders: Prince Edward Island's Historical Black Community* (Charlottetown, P.E.I.: Institute of Island Studies, 1991), 62–65. Elizabeth Hafkin Pleck, *Black Migration and Poverty: Boston 1855–1900* (New York, 1979), 128.

3. Louis Moore, "Fit For Citizenship: Black Sparring Masters, Gymnasium Owners, and the White Body, 1825–1886," *Journal of African American History* 96, no. 4 (Fall 2011): 448–73.

4. "Sporting Notes," *Boston Globe,* May 4, 1884.

5. "Professor Godfrey," *San Francisco Chronicle,* July 30, 1888.

6. "Latest Sporting Topics," *National Police Gazette,* January 31, 1891.

7. "Godfrey wants to go Europe," *Boston Globe,* November 8, 1887.

8. Elliott J. Gorn, *The Manly Art: Bare-Knuckle Prize Fighting in America* (Ithaca, N.Y.: Cornell University Press, 1986), 138; Michael S. Kimmel, *Manhood in America: A Cultural History,* 2nd ed. (New York: Oxford University Press, 2006), 94.

9. "A Chance for Godfrey," *Boston Globe,* November 16, 1887.

10. "Sporting News," *National Police Gazette,* November 10, 1883; "Athletic," *New Orleans Picayune,* January 17, 1884.

11. "Godfrey vs. Johnson," *Boston Herald,* May 11, 1884.

12. Theresa Runstedtler, *Jack Johnson Rebel Sojourner* (Berkeley: University of California Press, 2012), 9.

13. Howard P. Chudacoff, *The Age of the Bachelor: Creating An American Subculture* (Princeton, N.J.: Princeton University Press, 1999), 35.

14. Davarian Baldwin, *Chicago's New Negroes: Modernity, the Great Migration, and Black Urban Life* (Chapel Hill: University of North Carolina Press, 2007), 194.

15. "Boxers are Working," *Los Angeles Herald,* June 18, 1902.

16. "St. Paul News," *St. Paul Pioneer Press,* February 19, 1887; "Sporting Notes," *Omaha Bee,* September 4, 1887.

17. "Sporting Matters," *St. Paul Pioneer Press,* December 31, 1886. For other articles in which Johnson and Wilson sparred with each other in the press during December 1886, read: "The Sluggers," *St. Paul Pioneer Press,* December 9, 1886; "The Sluggers," *St. Paul Pioneer Press,* December 10, 1886; "The Heavy-Weight Boxers," *St. Paul Pioneer Press,* December 13, 1886; "Sporting Notes," *St. Paul Pioneer Press,* December 21, 1886.

18. "A One Sided Prize Fight," *Omaha Bee,* June 1, 1887.

19. Ibid.

20. Ibid.

21. "Challenge Accepted," *Omaha Bee,* June 3, 1887.

22. "In the Field of Sport," *Omaha Bee,* October 10, 1887.

23. "Dixon Whips Lyman," *Boston Globe,* January 3, 1888; "Topics in Sports," *Rocky Mountain News,* January 4, 1888.

24. Chudacoff, *Age of the Bachelor,* 187.

25. "Colored Champions," *Denver Times,* January 23, 1888.

26. "Boxing," *Spectator,* August 9, 1822.

27. "Lost on a Foul," *Rocky Mountain News,* January 26, 1888.

28. "Colored Champions," *Denver Times,* January 23, 1888.

29. Ibid.

30. "Lost on a Foul," *Rocky Mountain News,* January 26, 1888; "Prize Fight," *Denver Times,* January 25, 1888.

31. "Godfrey in Boston," *Boston Globe,* January 31, 1888.

32. "Lost on a Foul," *Rocky Mountain News,* January 26, 1888; "Prize Fight," *Denver Times,* January 25, 1888.

33. "George Godfrey's Challenge," *Boston Globe,* March 27, 1888; "Godfrey Wants Gore," *St. Paul Globe,* April 2, 1888.

34. Archie Moore, *The Archie Moore Story* (New York: McGraw Hill, 1960), 104.

35. "Rise of Colored Prizefighters," *Baltimore American,* July 18, 1910.

36. Jack Johnson, *In the Ring and Out: The Autobiography of Jack Johnson* (New York: Carol Publishing Group, 1992), 38–39.

37. Andrew M. Kaye, *The Pussycat of Prizefighting: Tiger Flowers and the Politics of Black Celebrity* (Athens: University of Georgia Press, 2004), 60.

38. "Battle Royal is Popular," *Minnesota Journal,* December 31, 1905.

39. Adelbert H. Roberts, "Of Double Significance," *Kalamazoo Gazette,* August 2, 1901.

40. Martin Summers, *Manliness and Its Discontents,* 3.

41. "Wealth for Negroes," *Kansas City Times,* May 8, 1892.

42. Theresa Runstedtler, *Jack Johnson Rebel Sojourner* (Berkeley: University of California Press, 2012), 12.

43. "Godfrey in Boston," *Boston Globe,* January 31, 1888.

44. Davarian Baldwin, *Chicago's New Negroes*, 195.

45. Ibid., 196.

46. For works on black manhood, see Summers, *Manliness and Its Discontents;* Marlon Ross, *Manning the Race: Reforming Black Men in the Jim Crow Era* (New York: New York University Press, 2004); Hazel V. Carby, *Race Men: The W.E. B. Du Bois Lectures* (Cambridge, Mass.: Harvard University Press, 1998); Kevin Gaines, *Uplifting the Race: Black Leadership, Politics, and Culture in the Twentieth Century* (Chapel Hill: University of North Carolina Press, 1996); Earnest Jenkins and Darlene Clark Hine, eds., *A Question of Manhood: A Reader in U.S. Black Men's History and Masculinity, vol. 2, The 19th Century: From Emancipation to Jim Crow* (Indianapolis: Indiana University Press, 2001); Donald R. Shaffer, *After the Glory: The Struggles of Black Civil War Veterans* (Lawrence: University Press of Kansas, 2004); Christopher Booker, *I Will Wear No Chain: A Social History of African American Males* (London: Praeger, 2000).

47. Summers, *Manliness and Its Discontents*, 4.

48. Gaines, *Uplifting the Race*, 2.

49. Ibid., 3.

50. Angela Hornsby-Gutting, *Black Manhood and Community Building in North Carolina, 1900–1930* (Gainesville: University Press of Florida, 2009), 7.

51. Hornsby-Gutting, *Black Manhood and Community Building*, 53.

52. "Black and White Ruffians," *New York Globe,* April 8, 1883; "Revival of Brutality," *New York Globe,* May 19, 1883. For biographical information on Fortune, see Emma Lou Thornbrough, *T. Thomas Fortune: Militant Journalist* (Chicago: University of Chicago Press, 1972).

53. Gaines, "Assimilationist Minstrelsy as Racial Uplift Ideology: James D Corrothers's Literary Quest for Black Leadership," *American Quarterly* 45, no. 3 (September 1993): 347.

54. "Arenic," *San Francisco Chronicle,* March 3, 1890.

55. Anthony Rotundo, *American Manhood: Transformations in Masculinity from the Revolution to the Modern Era* (New York: Basic Books, 1993), 222.

56. John F. Kasson, *Houdini, Tarzan, and the Perfect Man: The White Male Body and the Challenge of Modernity in America* (New York: Hill and Wang, 2001), 10.

57. Gail Bederman, *Manliness and Civilization: A Cultural History of Gender and Race in the United States, 1880–1917* (Chicago: University of Chicago Press, 1995), 14.

58. Rotundo, *American Manhood*, 222–32; Bederman, *Manliness and Civilization,* 20–31.

59. Michael S. Kimmel, *Manhood in America: A Cultural History*, 2nd ed. (New York: Oxford University Press, 2006), 82.

60. Kasson, *Houdini, Tarzan, and the Perfect Man,* 30.

61. Bederman, *Manliness and Civilization,* 8.

62. Jack London, "World's Fight Experts Congregate in Nevada," *San Francisco Chronicle,* June 24, 1910.

63. Gorn, 207–47; Kevin B. Wamsley and David Whitson, "Celebrating Violent Masculinities: The Boxing Death of Luther McCarty," *Journal of Sport History* 25, no. 3 (1998): 420–21.

64. "Jeffries wants to go Fishing," *Baltimore American,* April 23, 1905.

65. "The Color Line with Pugilists," *Baltimore American,* December 2, 1902.

66. Runstedtler, *Rebel Sojourner,* 7, 22.

67. "In Vigorous Training," *St. Paul Globe,* June 7, 1885.

68. George Dixon, *A Lesson in Boxing* (New York: George Dixon, 1893), 3.

69. Michael Oriard, *Reading Football: How the Popular Press Created an American Spectacle* (Chapel Hill: University of North Carolina Press, 1993), 17.

70. Steven A. Riess, *City Games: The Evolution of American Urban Society and the Rise of Sports* (Urbana: University of Illinois Press, 1989), 72.

71. John B. McCormick, *The Square Circle; Or, Stories of the Prize Ring, Being Macon's Description of Many Pugilistic Battles, Fought with Bare Knuckles or Boxing Gloves, with Numerous Anecdotes of Famous Fighters: To Which is Added, How to be Young at Fifty: A Treatise on the Proper Method of Living, of Great Value of All Me* (New York: Continental Publishing, 1897), 52.

72. Ibid., 230.

73. Martin E. Dann, *The Black Press, 1827–1890: The Quest for National Identity* (New York: G.P. Putnam's Sons, 1971), 13.

74. Charles A. Simmons, *The African American Press: With Special References to Four Newspapers, 1827–1965* (Jefferson, N.C.: McFarland, 1998), 20.

75. Simmons, 20.

76. "Revival of Brutality," *New York Globe,* May 19, 1883.

77. W.E.B Du Bois, *The Souls of Black Folk,* in John Hope Franklin, ed., *Three Negro Classics* (New York: Harper Collins Publishers, 1965), 244–46.

CHAPTER 1. BRING HOME THE BACON

1. See "Police Court," *Cincinnati Daily Gazette,* December 29, 1877; "A Thoroughly Bad Man," *Cincinnati Commercial Tribune,* April 25, 1878; "Third Street Station," *Cincinnati Commercial Tribune,* June 23, 1879; "Mysterious Shooting This Morning," *Cincinnati Commercial Tribune,* June 2, 1880; "A Bold Thief," *Cincinnati Daily Gazette,* July 22, 1880.

2. "Two Blowing Africans Contending for the Muscular Mastery," *Albany Evening Journal,* March 8, 1883.

3. "Black Boxers," *Troy Press,* March 8, 1883.

4. Nancy Bertaux in *Race and the City: Work, Community, and Protest in Cincinnati, 1820–1970,* ed. Henry Louis Taylor Jr. (Chicago: University of Illinois Press, 1993), 127.

5. Ibid., 144.

6. "Colored Colonization," *Cincinnati Daily Gazette,* August 8, 1887.

7. David A. Gerber, *Black Ohio and the Color Line, 1860–1915* (Chicago: University of Chicago Press, 1976), 64. Trotter, *River Jordan,* 68–69.

8. "Prize Ring," *Cincinnati Enquirer,* January 23, 1883.

9. "Why He Failed," *Cincinnati Inquirer,* January 29, 1883.

10. "Sporting News," *National Police Gazette,* January 19, 1884.

11. See, "Pugilism," *St. Paul Pioneer Press,* February 21, 1887; "Wilson-Woodson Fight," *St. Paul Pioneer Press,* February 24, 1887; "A Day's Sporting Record," *St. Paul Pioneer Press,* February 25, 1887; "Wilson Bests Woodson," *St. Paul Pioneer Press,* March 29, 1887; "Couldn't Knock Him Out," *St. Paul Pioneer Press,* April 12, 1887; "Scrap at the Olympic," *St. Paul Pioneer Press,* April 16, 1887; "Billy Wilson the Champion," *St. Paul Pioneer Press,* May 23, 1887.

12. "A Pugilist Shot Dead," *Chicago Tribune,* September 20, 1887; "The City," *Chicago Tribune,* September 21, 1887. Woodson was in Chicago to provide muscle at his mother's saloon, and had reportedly been drunk for three straight days.

13. "Chicago," *Western Appeal,* September 24, 1887.

14. "Keep Stepping," *The Evening News,* January 12, 1907.

15. William Gildea, *The Longest Fight: In the Ring with Joe Gans: Boxing's First African American Champion* (New York: Farrar, Straus and Giroux; 2012), 122.

16. "Sure to Get There," *Detroit Plain Dealer,* May 5, 1893.

17. "Rocky Road for Ring Champions," *Harrisburg Gazette,* January 6, 1912.

18. "Courier Journal," *Indianapolis Freeman,* June 17, 1893.

19. Rayford Logan, *The Negro in American Life and Thought: The Nadir, 1877–1901* (New York: Dial Press, 1954), 162.

20. "What Pugilists Once Did for a Living," *Cleveland Plain Dealer,* February 2, 1902.

21. "Home Life of Jeffries," *Los Angeles Express,* August 2, 1902.

22. "What Pugilists Once Did for a Living," *Cleveland Plain Dealer,* February 2, 1902.

23. "Denver Ed Puts Griffen [*sic*] to Sleep," *Los Angeles Times,* October 3, 1901; "Madden's Champion," *Los Angeles Herald,* January 28, 1903. His father was born in Alabama and his mother was born in Georgia.

24. "Too Much for Martin," *Los Angeles Express,* February 6, 1903.

25. "Won in One round," *Los Angeles Express,* September 16, 1903.

26. "Martin Best Puncher Man," *Los Angeles Times,* August 13, 1904.

27. "Hock Bones," *Spokane Press,* February 13, 1910.

28. "Slamowitz, Alias Brock, Got Start by Whipping Negroes," *Memphis Scimitar,* January 2, 1910.

29. "McVey's Rapid Rise," *Los Angeles Examiner,* October 24, 1903.

30. Johnson, *My Life and Battles,* 33–34.

31. Johnson, *My Life and Times,* 19.

32. "They Knew Jack When he was a Poor Man," *San Francisco Examiner,* July 7, 1910.

33. Johnson, *My Life and Battles*, 3.

34. "Life Story of Jack Johnson," *Oregonian*, May 9, 1909.

35. "Kid Broad to Meet Young Corbett," *The Republic*, May 11, 1902. Various accounts exist about this brutish battle, but they all have Johnson desperate for food before the fight—he borrowed 50 cents to eat—and easily defeating his adversaries.

36. Johnson, *My Life and Battles*, 6.

37. "Life Story of Jack Johnson," *Oregonian*, May 9, 1909.

38. "Jack Johnson Sticks to Schedule of Wages," *Anaconda Standard*, August 25, 1912.

39. "The Dinge: Jack Johnson Lucky Champ," *Los Angeles Times*, July 21, 1914.

40. "Jack Johnson Sticks to Schedule of Wages," *Anaconda Standard*, August 25, 1912.

41. "Editorial Afterthought," *New York Age*, December 31, 1908.

42. At this fight, the announcer referred to Wilson, who was "coffee colored," as a "jap." "The Ring," *Cincinnati Weekly Enquirer*, June 29, 1884. Wilson like other black heavyweights also traveled to New York in January 1883 to fight Professor Hadley for the colored heavyweight title. After his debut, the press referred to him as another "African claimant for the pugilistic honors." "Spring Hill Dick's Benefit," *Cincinnati Weekly Enquirer*, January 16, 1883. "Arenic," *San Francisco Chronicle*, March 24, 1890. Wilson was born in 1861 in Petersburg, Virgin Islands.

43. "The Local Fight," *St. Paul Pioneer Press*, June 14, 1885.

44. "Local Pugilistic Contest," *St. Paul Pioneer Press*, May 25, 1885.

45. "Thompson Knocked out," *St. Paul Pioneer Press*, May 26, 1885; "Only One Round," *St. Paul Globe*, May 26, 1885; "Pugilistic Talk," *St. Paul Pioneer Press*, May 27, 1885; Best, "Looking Evil in the Face," 244. To celebrate his victory, Wilson "paraded in a four-horse open barouche," but the celebration was disgusting to many of his friends. In St. Paul, riding around in a buggy was illegal for prostitutes. Evidently they did not like black men or prostitutes flaunting their accomplishments publicly.

46. "To-morrow's Prize fight," *St. Paul Pioneer Press*, June 13, 1885; "The Local Fight," *St. Paul Pioneer Press*, June 14, 1885; "Today's Prizefight," *Minneapolis Tribune*, June 14, 1885.

47. "Conquered by Cardiff," *St. Paul Pioneer Press*, June 15, 1885. Despite the fact the fight took place outside St. Paul city limits, the police waited for the fighters at the St. Paul docks to arrest them. Other sporting men who did not want to see their brethren arrested helped to lower down Cardiff and Wilson into a rowboat so they could row across the Mississippi River to avoid arrest. The tactic did not work as the police gave chase and arrested the fighters.

48. Taylor, "John Quincy Adams: St. Paul Editor and Black Leader," *Minnesota Historian* (Winter 1973): 284–85. This issue no longer exists. The first issue is from June 13, 1885. Also, after July 18, 1885, the dates on microfilm skip to March 5, 1887.

49. Charles A. Simmons, *The African American Press: With Special References to Four Newspapers, 1827–1965* (Jefferson, N.C.: McFarland, 1998), 20; David Vassar Taylor, "John Quincy Adams," *Minnesota Historian* (Winter 1973): 284. During the 1880s, African Americans started 504 newspapers, but only eight survived until 1914.

50. "Editorial," *Western Appeal*, June 13, 1885.

51. "Editorial," *Western Appeal*, June 20, 1885.

52. "Editorial," *Western Appeal*, July 18, 1885. Despite Parker's pleas, three years later this problem still persisted and John Quincy Adams complained, "They show their interest in the moral of the black men, by shutting their eyes to the fact that gambling is carried on by them, the same as if no law against gambling existed." "Editorial," *Western Appeal*, March 3, 1888.

53. Mary Lethert Wingerd, *Claiming the City: Politics, Faith, and the Power of Place in St. Paul* (Ithaca, N.Y.: Cornell University Press, 2001), 14.

54. Taylor, *Pilgrim's Progress*, 53.

55. Ibid., 58.

56. Jefferson advertised his sporting saloon in the *Western Appeal* as the only sporting saloon in the city. "Advertisements," *Western Appeal*, June 13, 1885. "The Prize Ring," *St. Paul Pioneer Press*, October 27, 1884. In October 1884, Jefferson first brought his fighters to Chippewa Falls and then to St. Paul, offering any local fighter $50 if they could stand up to Smith for four rounds. In the same article that the *Pioneer Press* announced that the Jefferson Combination was coming to the city, the newspaper also reported, "Matters pugilistic are now the absorbing topic of conversation in St. Paul sporting circles." See also "The Prize Ring," *St. Paul Pioneer Press*, November 24, 1884; "The Colored Champions," *St. Paul Pioneer Press*, December 29, 1884; "The Prize Ring," *St. Paul Pioneer Press*, January 5, 1885.

57. "Wilson Beats Woodson," *St. Paul Pioneer Press*, March 29, 1887; "Weekly Sporting Record," *St. Paul Pioneer Press*, April 11, 1887. In May 1887, Frank Taylor and the "Black Pearl" Harris Martin fought a thirty-seven-round fight for the "colored middleweight title."

58. "Nig-ger," *Western Appeal*, June 20, 1885. In my research of the *Tribune*'s article about the Cardiff–Wilson contest, I did not find them using "nigger," which raises questions about Parker's accuracy and intentions.

59. "Billy Wilson Beats Hadley," *St. Paul Pioneer Press*, March 22, 1885; "He was Desperate," *Minneapolis Tribune*, April 23, 1887. Lawrence Levine, *Black Culture and Black Consciousness: Afro-American Folk Thought From Slavery to Freedom* (New York: Oxford University Press, 1977) 102–3; Levine, 121–23. Levine contends that many records left behind by white masters complain that slaves "lied, cheated, stole, feigned illness, and loafed . . ." For more about the negro trickster after emancipation, see Levine, 370–86.

60. Jennifer C. Lena, "Voyeurism and Resistance in Rap Music Videos," in *That's the Joint: The Hip-Hop Studies Reader*, 2nd ed., ed. Murray Forman and Mark Anthony Neal (New York: Routledge, 2012), 464.

61. See "Market Hall's Hippodrome," *St. Paul Pioneer Press*, July 27, 1884; "Senator O'Brien's Bill," *St. Paul Pioneer Press*, January 12, 1885; "A Draw," *Minneapolis Tribune*, April 2, 1887.

62. "Broke His Hand," *Minneapolis Tribune*, April 16, 1887.

63. "He was Desperate," *Minneapolis Tribune*, April 23, 1887; "To a Finish," *Minneapolis Tribune*, May 3, 1887; "A Tough Slugging Match," *St. Paul Pioneer Press*, May

3, 1887; "Billy Wilson the Champion," *St. Paul Pioneer Press*, May 23, 1887. The chief of police did not let the two box in St. Paul city limits. Wilson knocked Woodson out in the thirteenth round.

64. "Editorial," *Western Appeal*, April 30, 1887.

65. "Editorial," *Western Appeal*, March 3, 1888. Adams mentioned recent fights involving "Cricket," Jackson, Andrew Miller, Joe Seawright, Tom Andrews, Harry Smith, and Black Frank.

66. Wiggins, *Glory Bound*, 143.

67. Ibid., 155.

68. "Muscle, Science, and Prejudice," *New York Age*, January 5, 1889; "Jackson Wins," *San Francisco Chronicle*, December 29, 1888.

69. "Editorial," *Western Appeal*, March 2, 1889.

70. "Jackson Wins," *San Francisco Chronicle*, April 27 1889.

71. "Editorial," *Western Appeal*, May 4, 1889.

72. "Editorial," *Indianapolis Freeman*, January 5, 1889.

73. "The Field of Sport," *Indianapolis Freeman*, April 26, 1890.

74. "Editorial," *Indianapolis Freeman*, May 17, 1890.

75. James Weldon Johnson, *Black Manhattan* (New York: Anthenum, 1968), 73.

76. "Editorial," *Indianapolis Freeman*, May 10, 1890.

77. "Frederick Douglass," *Cleveland Gazette*, September 10, 1892.

78. James Weldon Johnson, *Along This Way*, in *James Weldon Johnson, Writings* (New York: Library of America, 2004), 208.

79. "Editorial," *Indianapolis Freeman*, April 5, 1890; "Editorial," *Indianapolis Freeman*, July 12, 1890.

80. "Pugilism and Progress," *Cleveland Gazette*, July 5, 1890.

81. "The Prince of Jockeys," *New York Age*, July 5, 1890.

82. "In The College and the Prize Ring," *New York Age*, December 20, 1890.

83. "The Two Races," *Evening Call*, June 23, 1893.

84. Katherine C. Mooney, *Race Horse Men: How Slavery and Freedom Were Made at the Racetrack* (Cambridge, Mass.: Harvard University Press, 2014), 201.

85. Ibid., 202.

86. "Editorial," *Colored American*, February 24, 1900.

87. "Champion Gans in the City," *Indianapolis Freeman*, October 20, 1906.

88. "Joe Gans," *Broad Ax*, September 8, 1906.

89. "A Lesson From Joe Gans," *The Colored American Magazine*, October 1907, 252; "Throng Sees Gans Beat Jimmy Burns," *Los Angeles Times*, September 28, 1907; for information on the *Colored American Magazine*, see August Meier, "Booker T. Washington and the Negro Press: With Special Reference to the Colored American Magazine," *Journal of Negro History* 38, no. 1 (January 1953): 79–82.

90. "Achievement Better than Complaint," *Washington Bee*, June 27, 1907.

91. "Sermon on Jack Johnson," *Detroit Free Press*, June 7, 1909.

92. "The Superiority of the Black," *New York Age*, December 31, 1908.

93. W.E.B Du Bois, "The Conservation of Races," in Eric J. Sundquist, ed., *The Oxford W.E.B. Du Bois Reader* (New York: Oxford University Press, 1996), 46.

CHAPTER 2. RACE MAN OR RACE MENACE?

1. "Erne Went Down in First Round," *Baltimore American*, May 13, 1902.

2. "Gans and Rockefeller," *Baltimore Sun*, May 15, 1902.

3. "Turn out for Gans," *Baltimore Sun*, May 20, 1902.

4. "Gans to the Front," *Nashville Globe*, January 31, 1908.

5. "Pool Bet on McGovern," *Chicago Record*, December 15, 1900; "Fight Was a Raw Fake," *Chicago Journal*, December 14, 1900.

6. "Win Coin out West," *Chicago Daily News*, December 18, 1900.

7. "In the World of Sports," *Indianapolis Freeman*, August 18, 1906.

8. "Gans to the Front," *Nashville Globe*, January 31, 1908.

9. Summers, *Manliness and Its Discontents*, 4, 6.

10. Gaines, *Uplifting the Race*, 78.

11. "Tells Why Joe Gans, Now Rich, Quits Ring," *Fort Worth Telegram*, September 29, 1907.

12. "Gans to the Front," *Nashville Globe*, January 31, 1908.

13. "Griffin-Kennedy Fight," *Los Angeles Examiner*, June 26, 1901; "Hank Griffin has Perilous Bath," *Los Angeles Herald*, September 13, 1902.

14. "'Denver Ed' Puts Griffen to Sleep," *Los Angeles Times*, October 3, 1901.

15. "About the Boxers," *Los Angeles Herald*, March 6, 1903.

16. "Hank Griffin Would Like to Meet 'Lil Artha' He Says," *Ann Arbor Daily News*, January 19, 1909.

17. "The Bell Rings for Hank Griffin," *Ann Arbor Daily News*, May 2, 1911.

18. Runstedtler, *Jack Johnson, Rebel Sojourner*, 138–39.

19. "Says Paris is Crazy Over Negro Fighters," *Trenton Times*, May 30, 1909.

20. "Mr. Snowy Baker's Experiences," *Referee* (Sydney), April 29, 1914.

21. "Where are the Black Men?" *Referee*, January 15, 1919.

22. "Jersey City," *Pittsburgh Courier*, May 10, 1924.

23. "Prize Fighter Turns Garage Owner," *Michigan Chronicle*, January 4, 1947.

24. "Langford Draws the Color Line," *Salt Lake Herald*, November 26, 1914.

25. Allan Morrison, "Amazing Career of Sam Langford," *Ebony*, April 1956, 102.

26. "Sam Langford the Happiest Man," *Referee*, July 10, 1912.

27. "The Cherry Kids," *National Advocate*, July 12, 1912.

28. To see more on Sam Langford and his family, see Clay Moyle, *Sam Langford: Boxing's Greatest Uncrowned Champion* (Seattle: Bennett and Hastings Publishing, 2006.)

29. "Prize Fighter Turns Garage Owner," *Michigan Chronicle*, January 4, 1947.

30. Morrison, "Amazing Career of Sam Langford," 102.

31. "Gans Tells Story of Remarkable Ring Life," *Indianapolis Freeman*, February 2, 1907.

32. "Joe Gans Dies in Baltimore," *New York Age*, August 11, 1910.

33. "Wear Purple and Diamonds," *Los Angeles Times*, February 11, 1903.

34. "Planning More Fights," *Los Angeles Express*, February 28, 1903.

35. "Mother Made Him a Fighter," *Fort Worth Star Telegram*, January 1, 1909.

36. "Jack Johnson's Birthday Party," *Los Angeles Herald*, April 1, 1903.

37. "Life Story of Jack Johnson," *Oregonian*, May 9, 1909.

38. "Mack's Talk," *Memphis Scripter*, January 24, 1910.

39. "Life Story of Jack Johnson," *Oregonian*, May 9, 1909.

40. "Jack Johnson," *Cleveland Gazette*, November 20, 1909.

41. "Johnson in Elite Colony," *Kansas City Star*, December 22, 1912.

42. "Godfrey and Ashton," *Boston Globe*, September 19, 1887.

43. "Honored in Death," *Boston Morning Journal*, October 21, 1901.

44. "Latest Sporting Topics," *National Police Gazette*, January 31, 1891.

45. "Honored in Death," *Boston Morning Journal*, October 21, 1901; "Godfrey Training Hard," *Boston Globe*, October 17, 1892.

46. Bob Petersen, *Peter Jackson: A Biography of the Australian Heavyweight Champion, 1860–1901* (Jefferson, N.C.: McFarland, 2012), 139.

47. "Race Doings," *Cleveland Gazette*, July 2, 1892.

48. "Doings and Comments," *Cleveland Gazette*, February 21, 1891.

49. "'Old Chocolate,' Greatest of Negro Fighters," *Chicago Whip*, May 15, 1920.

50. "Joe Walcott Now Porter in New York Theatre," *Boston Globe*, May 20, 1928.

51. "Joe Choynski Defeated by Walcott," *Saturday Evening World*, February 24, 1900.

52. "Joe Walcott in a New Role," *Cleveland Gazette*, September 5, 1903.

53. "'Black Demon' Walcott to Run for Mayor," *Boston Journal*, October 11, 1904.

54. "Joe Walcott Kills Negro Companion in Dance Hall," *Boston Journal*, October 18, 1904.

55. Hal Coffman, "Good Fellows When they Had It," *El Paso Herald*, December 3, 1913.

56. Paul Purman, in "They were Good Fellows When they Had the Coin," *Bismarck Daily*, October 26, 1916.

57. "Sam Langford, Last of Trio of Colored Fighters, Counted Out," *Tulsa World*, April 21, 1918.

58. "Grape and High Life Soon Puts Quietus on Negro Pugilistic Champions," *Trenton Evening Times*, November 16, 1912.

59. "Colored Boxers Died in Poverty," *Philadelphia Inquirer*, April 28, 1918. The article mentioned George Dixon, Joe Walcott, Joe Gans, Peter Jackson, and Frank Craig, "The Harlem Coffee Cooler." In addition welterweight champion "Dixie Kid" Aaron Brown, and the great fighter Sam Langford also died broke.

60. "Editorial," *Western Appeal*, June 29, 1889.

61. "Negroes Say, 'Close Dens,'" *Los Angeles Times,* November 24, 1902.

62. "The Brick Block," *The Eagle,* September 3, 1903; "Editorial," *The Eagle,* September 3, 1903.

63. "Colored Boxers Died in Poverty," *Philadelphia Inquirer,* April 28, 1918.

64. "Most Prizefighters Poor When they Die," *Kalamazoo Gazette,* October 15, 1905.

65. "George Dixon is Now a Poor Man," *Philadelphia Inquirer,* August 12, 1900.

66. "Young Corbett Greatest," *National Police Gazette,* January 16, 1904; "George Dixon is Home and Broke," *Philadelphia Inquirer,* August 22, 1905. Dixon claimed, "the fighting game in England has gone away back. There are very few champions over there and the purses they give to the fighters are so small that I hate to think of the days when I fought around New York." The proud Dixon said, "just think of me fighting twenty rounds for a twenty-five or fifty dollar purse . . . I am really ashamed to tell you the money I made in England. I got such a small amount that I am sure I could go into any crap game and with a little luck with the bones in one evening I could come out of the place with more money than I got out of all fights I had in England."

67. Sullivan, "Only Friend of George Dixon, Who is Now Down and Out," *Wilkes Barre Record,* December 7, 1907.

68. Ibid.

69. John L. Sullivan "John L. Sullivan on the Financial Scare," *Oregonian,* December 8, 1907.

70. "Editorial," *Colored American,* August 30, 1902.

71. "The Time to 'Make Hay,'" *Colored American,* September 13, 1902.

72. "His Last Fight," *Nashville Globe,* January 10, 1908.

73. "George Dixon Dead," *Iowa State Bystander,* January 31, 1908.

74. "Council Strikes at Jack Johnson," *Chicago Tribune,* October 23, 1912.

75. "Negro Educator Scores Johnson," *Detroit Free Press,* October 21, 1912.

76. "White Hope Champion," *Philadelphia Tribune,* February 22, 1913.

77. "Champion Jack Johnson Denies Charges Against Him in Daily Newspapers," *Chicago Defender,* October 26, 1912.

78. "2,000 Citizens Condemn U.S. Judges," *Chicago Defender,* November 23, 1912.

79. Lester A. Walton, "Merit Not Color," *New York Age,* April 8, 1915.

CHAPTER 3. BLACK MEN AND THE BUSINESS OF BOXING

1. "Dobbs Now in Jail," *Boston Globe,* September 26, 1894.

2. "Sporting Notes," *Philadelphia Inquirer,* September 2, 1894; "Lynn," *Boston Globe,* September 14, 1894; "Pugilistic Gossip," *Boston Globe,* September 24, 1894.

3. Benton, however, tracked him down in Philadelphia and threatened to sue. Fortunately for Dobbs, he avoided a lawsuit, found another white manager, and proceeded with his career. "Fights at New Orleans," *Boston Globe,* September 23, 1894;

"Gossip of the Fighters," *Boston Globe,* September 27, 1894; "Corbett-Fitz Match," *Boston Globe,* October 28, 1894; "About the Boxers," *Boston Globe,* October 31, 1894.

4. "Very Yellow," *St. Paul Globe,* March 10, 1894.

5. Like most fighters of this era, Dobbs's background remains a mystery. Dobbs liked to age himself by ten years. He often told reporters he was born in Nashville, Tennessee, in 1859—he never stated free or slave—but toward the end of his life he claimed he was born in Georgia in 1868.

6. Dobbs's named first graced a newspaper while playing baseball in Colorado in 1889. "Colorado Springs," *Leavenworth Advocate,* June 8, 1889.

7. "Bobby Dobbs," *Afro American Ledger,* March 29, 1902; "Athletic Carnival," *Afro American Ledger,* June 7, 1902; "Athletic Carnival," *Afro American Ledger,* June 14, 1902; "Advertisement," *Afro American Ledger,* July 21, 1902; "Latest News of the Great Athletic Carnival," *Afro American Ledger,* June 28, 1902; "The Athletic Carnival," *Afro American Ledger,* July 5, 1902.

8. Runstedtler, *Rebel Sojourner.*

9. "Supples Trimmed Britton," *National Police Gazette,* August 18, 1903; "Boxing in England," December 12, 1903; "Dobbs Knocks Out Green," *National Police Gazette,* December 3, 1910; "Princes at Boxing Matches," *National Police Gazette,* March 11, 1911; "Boxing on Horseback," *National Police Gazette,* April 13, 1912; "German's Latest Sporting Fad, Boxing on Horse Back," *National Police Gazette,* April 14, 1912; "Damon Runyon Tells Story of Life of Bobby Dobbs, Veteran Colored Fighter Who Had Most Remarkable Career," *Grand Folks Daily Herald,* February 18, 1916. For information on Frank Craig in Europe, see "In the Squared Circle With Biddy Bishop," *Chicago Defender,* January 9, 1937; "Craig, Ex-Middleweight Champ in London Jail," *Chicago Defender,* November 13, 1937.

10. "Return of Bobby Dobbs," *New York Sun,* August 24, 1899.

11. Ibid.

12. "Bobby Dobbs Writes from England," *Indianapolis Freeman,* October 1, 1904.

13. "Bobby Dobbs Finds Cousin," *Chicago Defender,* February 16, 1916.

14. "C.A.C. Smith," *National Police Gazette,* August 4, 1883.

15. Roosevelt Samuel Ruffin, *Black Presence in Saginaw, Michigan, 1855–1900* (n.p., 1978), 47; Smith's decision to leave Saginaw might have been influenced by the success of local black barbers James J. Campbell and Abram Reno, who owned successful barbershops and owned a few thousand dollars' worth of property in Saginaw. Jeremy W. Kilar, "Black Pioneers in Michigan's Lumber Industry," *Journal of Forestry,* 24, no. 3 (July 1980): 144; 1880 *East Saginaw, Michigan City Directory.*

16. "Correspondents," *National Police Gazette,* February 26, 1881.

17. By 1883, Smith moved to Port Huron, Michigan, where he taught boxing, barbered, and ran a bathhouse, but he lacked national recognition of his skills. *1883 Port Huron, Michigan Directory.*

18. For a history of bare-knuckle prizefighting, see Gorn, *Manly Art*; Bob Mee, *Bare Fists: The History of Bare-Knuckle Prize-Fighting* (New York: Overlook Press, 2001.)

19. Chudacoff, *Age of the Bachelor,* 187–98.

20. "Pugilistic," *National Police Gazette,* November 24, 1888; "The Ring," *San Francisco Chronicle,* November 26, 1888. Graves challenged Jackson for a fight between $2,500 and $5,000. He even traveled to New York to fight Jackson, but Jackson never accepted his offer.

21. "The World of Sports," *National Police Gazette,* September 4, 1880. The following request from C.A.C. Smith represents a typical telegram challenge. "To the Sporting Editor of the Police Gazette—Sir: Please state in the sporting column of the Gazette that I am ready to meet any colored pugilist in America in a contest with hard gloves for $250 a side, Queensberry rules, with or without gloves for $500 a side. George Taylor the lightweight champion preferred." "Sporting News," *National Police Gazette,* January 19, 1884. Boxers also used the *Police Gazette* to respond to challenges to their honor. For instance, McHenry Johnson read in the *New York Daily News* that Charley Murphy, the black champion of Washington, D.C., wanted to fight Johnson, so he went to the *Police Gazette* offices with his response. Johnson replied "Sir—in response to Charley Murphy's (the colored pugilists) challenge please state that I will either fight or box Murphy for from $100 to $500 a side, the contest to be decided in New York in a time and place to be mutually agreed upon. To prove I mean business, my backer Mr. The. Allen has posted $50 forfeit with Richard K. Fox. Now, if Murphy and his backers mean business, let them cover the money Mr. Allen has posted and name a day to meet and the Police Gazette office to arrange a match."

22. "The Ring," *Cincinnati Weekly Enquirer,* April 29, 1884; "The Ring," *Cincinnati Weekly Enquirer,* May 1, 1884.

23. "The Ring," *Cincinnati Weekly Enquirer,* April 29, 1884; "The Ring," *Cincinnati Weekly Enquirer,* May 1, 1884.

24. Gorn, *Manly Art,* 142–44. Also see Chudacoff, *Age of the Bachelor,* 224–31.

25. Bertram Wyatt-Brown, *Southern Honor: Ethics and Behavior in the Old South* (New York: Oxford University Press, 1982), xv. Also see Gorn, *Manly Art,* 139–43.; Gorn, "Gouge and Bite, Pull Hair and Scratch": The Social Significance of Fighting in the Southern Backcountry," *American Historical Review* 90, no. 1 (February 1985): 18–43; Kenneth S. Greenburg, *Honor and Slavery* (Princeton, N.J.: Princeton University Press, 1996,); Joanne B Freeman, *Affairs of Honor: National Politics in the New Republic* (New Haven, Conn.: Yale University Press, 2001.)

26. Gorn, *Manly Art,* 141.

27. Ibid., 143.

28. "Sporting News," *National Police Gazette,* February 10, 1883; "The Black Diamond," *Cincinnati Weekly Enquirer,* March 8, 1883; "Harry Woodson, the Black Diamond," *National Police Gazette,* April 17, 1883.

29. "Ring and Pit," *Brooklyn Daily Eagle,* April 6, 1883.

30. "Sporting Matters," *Detroit Free Press,* April 19, 1883.

31. "Sporting News," *National Police Gazette,* May 5, 1883; "The Black Diamond Talks Business," *Cincinnati Weekly Enquirer,* April 19, 1883.

32. "Too Sick to Fight," *Boston Globe,* May 18, 1883. "Sporting News," *National Police Gazette,* June 9, 1883: "Sporting Brieflets," *Boston Herald,* May 20, 1883.

33. "The Day's Gleanings," *Saginaw Evening News,* May 25, 1883.

34. "Sporting News," *National Police Gazette,* June 9, 1883.

35. "Sporting News," *National Police Gazette,* June 30, 1883.

36. "Pugilistic Points," *Cincinnati Weekly Enquirer,* July 22, 1883. See Greenburg, *Honor and Slavery.*

37. "Sporting News," *National Police Gazette,* June 9, 1883; "Sporting News," *National Police Gazette,* June 23, 1883; "Sporting News," *National Police Gazette,* June 30, 1883.

38. "Sporting News, *National Police Gazette,* July 14, 1883; "Athletic," *New Orleans Picayune,* July 31, 1883. Reilly claimed that "he praised Smith in public, hoping to net enough in sparring exhibitions to reimburse him for about $500 expenses on Smith."

39. "Athletic," *New Orleans Picayune,* July 31, 1883.

40. "Sporting News," *National Police Gazette,* June 9, 1883; "Exciting Glove Fight," *New York Herald,* August 20, 1883.

41. "Sporting News," *National Police Gazette,* January 19, 1884.

42. Macon, "Pugilistic Points," *Cincinnati Weekly Enquirer,* July 22, 1883; "The Prize Ring," *Cincinnati Weekly Enquirer,* August 17, 1883; "With Soft Gloves," *Cleveland Leader,* March 11, 1884. In February Thompson knocked out Stewart in three rounds. "The Ring," *Cincinnati Weekly Enquirer,* March 19, 1884.

43. "The Prize Ring," *St. Paul Pioneer Press,* December 22, 1884; "The Prize Ring," *St. Paul Pioneer Press,* January 5, 1885. As the fight date neared the *Pioneer Press* predicted Smith would win and believed that Hafey was "no match for the colored heavyweight, and [would] be easily disposed of."

44. "The Fergus Falls Fiasco," *St. Paul Pioneer Press,* January 6, 1885; "Local Pugilist," *St. Paul Pioneer Press,* January 7, 1885; "The Prize Ring," *St. Paul Pioneer Press,* January 12, 1885; "From the Field at Large," *St. Paul Pioneer Press,* February 9, 1885. Jefferson argued that the fight was legitimate, and thus had to pay Hafey $200 in forfeit money. In order to restore his honor, Smith said he would raise $250 and fight Hafey in a private location. He also said he would travel to Winnipeg, Canada, to fight Ed McKeown. A month later Smith arranged a touring troop of local colored fighters that included a song and dance team and a comedian. There is no record about the success or failure of the show, but what is clear that after his reputation as a coward, a minstrel show was Smith's only option in St. Paul.

45. C.A.C. Smith, "Thunderbolt Smith," *Buffalo Courier,* February 18, 1898.

46. Smith died in 1904 in Chicago. "Town Talk," *Saginaw News,* August 23, 1904.

47. Gorn, *Manly Art,* 205.

48. "The Times Eagles," *Los Angeles Times,* September 11, 1892.

49. Alfred Henry Lewis, "Can't Change Men into Sheep; Hence we Have Prize Fights," *San Francisco Examiner,* June 29, 1910.

50. Clymer, "The Market in Male Bodies," 140.

51. "Pacific Coast," *Los Angeles Times,* August 25, 1888; "Godfrey Gives Up," *San Francisco Chronicle,* August 25, 1888.

52. "A Mighty Moke," *Los Angeles Times,* December 29, 1888; "Jackson Wins," *National Police Gazette,* May 11, 1889.

53. "A Great Fight," *San Francisco Chronicle,* May 22, 1891. "Declared a Draw," *Los Angeles Times,* May 22, 1891; "C.A.C. Smith," *National Police Gazette,* August 4, 1883. C.A.C. Smith, from Port Huron, Michigan, won $1,000 when he defeated the Canadian heavyweight champion Jack Stewart in 1883 in Michigan.

54. "White and Colored, Two Knock-outs at the Golden Gate Club," *San Francisco Chronicle,* June 20, 1889; "Beaten," *San Francisco Chronicle,* October 15, 1889; "A Lucky Blow," *San Francisco Chronicle,* April 26, 1890; "Turner Defeated," *San Francisco Chronicle,* May 28, 1891; "Nineteen Rounds," *San Francisco Chronicle,* March 1, 1892; "Charley Turner Wins," *San Francisco Chronicle,* April 22, 1892; "Turner Knocked Out," *San Francisco Chronicle,* November 18, 1892. He fought and beat the two black fighters he faced, Wiley Evans and the "Black Pearl" Harris Martin. When the state banned prizefighting in 1893, Turner headed to Nevada to work in the ring. After California legalized the fight game again, the Stockton native went back to work and continued to fight into his forties. He also trained his younger brother, the credible welterweight Rufe Turner. The 1900 federal census lists the forty-year-old Turner as a pugilist for his occupation. Fighting was all Charley Turner knew.

55. "Sportsmen Niche," *San Francisco Chronicle,* April 21, 1883.

56. George Siler, "Color Line in Prizefighting," *Chicago Tribune,* November 4, 1900.

57. "The Colored Man in the Ring," *Boston Globe,* April 19, 1891.

58. "A Tough City for the Loser," *Baltimore America,* November 20, 1906.

59. "Sporting News," *New York Globe,* January 26, 1884.

60. "Godfrey's Decision," *Boston Globe,* April 13, 1888.

61. "Godfrey Wouldn't Meet Ashton in Providence with a Gatlin Gun," *Boston Globe,* November 14, 1889.

62. "Dixon and Prejudice," *Cleveland Gazette,* March 12, 1892. In March of that year, a hotel in Buffalo, New York, drew the color line on the champion and refused him service in their restaurant. Dixon vigorously protested until the hotel served the champ with white guests.

63. Dale A. Somers, *The Rise of Sport in New Orleans, 1850–1900* (Baton Rouge: Louisiana State University Press, 1972), 179–83.

64. "Dixon and Jim Crow," *Cleveland Gazette,* September 10, 1892.

65. "Editorial," *Appeal,* September 10, 1892.

66. Somers, *Rise of Sports in New Orleans,* 181.

67. "Editorial," *Cleveland Gazette,* September 17, 1892.

68. "Dusky Fighters," *New Orleans Picayune,* March 1, 1892.

69. "Interstate Championship," *New Orleans Picayune,* March 5, 1893.

70. "Bob Harper and his Gold Medal," *Inter Ocean,* April 29, 1890.

71. "Harper Wins in the Fifth Round," *Chicago Tribune,* January 28, 1892. For another account of the fight, see George Siler, *Inside Facts of Pugilism* (Chicago: Laird & Lee, 1907), 34–48.

72. "Green Defeats Harper," *New Orleans Picayune,* March 7, 1893.

73. "Ike Rivers versus Unknown," *Inter Ocean,* June 28, 1892.

74. "Routing the Black King," *Chicago Tribune,* January 17, 1897. "Former Gambler and Politician Expires," *Chicago Tribune,* March 9, 1901.

75. "Former Gambler and Politician Expires," *Chicago Tribune,* March 8, 1901.

76. See St. Claire Drake and Horace R. Cayton, *Black Metropolis: A Study of Negro Life in a Northern City* (New York: Harcourt, Brace, 1945), 45; Allan H. Spear, *Black Chicago: The Making of a Negro Ghetto* (Chicago: University of Chicago Press, 1967), 71–89. Christopher Robert Reed, *Black Chicago's First Century;* Davarian L. Baldwin, *Chicago's New Negroes: Modernity, The Great Migration and Black Urban Life* (Chapel Hill: the University of North Carolina Press, 2007), 194–204; Robin F. Bachin, *Building the South Side: Urban Space and Civic Culture in Chicago* (Chicago: University of Chicago Press, 2004) 255–56.

77. "Colored Republicans," *Los Angeles Times,* October 21, 1898. Black leader Jacob Soars made speeches for the candidates and urged those at the Manhattan to vote for the Henry Gage for governor.

78. J. L. Edmonds, "Why are the Colored Voters Supporting the Union Ticket," *Los Angeles Herald,* October 16, 1898; "The Afro Americans," *Los Angeles Herald,* October 20, 1898; "A Colored Club," *Los Angeles Times,* November 3 1898; "Enthusiastic Meeting," *Los Angeles Times,* November 26, 1898.

79. "Renewed Activity," *Los Angeles Herald,* October 22, 1898.

80. "City Elections," *Los Angeles Times,* December 6, 1898.

81. "Police Shepherd Crooks," *Los Angeles Times,* April 26, 1899.

82. Kevin J. Mumford, *Interzones: Black/White Sex Districts in Chicago and New York in the Early Twentieth Century* (New York: Columbia University Press, 1997), xii; Berges, 25–26.

83. "The Raid on the Coons," *Los Angeles Herald,* June 26, 1899. "Dive Cases Disposes Of," *Los Angeles Times,* June 30, 1899.

84. "Peace Disturbances," *Los Angeles Times,* June 27, 1899. Simpson erased the names of the club members before the police could implicate others.

85. "Field of Sport," *Los Angeles Herald,* March 3, 1900.

86. "The Field of Sport," *Los Angeles Herald,* February 17, 1900; "Boxing," *Los Angeles Herald,* February 19, 1900; "The Ring," *Los Angeles Herald,* February 26, 1900.

87. "Talk of New Boxing Club," *Los Angeles Express,* March 13, 1901.

88. "Woods and Tremble," *Los Angeles Herald,* March 2, 1901.

89. Molina, *Fit to Be Citizens,* 1–14.

90. "How Peggy Stopped the Prize Fight," *Los Angeles Times,* March 16, 1901.

91. "Police Board," *Los Angeles Times,* March 27, 1901.

92. "Lawyer Luther Brown's Dark Brown Gang," *Los Angeles Times,* April 3, 1901.

93. Carroll also played catcher for and owned the local black baseball team, the Trilby's, which changed its name to the Alphas.

94. Michael Lomax, *Black Baseball Entrepreneurs: The Negro National and Eastern Colored Leagues, 1902–1931* (Syracuse, N.Y.: Syracuse University Press, 2014), xvii.

95. "The African American Congress," *Los Angeles Times,* August 6, 1898.

96. "Among the Boxing Clubs and Boxers," *Los Angeles Herald,* March 15, 1901; "Woods and Tremble," *Los Angeles Herald,* March 2, 1901.

97. "Among the Boxing Clubs and Boxers," *Los Angeles Herald,* March 15, 1901.

98. "Chance for Griffin," *Los Angeles Express,* May 15, 1901.

99. "Pugilistic Times During La Fiesta," *Los Angeles Times,* April 15, 1901.

100. "New Athletic Club Has Come to Stay," *Los Angeles Times,* April 29, 1901.

101. "Griffin and Kennedy in Readiness to Fight," *Los Angeles Herald,* May 6, 1901; "Griffin and Kennedy will Meet Tonight," *Los Angeles Herald,* May 7, 1901.

102. "Kennedy and Griffin Draw," *Los Angeles Herald,* May 8, 1901.

103. "Solomon and Dalton in Ten Round Preliminary," *Los Angeles Herald,* June 15, 1901.

104. "Baseball Notes," *Los Angeles Times,* July 1, 1901; "Sporting Notes," *Los Angeles Times,* September 2, 1901. Three years later, Carroll opened up a new athletic club in San Bernardino.

105. "Gardner May Come," *Los Angeles Herald,* June 24, 1902.

106. George Siler, "Color Line in Prizefighting," *Chicago Tribune,* November 4, 1900.

107. "The Rise of the Colored Prizefighter," *Baltimore American,* July 18, 1910.

108. "Colored Pugs are Easy Marks," *Salt Lake Herald,* March 24, 1907.

109. "Gans Means to Have a Fight," *Baltimore America,* October 17, 1905.

110. "Joe Gans Counted Out," *Anaconda Standard,* August 11, 1910.

111. "Walcott on his Dignity," *Boston Globe,* July 26, 1900; "O'Rourke Angry at Joe Walcott," *San Francisco Call,* October 1, 1901.

112. "Johnson is in Trouble," *Los Angeles Express,* January 1, 1903. To be sure, Johnson's proclamation of independence was partly prompted by his wife. Johnson, who would later be known as a womanizer who only dated or married white women, argued that his wife would leave him if he kept Carrillo as his manager. "I can get a manager any time I want one," he said, "but a wife is a different proposition. As I have a good wife I don't want to lose her, so if the club insists that I fight under the management of Mr. Carrillo, this coon will have to hike back to Chicago where there are numerous engagements waiting for me."

113. Johnson had to go to court the day after he beat Sam McVey and won $2,796.

114. "Abrams Received Johnson's Share," *Los Angeles Herald,* October 30, 1903.

115. "Reach No Decision On Referee For Big Fight," *Sacramento Star,* May 5, 1910; "Selection of Referee put Over Twelve Days," *San Francisco Examiner,* May 5, 1910.

116. "Johnson says He Requires No Manager," *San Francisco Examiner,* June 7, 1910.

117. "Inside Facts of Tham Langford," *Los Angeles Times,* May 30, 1913.

CHAPTER 4. COLORED CHAMPIONSHIP AND COLOR LINES

1. "Sporting News," *National Police Gazette,* December 23, 1882.

2. "Prizefight," *New York Herald,* April 1, 1881; "Life in New York City," *Brooklyn Daily Eagle,* April 27, 1884.

3. "Hadley's Retirement," *St. Paul Globe,* August 31, 1885.

4. "Sporting News," *National Police Gazette,* December 23, 1882.

5. "Prizefight," *New York Herald,* April 1, 1881. Cooley was born in 1845 in Providence, Rhode Island.

6. "Events in the Metropolis," *New York Times,* December 8, 1882; "The Ring," *New York Clipper,* December 8, 1882. Charles Cooley had been in a number of scrapes and run-ins with the law. In 1878 he was arrested with four other black men for beating up boxer Paddy Ryan. Cooley also was arrested in 1881 for pulling a gun on another man. "City and Suburban News," *New York Times,* June 25, 1878; "City and Suburban News," *New York Times,* August 11, 1881.

7. Charles Hadley, "Professor Hadley's Reply to His Challengers," *New York Herald,* January 8, 1882.

8. "Gigantic Black Buffers," *New York Herald,* January 7, 1882. They fought a draw.

9. Isenberg, *John L. Sullivan,* 96–97.

10. "Mack's Melange," *New Orleans Picayune,* January 5, 1902.

11. Gail Bederman, *Manliness and Civilization,* 8.

12. "John L. Sullivan," *Philadelphia Inquirer,* December 1, 1889.

13. "Sporting," *Cincinnati Weekly Inquirer,* January 26, 1883.

14. "The Man From Troy," *New York Herald,* March 18, 1882.

15. "Godfrey and Sullivan," *Boston Globe,* October 10, 1900.

16. Macon, "Pugilistic Points," *Cincinnati Enquirer,* July 22, 1883. He also noted, "If Sullivan is a true Bostonian he will not persist in a determination not to slug a man merely because of his color."

17. "Mervine Thompson's History," *Cleveland Herald,* February 11, 1884; "Macon's Description of Sullivan's Great Rival," *Cincinnati Enquirer,* February 27, 1884; "The Sturdy Canadian Who is Seeking Sullivan," *Boston Globe,* June 10, 1883. In 1883, Thompson used the name Patrick O'Donnell in several wrestling tournaments. He also challenged Sullivan to a fight in 1883 using that name.

18. Federal Census Records, 1870 and 1880, www.ancestry.com. According to both records, he was born in 1854. When searching this site for the 1870 census search under "Marvin Thompson," and for 1880 search under "Mervin Thompson." "Ring Veteran Sullivan Foe, Visits Batavia," *Batavia Daily News,* April 11, 1936. Thompson indicated several times that his family moved to Rochester, New York, so that his family could fight in the war. In the 1930s, in several interviews he claimed his father and three brothers fought for the Union, placing them in white troops. According to an eighty-year-old Thompson they "were living in New York when the Civil War broke out. My mother died and my father and all three of my brothers joined the

Army." He noted that after his mother's death "I ran away from home before my seventh birthday and during the war I traveled all around the South, sometimes with the Union soldiers and sometimes with the rebels. I remember once when I'd lost my shoes the rebel soldiers broke into a store to get a pair for me. I guess I was a sort of a mascot for both armies." His dad and one brother lost their lives during the Second Battle of Bull Run (Second Manassas) in 1862—before black troops entered the war—and he noted, "Two brothers were killed later fighting Indians will General Custer." After the war, Thompson went down south with his brother William, "gathering up the dead and burying them in cemeteries." William then sent Mervine to live with Reverend Eliphalet Owen of Wyoming, New York. Owen fought for the all-white 136th Infantry Regiment from New York, with only one Thompson, Henry Thompson.

19. Davis, *City of Quartz*, 11–12; 1870 Federal Census, www.ancestry.com.

20. 1880 Federal Census, www.ancestry.com.

21. "In and Outdoor Sports," *Cleveland Plain Dealer*, February 5, 1884. "Stewart Knocked Out," *Cleveland Herald*, February 6, 1884; "Has Not heard from Sullivan," *Cincinnati Weekly Enquirer*, February 26, 1884; "Mervine Thompson's History," *Cleveland Herald*, February 11, 1884 The *Cleveland Herald* chimed in on the race issue, protecting Thompson's whiteness, saying, "this [Sullivan's assertion] is false in every particular." It is not clear who told Sullivan, but for some reason Thompson's manager, Duncan Ross, had been blamed. In response to this accusation, Ross asserted, "I have never told this to any newspaperman and have not heard from Sullivan." Fans waited for Sullivan's judgment, and Thompson waited for his ruling, because Sullivan had the social power to make that determination. A month prior, for example, Canadian heavyweight Jack Stewart refused to fight Thompson and claimed Thompson had black blood, but the press, and the sporting public, blew off those assertions and continued to insist Thompson was a white man. In other words, Stewart did not have the social power of the heavyweight champion, and whites deemed his claim as cowardly. "General Notes," *Cleveland Herald*, January 27, 1884; "Pugilism," *Cleveland Herald*, January 22, 1884; "Pugilism," *Cleveland Herald*, February 1, 1884; "In and Outdoor Sports," *Cleveland Plain Dealer*, February 5, 1884. "Stewart Knocked Out," *Cleveland Herald*, February 6, 1884; "Pugilism" *Cleveland Herald*, February 14, 1884; in 1883, there were some other occasions where fans marked Thompson as not white. "Active Athletes," *Buffalo Daily Courier*, July 1, 1883; "A Challenge," *Buffalo Daily Courier*, July 1, 1883; "The Glove Fight Arranged," *Buffalo Daily Courier*, July 3, 1883; "Thompson and Baker," *Buffalo Daily Courier*, July 6, 1883; "No Slugging," *Buffalo Daily Courier*, July 7, 1883. City officials tried to halt the match, claiming "these men have shown so much bad blood that I will not permit even a sparring match between the men," but the law could not stop the fighters. To avoid the police, the two battled on Navy Island near Niagara Falls. On Sunday morning July 15, at two o'clock, nearly three hundred men arrived at a port to take a "river excursion" to the match. The crowd was "one of the roughest, toughest, and most disreputable crowds

that ever disgraced a city," and threatened Thompson with harm if he won. Baker, who weighed only 168 pounds, knocked Thompson out in the eighth round. With that loss it seemed Thompson would never get his shot at Sullivan. The *Buffalo Daily Courier* observed, "Thompson will do well to never put up his hands in another contest until he is better qualified to cope with a settled antagonist. . . ." The paper also added, "He has plenty of 'sand' and endurance, but is exceedingly deficient in execution, science, and delivery and has much to learn yet as to how he should use his hands." "Knocked Silly," *Buffalo Daily Courier,* July 16, 1883; "Thompson Goes Down," *Buffalo Evening News,* July 16, 1883.

22. "Colored Sluggers," *St. Louis Democrat-Globe,* February 10, 1884; "Sporting," *St. Louis Daily Globe-Democrat,* February 25, 1884.

23. "A Glove Fight," *St. Paul Globe,* March 11, 1884; "A White Knocks out a Negro at Cleveland," *Omaha Bee,* March 11, 1884; "A Rough and Tumble Sparring Match in Ohio Between a White Man and a Negro," *Fort Worth Gazette,* March 12, 1884; "Photographs of Thompson," *National Police Gazette,* April 12, 1884.

24. "A Talk With the Best Man," *Louisville Courier Journal,* May 4, 1884. In the interview he added, "They won't let us spar in Ohio; I'll do this: Chicago is about 800 miles from Cleveland and I'll pay Thompson's expenses there and give him $1,000 and the gate receipts if he will stand up in front of me. He wants the right to use wrestling powers. Well, I'll give him that too. I'll fight by the London rules and lick him."

25. For information on libel and race, see Thomas Stephenson, *Race Distinctions in American Law* (New York: Negro University Press, 1969), 26–34; Kentucky did not legalize the "one drop rule" until 1911. See Charles Staples Mangum, *The Legal Status of the Negro* (Chapel Hill: University of North Carolina Press, 1944), 12; "Sporting Notes," *Boston Globe,* May 4, 1884; "Sporting News," *Cincinnati Enquirer,* May 9, 1884; "Wrestling Matches," *Cincinnati Commercial Gazette,* June 16, 1884; "Miscellaneous," *Cleveland Plain Dealer,* June 16, 1884; "Pugilistic News," *National Police Gazette,* February 20, 1886; "Very Tame Slugging," *Washington Post,* April 8, 1887; "Sports and Pastimes," *Syracuse Standard,* November 19, 1887; "Merve Thompson Wants a Farm," *Batavia Daily News,* October 15, 1901; "The Glove Artists," *St. Paul Globe,* November 19, 1887. Thompson fought more black fighters than his counterparts, possibly because he wanted to highlight his white skin. Thompson fought the following black fighters: C.A.C. Smith, Billy Wilson, Charles Hadley, George Peters, and "Big Six" Alfred Walker. For the most part, the color contrast helped him pass. This aspect was most noticeable in his fight against the black fighter George Peters of Detroit. Peters, who weighed 160 pounds, knocked Thompson out in January 1888, and after the fight the *Cleveland Herald-Leader* wrote, "Peters looked like a pigmy by the side of the big Cleveland heavyweight," and Thompson "looked as strong as a lion, but as clumsy as a whale." Newspapers around the country captured the same disparity in size and color in their headlines. One read, "Thompson 'The Thunder Bolt' Knocked out in Five Rounds by a Coon," another noted, "'The Thunderbolt'

Knocked out by a small but Agile Senegambian," while a third observed, "Whirlwind Thompson Slaughtered by a small Sized Coon." "The World of Sport," *Cleveland Leader,* January 17, 1888; "Thompson 'The Thunder Bolt' Knocked out in Five Rounds by a Coon," *Omaha Herald,* January 17, 1888; "'The Thunderbolt' Knocked out by a small but Agile Senegambian," *St. Paul Globe,* January 17, 1888; "Whirlwind Thompson Slaughtered by a small Sized Coon," *Wheeling Register,* January 18, 1888. Despite the fact Thompson publically claimed he was white, lived his life as a white man after his athletic career, and eventually died as a white man, because of Sullivan's words Thompson is remembered as a black fighter. By drawing the color line against a man who was not quite visibly white, Sullivan used his championship status to claim power, manliness, and authority as a white right.

26. "Latest Sporting Topics," *National Police Gazette,* January 31, 1891.

27. "Pugilistic News," *National Police Gazette,* October 8, 1887.

28. "Two Fistic Combats," *National Police Gazette,* November 23, 1889. The fight took place on November.

29. "Godfrey in Boston," *Boston Globe,* January 31, 1888; "Godfrey Wants to Meet Lannon," *Boston Globe,* January 1, 1889; "Cardiff Quit," *Boston Globe,* May 9, 1890; "He was Game," *Boston Globe,* November 26, 1890; "Kilrain the Victory," *San Francisco Chronicle,* March 14, 1891; "Godfrey's Fight," *Boston Globe,* May 17, 1892; "Choynski the Victory," *San Francisco Chronicle,* November 1, 1892.

30. "Black Cloud on the Pacific," *New York Sun,* January 4, 1889.

31. "World of Sport," *Inter Ocean,* July 14, 1889.

32. Gerald Early, *The Culture of Bruising: Essays on Prizefighting, Literature, and Modern American Culture* (Hopewell, N.J.: Ecco Press, 1994), 15.

33. Trevor Wignall, *The Story of Boxing* (London: Hutchinson, 1923), 253, 257; Trevor Wignall, *The Sweet Science* (London: Chapman and Hall), 195.

34. "New Orleans Notes," *Indianapolis Freeman,* July 5, 1890.

35. "Editorial," *Indianapolis Freeman,* June 11, 1892; "Editorial," *Indianapolis Freeman,* January 5, 1889.

36. Wiggins, *Glory Bound,* 44–46.

37. "Jackson and Corbett," *New York Herald,* October 16, 1892.

38. "Jim and Joe Clash," *Chicago Tribune,* January 10, 1893; "Jackson Challenges Corbett," *Chicago Tribune,* February 12, 1892.

39. "Corbett Caught Up," *Chicago Tribune,* July 11, 1892.

40. "Says America is the Ground," *Chicago Tribune,* March 27, 1894.

41. "Corbett Signs Articles," *New York Herald,* September 9, 1894.

42. "Jackson Branded a Coward," *Los Angeles Herald,* September 13, 1894.

43. Bob Armstrong, "When Fighters Really Fought," *Chicago Defender,* February 27, 1927.

44. "Prospect in England Much Better," *Chicago Tribune,* August 1, 1897; "See Armstrong and Jimmy Barry," *Chicago Tribune,* May 31, 1897.

45. "General Sporting News," *Duluth Times,* August 21, 1896.

46. "Parson Davies' Colored Hercules," *San Francisco Call,* March 20, 1897.

47. "Armstrong to Fight Here," *Philadelphia Inquirer,* March 17, 1900.

48. "Prospect in England Much Better," *Chicago Tribune,* August 1, 1897; "See Armstrong and Jimmy Barry," *Chicago Tribune,* May 31, 1897.

49. "A Hurricane Battle," *San Francisco Chronicle,* February 16, 1893. "Markham Signs Prize Fight Bill," *Los Angeles Times,* March 11, 1893.

50. "Big Blacks," *Cincinnati Enquirer,* March 4, 1898.

51. "Childs," *Cincinnati Enquirer,* March 5, 1898.

52. "Childs Proves a Surprise," *Chicago Daily News,* January 31, 1898.

53. "The Prize Ring," *Memphis Commercial Appeal,* November 29, 1900; "A One-Eyed Fighter," *Memphis Commercial Appeal,* December 28, 1900.

54. "Pugilist Childs in Training," *Los Angeles Express,* October 18, 1902; "Childs is Betting Favorite," *Los Angeles Express,* October 21, 1902.

55. Johnson, *My Life and Times,* 20–21.

56. "McCarey's Big Task," *Los Angeles Express,* October 1, 1903.

57. Jack Johnson, *My Life and Battles,* ed. and trans. Christopher Rivers (Westport, Conn.: Praeger, 2007), 39–40.

58. "Colored Champion Says He is Much Better Than Ever," *Los Angeles Herald,* October 1, 1903.

59. "It's 'Up to You' Champion Jeffries," *Los Angeles Times,* October 29, 1903.

60. "Public Refuses to Accept Color Line," *Los Angeles Times*, October 22, 1903.

61. "Jim Jeffries Turns Down Offer to Fight Big Jack Johnson," *New York Evening News,* December 18, 1903.

62. "Jeffries Won't Fight Johnson," *Philadelphia Inquirer,* February 6, 1904.

63. "Marvin Hart's Home Coming," *Salt Lake Tribune,* July 16, 1906.

64. See, Roberts, *Papa Jack*; Ward, *Unforgivable Blackness*; Runstedtler, *Rebel Sojourner.*

65. "Pittsburg Boxer Stops in Seventh," *New York Times,* March 14, 1911; "Jeannette Defeats Barry in Dull Bout," *New York Times,* March 17, 1911. Leading up to the fight, across the country whites had pinned hopes on Moran because he was touted as "a promising heavyweight with speed and punch."

66. "White Hopes not Same Until Langford is in Jail," *Philadelphia Tribune,* May 24, 1913.

67. J. Alex Sloan, "Where We Get Off," *Los Angeles Times,* June 11, 1911.

68. "White Hopes Fade Away" *New York Times,* April 23, 1911.

69. "White Hope, Lost Hope, says *New York Globe*," *Indianapolis Freeman,* January 27, 1912.

70. "Search for a 'White Hope,'" *New York Age,* September 21, 1911.

71. "'White Hopes' Scarce," *Philadelphia Tribune,* July 13, 1912.

72. "White Hopes not Same Until Langford is in Jail," *Philadelphia Tribune,* May 24, 1913; "Other Black Boxers Better Than Pale Skins," *Philadelphia Tribune,* August 10, 1912.

73. J. P. Garvey, "Jack Johnson's Successor Will Probably not be a White Man," *Cleveland Plain Dealer*, August 4, 1912.

74. Quoted in "Joe Jeannette Retires," *New York Age*, September 16, 1915.

75. "The Johnson-Jeannette Bout," *New York Age*, August 22, 1912.

76. "Joe Jeannette After Johnson," *New York Times*, December 25, 1911. In their previous bouts they fought a limited number of rounds, but Jeannette wanted a long, drawn-out fight.

77. "Carl Morris and Kennedy," *New York Times*, December 27, 1911.

78. Quoted in Clay Moyle, *Sam Langford: Boxing's Greatest Uncrowned Champion* (Seattle: Bennett and Hastings, 2008), 187.

79. "Langford Boxed for George V.," *Los Angeles Times*, November 2, 1914.

80. "Just Ask Texas Brown if Langford Can Hit," *Memphis Scimitar*, January 8, 1910.

81. "Boxers Rest for Big Bout," *Memphis Commercial Appeal*, January 10, 1910.

82. "Negroes Will Give Fighters Banquet," *Memphis Scimitar*, January 5, 1910.

83. Bederman, *Manliness and Civilization*, 8–9.

84. "Langford Didn't Try for Hotel Lodging," *Memphis Scimitar*, January 8, 1910.

85. "Mack's Melange," *New Orleans Picayune*, September 1, 1912.

86. "The Johnson-Jeannette Bout," *New York Age*, August 22, 1912.

87. "Sam Langford to Sell," *Chicago Defender*, August 13, 1910; "Langford to be Used as Cats Paw: Afro-Americans are Afraid of Sam Langford," *Chicago Defender*, July 11, 1914.

CHAPTER 5. SAMBOS, SAVAGES, AND THE SHAKINESS OF WHITENESS

1. "Langford Works Well," *Los Angeles Times*, November 2, 1907.

2. "Langford Won in the Third Round," *Memphis Commercial Appeal*, January 11, 1910.

3. "Like to Bulls the Fighters," *Los Angeles Times*, December 16, 1905.

4. Jack London, "Thirst for Prize Fighting Deep-Seated in Human Race," *The Los Angeles Times*, June 29, 1910.

5. "Obstacles in Way of Burns-Langford Bout," *San Francisco Examiner*, April 2, 1910.

6. Carr, "Cold, Gory Horror, Pitiful Revolting," *Los Angeles Times*, March 18, 1910.

7. Ronald L. Jackson, *Scripting the Black Masculine Body: Identity, Discourse, and Racial Politics in Popular Media* (New York: State University of University Press, 2006), 12.

8. Richard Dyer, *White*, 148.

9. Ibid., 146.

10. Harry S. Carr, "The Cave Man They all Fear," *Los Angeles Times*, February 6, 1910. Carr also gave Langford an "Indian" name, calling him "Young-Man-The-Sight-Of-Whose-Fists-Gives-Prizefighters-The-Shivering-Willies." "When Sam's About: Drawing Color line is a Favorite Sport," *Los Angeles Times*, December 5, 1908.

11. See, Lee D. Baker, *From Savage to Negro: Anthropology and the Construction of Race, 1896–1954* (Berkeley: University of California Press, 1998).

12. Gorn, *The Manly Art*, 179–206; Isenberg, *John L. Sullivan and His America*, 62–74. "Professional boxing," Jeffory Clymer has argued "with its crowds buying tickets and pouring through the turnstiles to view two fighting men, represents an important way in which male bodies and capital converge." Jeffory Clymer, "The Market in Male Bodies: Henry James's *The American* and Late Nineteenth Century Boxing," *Henry James Review* 25 (2004): 136.

13. "The Proposed Battle," *Los Angeles Daily Herald,* March 18, 1884; "Ross and Thompson Home," *Cleveland Herald,* March 7, 1884; "Sporting Notes," *Cleveland Herald,* March 15, 1884; "Sullivan-Thompson," *Cleveland Herald,* March 16, 1884; "In and Outdoor Sports," *Cleveland Plain Dealer,* March 17, 1884.

14. "Macon's Description of Sullivan's Great Rival," *Cincinnati Weekly Enquirer,* February 27, 1884.

15. Kimmel, *History of Men,* 93–94.

16. Ibid., 56.

17. "Sporting Matters," *Boston Globe,* January 12, 1883.

18. "Science," *Chicago Tribune,* November 17, 1883.

19. Gorn, *The Manly Art,* 229.

20. "In the Pink of Condition," *Detroit Free Press,* May 19, 1892.

21. Valerie Babb, *Whiteness Visible: The Meaning of Whiteness in American Literature and* Culture (New York: New York University Press, 1998), 128–29.

22. "Advertisement," *Inter Ocean,* June 19, 1893.

23. Bederman, *Manliness and Civilization,* 35.

24. Baker, *From Savage to Negro,* 78–80.

25. George Frederickson, *The Black Image in the White Mind: The Debate on Afro-American Character and Destiny, 1817–1914* (Wesleyan, Conn.: Wesleyan University Press, 1987), 246–47.

26. Quoted in, "The Negro as a Prize Fighter," *Indianapolis Freeman,* July 19, 1890.

27. "A Color Line for the Ring," *Anaconda Standard,* January 6, 1896.

28. "With the Boxers," *Memphis Commercial Appeal,* January 17, 1901.

29. "News of the Boxers," *Memphis Commercial Appeal,* January 18, 1901.

30. "With the Boxers," *Los Angeles Times,* May 25, 1896.

31. "Two Ideas of Jim Jeffries," *Los Angeles Herald,* May 28, 1903.

32. Ibid.

33. E. Anthony Rutondo, *American Manhood: Transformations in Masculinity from the Revolution to the Modern Era* (New York: Basic Books, 1993), 222–32; Bederman, *Manliness and Civilization,* 22–23.

34. "The Ring," *Los Angeles Herald,* October 9, 1899.

35. Kristin L. Hoganson, *Fighting for American Manhood: How Gender Politics Provoked the Spanish-American and Philippine-American Wars* (New Haven, Conn.: Yale University Press, 1998), 110.

36. "Match for Kelly and McVey," *Los Angeles Express,* December 6, 1902; "Banking on Burns," *Los Angeles Express,* December 15, 1902; "Now Counting on Kelly," *Los Angeles Express,* December 20, 1902

37. "Kelly is a Dough Boy," *Los Angeles Express,* January 7, 1903.

38. Within two years, 1900–1902, he battled Frank Childs, "Denver" Ed Martin, Hank Griffin, Sam McVey, and Jack Johnson, only defeating Griffin in a controversial decision.

39. "Russell Boxes for Picnic Reporter," *Los Angeles Times,* September 9, 1902.

40. "Russell Gets the Decision After Foul Play," *Los Angeles Herald,* September 13, 1902; "Jeffries Will be There," *Los Angeles Express,* September 12, 1902.

41. "Russell Fouls Griffin," *Los Angeles Express,* September 13, 1902.

42. "McVey is a Wonder," *Los Angeles Express,* November 3, 1902.

43. "Russell is a Bad One," *Los Angles Express,* December 5, 1902; "Johnson is Winner," *Los Angeles Herald,* December 5, 1902. "Furious Mob At Ringside," *Los Angeles Times,* December 5, 1902.

44. "Pugilist is not a Vagrant," *Los Angles Express,* December 11, 1902.

45. Kasson, *Houdini, Tarzan, and the Perfect Man,* 10.

46. "Tremendous Interest," *Los Angeles Times,* May 7, 1901.

47. "Denver Ed Puts Griffen [*sic*] to Sleep," *Los Angeles Times,* October 3, 1901.

48. "Johnson has Shown Class," *Los Angeles Times,* October 18, 1904.

49. Baker, *From Savage to Negro,* 12–13.

50. "Jack Johnson's Change of Mind," *Los Angeles Herald,* September 28, 1903.

51. "Harry Stuart, "Young Fighter of Promise," *Los Angeles Herald,* October 13, 1902.

52. "Oxnard Loyal to Wonder," *Los Angeles Express,* November 13, 1902.

53. "McVey won from Kelly," *Los Angeles Times,* January 7, 1903; "Martin Best Puncher Man," *Los Angeles Times,* August 13, 1904; "Johnson, Sah Remains 'It,'" *Los Angeles Times,* February 27, 1903.

54. "Both Sides of the Colored Argument," *Los Angeles Herald,* October 23, 1903.

55. Tip Wright, "Tip Wright's Column," *Tacoma Times,* May 1, 1909.

56. William H. Wiggins Jr. "Boxing's Sambo Twins: Racial Stereotypes in Jack Johnson and Joe Louis Newspaper Cartoons, 1908 to 1938," *Journal of Sports History* 15, no. 3 (Winter 1988): 242–54. The boxing battle royals also helped pacify blacks, because the events demonstrated how blacks would humiliate themselves for some small change and white entertainment. Andrew M. Kaye, "'Battle Blind': Atlanta's Taste for Black Boxing in the Early Twentieth Century," *Journal of Sports History* 28, no. 2 (2001): 213–32.

57. Joseph Boskin, *Sambo: The Rise and Demise of an American Jester* (New York: Oxford University Press, 1986), 13–14.

58. Litwack, *North of Slavery,* 184–85.

59. "Black Men in the Ring," *Chicago Tribune,* December 29, 1889.

60. "Class Division in Fistiana," *Desert Evening News,* February 27, 1904.

61. Ibid.

62. "The Black's Superiority as a Fighting Machine is Established," *Wilkes-Barre Times*, January 5, 1907.

63. "What Makes the Negro Such a Fighter?" *Duluth Times*, September 6, 1908.

64. "M'Mahon and Langford Are to Battle Tonight," *Los Angeles Times*, November 10, 1914.

65. "Burns Tells of Plans after Australian Fights," *Anaconda Times*, June 30, 1908.

66. For more on Burns-Johnson, see Roberts, *Papa Jack*; Runstedtler, *Rebel Sojourner*.

67. "The Superiority of the Black," *New York Age*, December 31, 1908.

68. Bederman, *Manliness and Civilization*, 8.

69. "Jack London Describes the Fight and Jack Johnson's Golden Smile," *San Francisco Call*, December 27, 1908.

70. "Mack's Talk," *Memphis Scimitar*, December 5, 1909.

71. "Fights to Wrest Title from Negro," *Memphis Scimitar*, December 17, 1909.

72. "Two Fighters Unlike as Black and White," *San Francisco Chronicle*, July 2, 1910.

73. Jack London, "Winner of Battle Needs Energy of Abysmal Brute," *San Francisco Chronicle*, June 27, 1910.

74. Jack London, "World's Fight Experts Congregate in Nevada," *San Francisco Chronicle*, June 24, 1910.

75. "Ready for a Fight Within Three Weeks," *San Francisco Examiner*, March 22, 1910.

76. "Two Fighters Unlike as Black and White," *San Francisco Chronicle*, July 2, 1910.

77. "Big Fellow's Love for the Open will prove Savior," *Oakland Tribune*, May 5, 1910.

78. *Sacramento Star*, May 13, 1910.

79. "Physical Culture Expert Declares Johnson is an Athletic Marvel," *Salt Lake Telegram*, April 30, 1910.

80. "Jack Johnson Great Talker," *Sacramento Star*, April 26, 1910.

81. "Tad Visits Jack Johnson," *San Francisco Examiner*, June 4, 1910; "I Would Rather Die Than Quit. Says the Serious Mr. Johnson," *San Francisco Examiner*, June 30, 1910.

82. W. W. Naughton, "Good Nature and Light Boxing in Veteran Bout," *San Francisco Examiner*, June 12, 1910.

83. "Johnson will Ease Up on His Trained Stunts," *Oakland Tribune*, June 10, 1910.

84. C. E. Van Loan, "Training Camp," *San Francisco Examiner*, June 27, 1910.

85. "Jeffries Feels Somber Energy of Battle, Johnson Waits with Stolid Concern," *San Francisco Examiner*, July 1, 1910.

86. "Ring Gladiators Resting for Worlds Great Go," *Oakland Tribune*, July 3, 1910.

87. "Temperaments of Jeff and Johnson Compared," *San Francisco Chronicle*, June 25, 1910.

88. "I'll Rush from the Start," *San Francisco Examiner*, June 26, 1910.

89. "Preparing Jeff's Camp," *Sacramento Star*, April 6, 1910. Although churches and reformers attacked boxing, especially outside the West, they had primarily stayed in the shadows of protest and had not come out in full force until the Jeffries-Johnson affair.

90. "How can a man 'Come Back': He's Never been Away," *Sacramento Star*, May 27, 1910.

91. "How The California Grizzly Went Down And Out At Reno," *Los Angeles Times*, July 4, 1910.

92. Rex Beach, "The Spark had Died," *Los Angeles Times*, July 5, 1910.

93. "Remarks by the Staff," *Los Angeles Times*, July 6, 1910.

94. "Vision of Brutal, Grinning Gorilla, Defeated Jeffries," *Oakland Tribune*, July 10, 1910.

95. Hugh D. McIntosh, "The Black Boxers," *Daily Herald*, July 5, 1912.

CHAPTER 6. FOLLOWING THE COLOR LINE

1. "To Restrict Boxing Clubs," *Louisville Courier Journal*, March 14, 1902.

2. "Hero of Four Hundred Battles," *Indianapolis Freeman*, January 18, 1913; *Life Behind a Veil: Blacks in Louisville, Kentucky, 1865–1930* (Baton Rouge: Louisiana State University Press, 1985), 77, 81. By 1910, for example, the first year the census counted waiters, 421 of the 545 waiters in Louisville were black.

3. For his record, see "Sport," *Indianapolis Freeman*, May 25, 1901; "Evening Breezes," *Bay City Times*, April 25, 1901; "Jim Watt's Record," *Cleveland Plain Dealer*, July 18, 1900.

4. "Early Life of Marvin Hart," *Buffalo Courier*, January 17, 1906.

5. "Colored Boys Win," *Louisville Courier Journal*, May 25, 1897.

6. "Stopped by Police," *Augusta Chronicle*, January 29, 1898; "A Vicious Fight, *Oregonian*, March 19, 1898.

7. "Watts to Quit Louisville," *Louisville Courier Journal*, March 16, 1902.

8. "Sporting News," *Jackson Daily Patriot*, January 7, 1904.

9. "Hero of Four Hundred Battles," *Indianapolis Freeman*, January 18, 1913.

10. "Negro Boxers Barred," *Trenton Times*, March 2, 1902; "Barring the Black Boxer," *Boston Globe*, February 5, 1904; "Black Boxers May Sue," *Chicago Tribune*, February 11, 1904; "Colored Boxers Becoming Scarce," *National Police Gazette*, November 3, 1906; "Seconds Often Save Fights," *Springfield Republican*, January 30, 1910; "Jack Johnson Cannot Fight in New York," *Salt Lake Herald*, August 23, 1912; "Negro Pugilists Barred Hereafter," *New Orleans Picayune*, January 19, 1913.

11. "Editorial," *Marysville Daily Appeal*, July 1, 1910.

12. "Gameness that Worried Gans," *Baltimore America*, November 15, 1902.

13. "Is Boxing Doomed Here?" *Baltimore Sun*, November 18, 1902.

14. "Gives Gans Hard Fight," *Baltimore Sun*, November 15, 1902.

15. "Is Boxing Doomed Here?" *Baltimore Sun*, November 18, 1902.

16. "Local Boxers take the Count," *Baltimore American*, December 4, 1902.

17. For a history of housing segregation and reform in the city, see Antero Pietila, *Not in My Neighborhood: How Bigotry Shaped a Great American City* (Chicago: Rowan and Littlefield, 2010).

18. Jack Temple Kirby, *Darkness at Dawning: Race and Reform in the Progressive South* (New York: J.B. Lippincott, 1972), 4.

19. "White Man's Government in Maryland," *Semi-Weekly Messenger,* April 18, 1899.

20. "A Great Meeting," *Baltimore Sun,* April 14, 1899.

21. "Cheers for the Sun," *Baltimore Sun,* April 18, 1899.

22. "Ladies Interested," *Baltimore Sun,* April 7, 1899.

23. "The Boxing Question," *Baltimore Sun,* November 20, 1902.

24. "A Boxer Defends Boxing," *Baltimore Sun,* November 21, 1902; "The Difference in Boxing," *Baltimore Sun,* November 24, 1902.

25. "Boxing Hangs in the Balance," *Baltimore American,* December 6, 1902.

26. "What Joe Gans Thinks of It," *Baltimore Sun,* December 14, 1902.

27. "Final Blow to Boxer's Game," *Baltimore American,* January 1, 1903.

28. "Boxing Likely to be Resumed," *Baltimore American,* July 9, 1903.

29. "Big Fight May Come Off in Los Angeles," *Los Angeles Herald,* February 4, 1901.

30. Mark Wild, *Street Meeting: Multiethnic Neighborhoods in Early Twentieth Century Los Angeles* (Berkeley: University of California Press, 2005), 38–39.

31. Wild, *Street Meeting,* 15–16.

32. Jim Jeffries, "My Story of My Life," *Oregonian,* March 20, 1910. His family on his father's side had colonial roots dating back to the seventeenth century. Jeffries's great grandfather, William, had a large plantation and owned thirty slaves in Virginia. The Jeffries bloodline had also fought in the American Revolution, the War of 1812, and against Indians. Eventfully, his great grandfather sold his slaves—to cover expenses—and moved to the Ohio frontier.

33. Natalia Molina, *Fit to be Citizens: Public Health and Race in Los Angeles, 1879–1939* (Berkeley: University of California Press, 2006), 34.

34. Jim Jeffries, "My Story of My Life," *Oregonian,* March 20, 1910.

35. "Pugilists want to Make Matches," *Los Angeles Times,* 25 March 1901. Another article observed, "The fact that the Alpha Athletic Club has been making good money has served as no small incentive to its more rapid progress." "Griffin is Matched with Kennedy," *Los Angeles Times,* April 14, 1901.

36. "Burns Agrees to Come," *Los Angeles Herald,* December 10, 1902.

37. "Pugilism," *Los Angeles Times,* June 19, 1902; "Men are Now Ready," *Los Angeles Herald,* June 20, 1902. McCarey also banked on the colored heavyweight championship to build his coffers. Between 1901 and 1903, he hosted five battles for the colored heavyweight championship. McCarey wanted Jeffries to fight one of these black challengers during La Fiesta, but Jeffries would not fight black men for the title.

38. "Three Cyclonic Fights," *Los Angeles Express,* June 20, 1902.

39. "Color line Only a Ruse," *Los Angeles Express,* February 18, 1903.

40. "Neill Now Willing," *Los Angeles Herald,* January 3, 1903.

41. "Contests of Two Jacks," *Los Angeles Express,* May 17, 1902.

42. "Pink Furies Blaze Away," *Los Angeles Times,* May 17, 1902.

43. Lawrence B. De Graaf, "The City of Black Angels: Emergence of the Los Angeles Ghetto, 1890–1930," *Pacific Historic Review* 39, no. 3 (August 1970): 327. Lonnie G. Bunch III, "'The Greatest State for the Negro,' Jefferson L. Edmonds, Black Propagandist of the California Dream," in *Seeking El Dorado: African Americans in California,* ed. Lawrence B. De Graaf, Kevin Mulroy, and Quintard Taylor (Seattle: University of Washington Press, 2001), 130–31.

44. De Graaf, "The City of Black Angels," 329.

45. Lonnie G. Bunch III, "The Greatest State for the Negro," Jefferson L. Edmonds Black Propagandist of the California Dream," in *Seeking El Dorado: African Americans in California,* ed. Lawrence B. De Graaf, Kevin Mulroy, and Quintard Taylor (Seattle: University of Washington Press, 2001), 130–31.

46. De Graff, "The City of Black Angels," 327.

47. "Negroes are Coming," *Los Angeles Herald,* March 20, 1903.

48. "Johnson, Sah, Remains 'It,'" *Los Angeles Times,* February 27, 1903; "Nearly a thousand Negro Colonists," *Los Angeles Times,* February 27, 1903.

49. "Not One Went the Limit," *Los Angeles Express,* March 19, 1903.

50. "Joe Walcott Will Come," *Los Angeles Herald,* March 3, 1903; "About the Boxers," *Los Angeles Herald,* March 6, 1903; "Mississippi is in Town," *Los Angeles Herald,* March 17, 1903; "Another Dixon Born," *Los Angeles Herald,* March 19, 1903.

51. "Interest in Coming Mill," *Los Angeles Herald,* April 30, 1903.

52. "Carter Knocked out" *Los Angeles Herald,* May 5, 1903.

53. "Card is Changed Again," *Los Angeles Herald,* May 7, 1903.

54. "Gets Decision over Woods in Fourth Round over Ugly Foul," *Los Angeles Times,* June 10, 1903; "How it Happened," *Los Angeles Times,* June 10, 1903. The first fight of the night between Kid Williams (Mexican) and Frank Fields (white) was an exciting ten-round fight with no problems.

55. "Colored Boy is Compared with Al Neill," *Los Angeles Herald,* January 19, 1903; "Who is the Winner," *Los Angeles Herald,* April 2, 1903; "Both on Their Feet," *Los Angeles Herald,* April 3, 1903.

56. "Banking on Burns," *Los Angeles Express,* December 15, 1902.

57. "Gets Decision over Woods in Fourth Round over Ugly Foul," *Los Angeles Times,* June 10, 1903; "How it Happened," *Los Angeles Times,* June 10, 1903.

58. "Gets Decision over Woods in Fourth Round over Ugly Foul," *Los Angeles Times,* June 10, 1903; "How it Happened," *Los Angeles Times,* June 10, 1903.

59. "Twisted his Neck," *Los Angeles Herald,* June 10, 1903.

60. Gerald Woods, "A Penchant for Probity," 105.

61. Robert Fogelson, *The Fragmented Metropolis: Los Angeles, 1850–1930* (Cambridge, Mass.: Harvard University Press, 1968), 145.

62. "About Prize Fights," *Los Angeles Times,* June 11, 1903.

63. "No More Mixed Matches," *Los Angeles Herald*, June 13, 1903.

64. "Ministers Hit Pugs," *Los Angeles Express*, October 26, 1903.

65. "No Prize Fighting in Residence Sections," *Los Angeles Times*, October 17, 1903; "Prize Fight Not Wanted," *Los Angeles Times*, October 18, 1903; "Prize Fighting: 'Pugs,'" *Los Angeles Times*, "Driven Into Corner," *Los Angeles Times*, October 20, 1903.

66. "Council May Stop Johnson-McVey Mill," *Los Angeles Times*, October 25, 1903.

67. "Council May Stop Johnson-McVey Mill," *Los Angeles Times*, October 25, 1903; "At the City Hall, Medley of Views on the Prize fight," *Los Angeles Times*, October 29, 1903; "Big Money in Johnson Bill," *Los Angeles Times*, October 29, 1903. Many members of the council, the same council who opposed the morality of boxing, went to the match and did not like what they saw. They watched Jack Johnson, a man the paper supported in his stance to get Jeffries to break the color line, pummel McVey for twenty rounds.

68. "Prize Fighting Prohibited," *Los Angeles Times*, November 4, 1903; "Boxing game rises Again," *Los Angeles Times*, May 28, 1904; "Editorial," *Los Angeles Times*, May 29, 1904. In May 1904, a local judge ruled the city ordinance unconstitutional because it made illegal what the state law made legal.

69. "Big Battle is Possible," *Los Angeles Times*, June 15, 1904.

70. "Big Darkies Coming Next," *Los Angeles Times*, September 18, 1904.

71. "Fighters at Work," *Los Angeles Herald*, June 19, 1907.

72. "Featherweight Championship Battlers are Fit and Ready," *Los Angeles Herald*, December 11, 1908.

73. See Roberts, *Papa Jack*; Runstedtler, *Rebel Sojourner*; Ward, *Unforgivable Blackness*.

74. "After Dixie's Scalp," *Memphis Commercial Appeal*, October 15, 1909.

75. "Coleman Here for His Go Against Hock Bones," *Memphis Scimitar*, January 27, 1910.

76. See, "After Dixie's Scalp," *Memphis Commercial Appeal*, October 15, 1909; "Congo Kid Favorite," *Memphis Commercial Appeal*, October 23, 1909; "Dixie Kid Gets Another Decision," *Memphis Commercial Appeal*, November 16, 1909; "Fight Clubs Won't Combine," *Memphis Commercial Appeal*, January 3, 1910.

77. For information on Mayor Crump, race, and reform, see Kirby, *Darkness at the Dawning*, 47–49; G. Wayne Dowdy, *Mayor Crump Don't Like It: Machine Politics in Memphis* (Jackson: University of Mississippi Press, 2006.)

78. "Color Line is Drawn Again," *Memphis Commercial Appeal*, November 3, 1909.

79. "Whirlwind was Part Whirlwind but was Most Zephyr-Like" *Memphis Scimitar*, November 30, 1909.

80. "Color Line for M.A.C. Features," *Memphis Commercial Appeal*, January 16, 1910.

81. "Crump Denies Weird Story," *Memphis Scimitar*, January 19, 1910; "Mack's Talk," *Memphis Scripter*, January 18, 1910.

82. "Langford Beat Jim Crow Law," *Memphis Commercial Appeal*, January 19, 1910.

83. "Brock's Backers Thinks He'll Win," *Memphis Commercial Appeal,* January 28, 1910.

84. "Local Betting is Light," *Memphis Commercial Appeal,* July 4, 1910.

85. "That Fight," *Memphis Commercial Appeal,* July 5, 1910.

86. "Negro Boxers Barred," *Pawtucket Times,* July 11, 1910.

87. "May Bar Mixed Bouts," *New York Times,* September 13, 1913.

88. "News of the Boxing World," *Alaska Daily,* May 21, 1914.

89. "Gibson Calls off Langford Smith Go," *Trenton Evening Times,* September 25, 1913; "Another Ruling on Mixed Bouts," *New York Tribune,* September 25, 1913.

90. "Sam McVey is to Fight Law," *Los Angeles Times,* December 22, 1914.

91. "Joe Jeannette is Barred," *New Orleans Picayune,* June 15, 1913.

92. In 1913 Jeannette battled in the South three times. He fought Harry Wills in New Orleans, and meal-ticket fighters Nat Dewey and Jeff Clarke in Savannah and Memphis, respectively.

93. "Jeannette-Clarke," *Memphis Commercial Appeal,* June 24, 1913.

94. "Jeannette Hopes that the Commission Will Reinstate Him Soon," *Grand Folks Daily Herald,* February 12, 1916.

95. "With and Without Decisions," *Duluth News,* August 16, 1914; "Will Forsake the Feathers," *Cleveland Plain Dealer,* August 23, 1914.

96. "Negro Boxers Slowly Losing Grip in Ring," *New York Tribune,* January 15, 1915.

97. Lucien H. White, "Status of Negro Boxer," *New York Age,* January 21, 1915.

98. "Joe Jeannette Quits the Ring," *Trenton Evening Times,* September 12, 1915.

99. "Where are the Black Men?" *Referee,* January 15, 1919.

EPILOGUE

1. For information on Jack's career, see "Beau Jack" in Peter Heller, *In This Corner: The Candid View of the Champion's Corner* (New York: A Dell Books, 1973), 256–62; Gene Tunney, "The Facts About Beau Jack" *Sport,* February 1955, 12–13, 86–87.

2. Quoted in Red Smith, *The Red Smith Reader* (New York: Vintage Books, 1982), 276.

3. Beau Jack, "How I was Cheated out of $500,000," *Ebony,* February 1949, 40.

4. Quoted in "Couldn't Fight Wills Because of Race," in *Jet* 18, no. 12, 52.

5. Dan Burley, "Harry Wills," *Ebony,* September 1946, 25.

6. Dan Burley, "The Tragic Saga of Kid Chocolate," *Chicago Tribune,* May 19, 1959.

7. William Dettloff, *A Boxing Life: Ezzard Charles* (New York: McFarland, 2015), 10.

8. Quoted in A. S. Young, "Why Do Boxers Go Broke?" *Negro Digest,* June 1962, 11.

9. "Henry Armstrong," in Heller, *In This Corner,* 194.

10. "Henry Armstrong," in Heller, *In This Corner,* 196.

11. Joe Bostic, "Meet George Moore," *The People's Voice,* April 10, 1943.

12. "Henry Armstrong Buys L.A. Building In $25,000 Deal," *Chicago Tribune,* December 5, 1942.

13. Mike Tyson with Larry Sloman, *Mike Tyson: Undisputed Truth* (New York: Blue Rider Press, 2013), 335–57.

14. Dan Burley, "Confidentially Yours," *New York Amsterdam News,* February 19, 1944.

15. Barney Nagler, "Ike is Boxing's Businessman," *Sport,* January 1950, 44–47, 78–79.

16. "Ike Williams," in Heller, *In This Corner,* 267.

17. Ibid.

18. Ray Robinson, "Why I'm the Bad Boy of Boxing," *Ebony,* November 1950, 72–79.

19. "Sugar Ray Robinson Denies He's Bankrupt," *Baltimore Afro American,* November 5, 1955.

20. Kurt Badenhausen, "Floyd Mayweather: By the Numbers," *Forbes,* May 2, 2015. Accessed at http://www.forbes.com/sites/kurtbadenhausen/2015/05/02/25-floyd-mayweather-numbers-to-know-ahead-of-his-pacquiao-fight/#49a17a1759d9.

21. For a good account of the Ali Act, see Patrick Connor, "Bigger Than Antitrust: Boxing and the Ali Act." *SB Nation,* May 19, 2015. Accessed at http://www.badlefthook.com/2015/5/19/8627119/bigger-than-antitrust-boxing-and-the-ali-act.

BIBLIOGRAPHY

BOOKS

Archer-Straw, Petrine. *Negrophilia: Avant-Garde Paris and Black Culture in the 1920s.* New York: Thames and Hudson, 2000.

Bachin, Robin F. *Building the South Side: Urban Space and Civic Culture in Chicago.* Chicago: University of Chicago Press, 2004

Baker, Lee D. *From Savage to Negro: Anthropology and the Construction of Race, 1896–1954.* Berkeley: University of California Press, 1998.

Baldwin, Davarian L. *Chicago's New Negroes: Modernity, The Great Migration, and Black Urban Life.* Chapel Hill: University of North Carolina Press, 2007.

Batchelor, Denzil. *Jack Johnson and His Times.* London: Phoenix Sports Books, 1956.

Bederman, Gale. *Manliness and Civilization: A Cultural History of Gender and Race in the United States, 1880–1917.* Chicago: University of Chicago Press, 1995.

Benson, Peter. *Battling Siki: A Tale of Ring Fixes, Race, and Murder in the 1920s.* Fayetteville: University of Arkansas Press, 2006.

Bergs, Marshall. *The Life and Times of Los Angeles: A Newspaper, a Family, and a City.* New York: Atheneum, 1984.

Black, Daniel P. *Dismantling Black Manhood: An Historical and Literary Analysis of the Legacy of Slavery.* New York: Garland Publishing, 1997.

Bolster, Jeffrey W. *Black Jacks: African American Seamen in the Age of Sail.* Cambridge, Mass.: Harvard University Press, 1997.

Bontemps, Arna. *God Sends Sunday.* New York: Washington Square Press, 2005.

Booker, Christopher. *I Will Wear No Chain: A Social History of African American Males.* London: Praeger, 2000.

Boskin, Joseph. *Sambo: The Rise and Demise of an American Jester.* New York: Oxford University Press, 1986.

Brady, William A. *The Fighting Man*. Indianapolis: Bobbs-Merrill, 1916.

Callow, Alexander B., Ed. *American Urban History: An Interpretive Reader with Commentaries,* 3rd ed. New York: Oxford University Press, 1982.

Carby, Hazel V. *Race Men: The W.E.B. Du Bois Lectures*. Cambridge, Mass.: Harvard University Press, 1998.

Carr, Harry. *Los Angeles: City of Dreams*. New York: D. Appleton-Century, 1935.

Cayton, Horace M., and St. Claire Drake. *Black Metropolis: A Study of Negro Life in a Northern City*. New York: Harcourt, Brace, 1945.

Chudacoff, Howard P. *The Age of the Bachelor: Creating an American Subculture*. Princeton, N.J.: Princeton University Press, 1999.

Corrothers, James. *The Black Cat Club*. New York: Funk and Wagnalls, 1902.

Cromwell, Adelaide M. *The Other Brahmins: Boston's Black Upper Class, 1750–1950*. Fayetteville: University of Arkansas Press, 1994.

Daniels, Douglas Henry. *Pioneer Urbanites: A Social and Cultural History of Black San Francisco*. Philadelphia: Temple University Press, 1980.

Daniels, John. *In Freedom's Birthplace: A Study of the Boston Negroes*. Boston: Houghton Mifflin, 1914.

Dann, Martin E. *The Black Press, 1827–1890: The Quest For National Identity*. New York: G.P. Putnam's Sons, 1971.

Davis, Mike. *City of Quartz: Excavating the Future in Los Angeles*. New York: Verson, 2006.

De Graaf, Lawrence B., Kevin Mulroy, and Quintard Taylor, eds. *Seeking El Dorado: African Americans in California*. Seattle: University of Washington Press, 2001.

Deverell, William, and Thomas Sitton, eds. *California Progressivism Revisited*. Berkeley: University of California Press, 1994.

Dixon, George. *A Lesson in Boxing*. New York: George Dixon, 1893.

Dulaney, Marvin W. *Black Police in America*. Indianapolis: Indiana University Press, 1996.

Dyer, Richard. *White*. New York: Routledge, 1995.

Early, Gerald. *The Culture of Bruising: Essays on Prizefighting, Literature, and Modern American Culture*. Hopewell, N.J.: Ecco Press, 1994.

Ebner, Michael H., and Eugene M. Tobin, eds. *The Age of Urban Reform: New Perspectives on the Progressive Era*. Port Washington, N.Y.: Kennikat Press, 1977.

Farr, Finnis. *Black Champion: The Life and Times of Jack Johnson*. New York: Charles Scribner's Sons, 1964.

Flamming, Douglas. *Bound For Freedom: Black Los Angeles in Jim Crow America*. Berkeley: University of California Press, 2005.

Fleischer, Nat. *Black Dynamite: The Story of the Negro in the Prize Ring from 1782–1938*. *Vol. 1–5*. New York: C.J. O'Brien, 1938.

———. *The Heavyweight Championship: An Informal History of Heavyweight Boxing from 1719 to the Present Day*. New York: G.P. Putnam Son's, 1961.

———. *Fifty Years at Ringside*. New York: Greenwood Press, 1940. Reprint, 1969.

Fogelson, Robert. *The Fragmented Metropolis: Los Angeles, 1850–1930*. Cambridge, Mass.: Harvard University Press, 1968.

Foner, Eric. *A Short History of Reconstruction*. New York: Harper and Row, 1984.

———. *The Story of American Freedom*. New York: W.W. Norton, 1998.

Forman, Murray, and Mark Anthony Neal, eds. *That's the Joint: The Hip-Hop Studies Reader*. New York: Routledge, 2012.

Fox, Richard Kyle. *The Black Champions of the Prize Ring, From Molineaux to Jackson*. New York: Franklin Square, 1890.

———. *The Life and Battle of Jack Johnson, Champion Pugilist of the World*. New York: Fox's Athletic Library, 1912.

Franklin, John Hope, ed. *Three Negro Classics*. New York: Avon Books, 1999.

Frederickson, George M. *The Black Image in the White Mind: The Debate on Afro-American Character and Destiny, 1817–1914*. Wesleyan, Conn.: Wesleyan University Press, 1987.

Freeman, Joanne B. *Affairs of Honor: National Politics in the New Republic*. New Haven, Conn.: Yale University Press, 2001.

Gaines, Kevin. *Uplifting the Race: Black Leadership, Politics, and Culture in the Twentieth Century*. Chapel Hill: University of North Carolina Press, 1996.

Gatewood, William B., Jr. *"Smoked Yankees" And the Struggle for Empire: Letters From Negro Soldiers, 1898–1902*. Urbana: University of Illinois Press, 1971.

Gems, Gerald. *Windy City Wars: Labor, Leisure, and Sport in the Making of Chicago*. Lanham, Md.: Scarecrow Press, 1997.

Gerber, David A. *Black Ohio and the Color Line, 1860–1915*. Chicago: University of Chicago Press, 1976.

Gildea, William. *The Longest Fight: In the Ring With Joe Gans: Boxing's First African American Champion*. New York: Farrar, Straus and Giroux, 2012.

Gilmore, Al-Toney. *Bad Nigger!: The National Impact of Jack Johnson*. Port Washington, N.Y.: Kennikat Press, 1975.

Glenn, Evelyn Nakano. *Unequal Freedom: How Race and Gender Shaped American Citizenship and Labor*. Cambridge, Mass.: Harvard University Press, 2002.

Gordon-Reed, Annette, ed. *Race on Trial: Law and Justice in American History*. New York: Oxford University Press, 2002.

Gorn, Elliott J. *The Manly Art: Bare-Knuckle Prize Fighting in America*. Ithaca, N.Y.: Cornell University Press, 1986.

Gosnell, Harold F. *Negro Politicians: The Rise of Negro Politics in Chicago,* 3rd ed. Chicago: University of Chicago Press, 1969.

Greenblatt, Stephen. *Marvelous Possessions: The Wonder of the New World*. Chicago: University of Chicago Press, 1991.

Greenburg, Kenneth S. *Honor and Slavery*. Princeton, N.J.: Princeton University Press, 1996.

Greene, Lorenzo J., and Carter G. Woodson. *The Negro Wage Earner,* 2nd ed. New York: Russell & Russell, 1969.

Grossman, James R. *Land Of Hope: Chicago, Black Southerners and the Great Migration*. Chicago: University of Chicago Press, 1989.

Grossman, Lawrence. *The Democratic Party and the Negro: Northern and National Politics, 1868–92*. Chicago: University of Illinois Press, 1976.

Hardy, Stephen. *How Boston Played: Sport, Recreation, and Community, 1865–1915*. Boston: Northeastern University Press, 1982.

Harrison, Carter H. *Stormy Years: The Autobiography of Carter H. Harrison, Five Times Mayor of Chicago*. Indianapolis: Bobbs-Merrill, 1935.

Hearn, Jeff, and David Morgan, eds. *Men, Masculinities, and Social Theory*. Boston: Unwin Hyman, 1990.

Helg, Aline. *Our Rightful Share: The Afro-Cuban Struggle for Equality, 1886–1912*. Chapel Hill: University of North Carolina Press, 1995.

Heller, Peter. *In This Corner: The Candid View of the Champion's Corner*. New York: A Dell Book, 1973.

Hietla, Thomas R. *The Fight of the Century: Jack Johnson, Joe Louis, and the Struggle for Racial Equality*. Armonk, N.Y.: M.E. Sharpe, 2002.

Hine, Darlene Clark, and Earnest Jenkins, eds. *A Question of Manhood: A Reader in U.S. Black Men's History and Masculinity, Vol. 2, The 19th Century: From Emancipation to Jim Crow*. Indianapolis: Indiana University Press, 2001.

Hoberman, John. *Darwin's Athletes: How Sport Has Damaged Black America and Preserved the Myth of Race*. Boston: Houghton Mifflin, 1997.

Hoganson, Kristin L. *Fighting for American Manhood: How Gender Politics Provoked the Spanish-American and Philippine-American Wars*. New Haven, Conn.: Yale University Press, 1998.

Hornby, Jim. *Black Islanders: Prince Edward Island's Historical Black Community*. Charlottetown, P.E.I.: Institute of Island Studies, 1991.

Hornsby-Gutting, Angela. *Black Manhood and Community Building in North Carolina, 1900–1930*. Gainesville: University Press of Florida, 2009.

Horton, James Oliver. *Free People of Color: Inside the African American Community*. Washington: Smithsonian Institute Press, 1993.

Hotaling, Edward. *The Great Black Jockeys: The Lives and Times of the Men Who Dominated America's First National Sport*. Rocklin, Calif.: Prima Publishing, 1999.

Isenberg, Michael T. *John L. Sullivan and His America*. Urbana: University of Illinois Press, 1994.

Johnson, David R. *Policing the Urban Underworld: The Impact of Crime on the Development of the American Police, 1800–1887*. Philadelphia: Temple University Press, 1979.

Johnson, Jack. *Jack Johnson: In the Ring and Out*. Chicago: National Sports Publishing, 1927.

———. *Jack Johnson is a Dandy: An Autobiography*. New York: Chelsea House Publishers, 1969.

———. *My Life and Battles,* edited and translated by Christopher Rivers. London: Praeger, 2007.

Johnson, James Weldon. *Black Manhattan.* New York: Anthenum, 1968.

———. *Along This Way,* in *James Weldon Johnson, Writings.* New York: Library of America, 2004.

Kasson, John F. *Houdini, Tarzan, and the Perfect Man: The White Male Body and the Challenge of Modernity in America.* New York: Hill and Wang, 2001.

Kaye, Andrew M. *The Pussycat of Prizefighting: Tiger Flowers and the Politics of Black Celebrity.* Athens: University of Georgia Press, 2004.

Kelley, Robin D. G. *Race Rebels: Culture, Politics, and the Black Working Class.* New York: The Free Press, 1994.

Kimmel, Michael S. *The History of Men: Essays on the History of American and British Masculinities.* Albany: State University of New York Press, 2005.

———. *Manhood in America: A Cultural History,* 2nd ed. New York: Oxford University Press, 2006.

Kogan, Herman, and Lloyd Wendt. *Lords of the Levee: The Story of Bathhouse John and Hinky Dink.* Indianapolis: Bobbs-Merrill, 1943.

Kusmer, Kenneth L. *A Ghetto Takes Shape, Black Cleveland, 1870–1930.* Urbana: University of Illinois Press, 1978.

Lane, Roger. *William Dorsey's Philadelphia and Ours: On the Past and Future of the Black City in America.* Oxford, U.K.: Oxford University Press, 1991.

Lardner, John. *White Hopes and Other Tigers.* Philadelphia: J.B. Lippinicott, 1951.

Levine, Lawrence. *Black Culture and Black Consciousness: Afro-American Folk Thought From Slavery to Freedom.* New York: Oxford University Press, 1977.

Litwack, Leon. *North of Slavery: The Negro in the Free States, 1790–1860.* Chicago: University of Chicago Press, 1961.

———. *Been in the Storm So Long: The Aftermath of Slavery.* New York: Vintage Books, 1979.

Logan, Rayford W. *The Negro in American Life and Thought: The Nadir, 1877–1901.* New York: Dial Press, 1954.

———. *The Betrayal of the Negro: From Rutherford B. Hayes to Woodrow Wilson,* 3rd ed. New York: Collier Books, 1968.

Lomax, Michael. *Black Baseball Entrepreneurs, 1902–1931: The Negro National Leagues.* Syracuse, N.Y.: Syracuse University Press, 2014.

London, Jack. *The Abysmal Brute.* Lincoln: University of Nebraska Press, 2000.

———. *The Game.* Lincoln: University of Nebraska Press, 2001.

Lynch, Buhon. *Knuckles and Gloves.* New York: Henry Holt, 1923.

Mangum, Charles Staples. *The Legal Status of the Negro.* Chapel Hill: University of North Carolina Press, 1944.

Matthews, Victoria Earle, ed. *Black-Belt Diamonds: Gems from the Speeches, Addresses and Talks to Students of Booker T. Washington Principal of Tuskegee Institute, Tuskegee, Ala.* New York: Fortune and Scott Publishers, 1898.

McCallum, John D. *The World Heavyweight Boxing Championship: A History*. Radnor, Pa.: Chilton, 1974.

McCormick, John B. *The Square Circle; Or, Stories of the Prize Ring, Being Macon's Description of Many Pugilistic Battles, Fought with Bare Knuckles or Boxing Gloves, with Numerous Anecdotes of Famous Fighters: To Which is Added, How to be Young at Fifty: A Treatise on the Proper Method of Living, of Great Value of All Me*. New York: Continental Publishing, 1897.

Mead, Frank J., and Alix J. Muller. *History of the Police and Fire Departments of the Twin Cities: Their Origin in Early Village Days and Progress to 1900*. St. Paul, Minn.: American Land and Title Register Association Publishers, 1900.

Mee, Bob. *Bare Fists: The History of Bare-Knuckle Prize-Fighting*. New York: Overlook Press, 2001.

Meier, August. *Negro Thought in America, 1880–1915: Racial Ideologies in the Age of Booker T. Washington*. Ann Arbor: University of Michigan Press, 1963.

Merriner, James L. *Grafters and Googoos: Corruption and Reform in Chicago, 1833–2003*. Carbondale: Southern Illinois University Press, 2004.

Messner, Michael A., and Donald F. Sabo, eds. *Sport, Men, and the Gender Order: Critical Feminist Perspectives*. Champaign, Ill,: Human Kinetics Books, 1990.

Miles, Henry Downes. *Pugilistica: Being One Hundred and Forty-Four Years of the History of British Boxing*. London: Weldon, 1880.

Miletich, Leo N. *Dan Stuart's Fistic Carnival*. College Station: Texas A&M University Press, 1994.

Molina, Natalia. *Fit to be Citizens: Public Health and Race in Los Angeles, 1879–1939*. Berkeley: University of California Press, 2006.

Moore, Archie. *The Archie Moore Story*. New York: McGraw-Hill, 1960.

Mumford, Kevin J. *Interzones: Black/White Sex Districts in Chicago and New York in the Early Twentieth Century*. New York: Columbia University Press, 1997.

Myler, Patrick. *A Century of Boxing Greats: Inside the Ring with the Hundred Best Boxers*. Park West, N.Y.: Robinson Books, 1997.

Nell, William C. *Colored Patriots of The Revolution, With Sketches of Several Distinguished Colored Persons: To Which is added a Brief Survey of the Condition and Prospects of Colored Americans*. Boston: Robert F. Wallcut, 1855.

Nelson, Bruce. *Divided We Stand: American Workers and the Struggle for Black Equality*. Princeton, N.J.: Princeton University Press, 2001.

Odd, Gilbert. *Great Moments in Sport: Heavyweight Boxing*. New York: Pelham Books, 1973.

Oriard, Michael. *Reading Football: How the Popular Press Created an American Spectacle*. Chapel Hill. University of North Carolina Press, 1998.

Osofsky, Gilbert. *Harlem: The Making of a Ghetto*. New York: Harper & Row, 1966.

Philpott, Thomas Lee. *The Slum and the Ghetto: Immigrants, Blacks and Reformers in Chicago, 1880–1930*. Belmont, Calif.: Wadsworth Publishing, 1979.

Pleck, Elizabeth. *Black Migration and Poverty: Boston 1855–1900.* New York: Academic Press, 1979.

Pope, S. W., ed. *The New American Sport History: Recent Approaches and Perspectives.* Chicago: University of Illinois Press, 1997.

Ransom, Reverdy C. *The Pilgrimage of Harriet Ransom's Son.* Nashville, Tenn.: Sunday School Union, n.d.

Reed, Christopher Robert. *Black Chicago's First Century: Volume 1, 1833–1900.* Columbia: University of Missouri Press, 2005.

Riess, Steven A. *City Games: The Evolution of American Urban Society and the Rise of Sports.* Urbana: University of Illinois Press, 1989.

Roberts, Randy. *Papa Jack: Jack Johnson and the Era of White Hopes.* New York: The Free Press, 1983.

Roediger, David R. *The Wages of Whiteness: Race and the Making of the American Working Class.* New York: Verso, 1999.

Ross, Marlon. *Manning the Race: Reforming Black Men in the Jim Crow Era.* New York: New York University Press, 2004.

Rotundo, E. Anthony. *American Manhood: Transformations in Masculinity from the Revolution to the Modern Era.* New York: Basic Books, 1993.

Ruck, Rob. *Sandlot Seasons: Sport in Black Pittsburgh.* Chicago: University of Illinois Press, 1993.

Ruffin, Roosevelt Samuel. *Black Presence in Saginaw, Michigan, 1855–1900.* N.p., 1978.

Runstedtler, Theresa. *Jack Johnson Rebel Sojourner.* Berkeley: University of California Press, 2012.

Sammons, Jeffrey T. *Beyond the Ring: The Role of Boxing in American Society.* Urbana: University of Illinois Press, 1990.

Schneider, Mark R. *Boston Confronts Jim Crow, 1890–1920.* Boston: Northeastern University Press, 1997.

Shaffer, Donald R. *After the Glory: The Struggles of Black Civil War Veterans.* Lawrence: University Press of Kansas, 2004.

Simmons, Charles A. *The African American Press: With Special References to Four Newspapers, 1827–1965.* Jefferson, N.C.: McFarland, 1998.

Smith, Kevin R. *Black Genesis: The History of the Black Prizefighter 1760–1870.* New York: iUniverse, 2003.

———. *The Sundowners: The History of the Black Prizefighter, 1870—1930, Volume II, Part One.* Boston: CCK Publications, 2006.

Somers, Dale A. *The Rise of Sports in New Orleans, 1850–1890.* Baton Rouge: Louisiana State University Press, 1972.

Spalding, William Andrew. *William Andrew Spalding: Los Angeles Newspaperman.* San Marino, Calif: Huntington Library, 1961.

Spear, Allan H. *Black Chicago: The Making of a Negro Ghetto.* Chicago: University of Chicago Press, 1967.

Spivey, Donald, ed. *Sport in America: New Historical Perspectives*. Westport, Conn.: Greenwood Press, 1985.

Stead, William T. *If Christ Came to Chicago!* Chicago: Laird and Lee Publishers, 1894.

Stearns, Peter N. *Be a Man! Males in Modern Society*. New York: Holmes and Meier, 1990.

Stephenson, Thomas. *Race Distinctions in American Law*. New York: Negro University Press, 1969.

Sullivan, John L. *Life and Reminiscences of a 19th Century Gladiator*. Boston: Jas. A. Hearn, 1892.

Summers, Martin. *Manliness and Its Discontents: Marlon Ross, Manning the Race: Reforming Black Men in the Jim Crow Era*. New York: New York University Press, 2004.

Sundquist, Eric J. *The Oxford W.E.B. Du Bois Reader*. New York: Oxford University Press, 1996.

Taylor, David Vasser. *Pilgrim's Progress: Black St. Paul and the Making of an Urban Ghetto, 1870–1930*. PhD diss., University of Minnesota, 1977.

———. *African Americans in Minnesota*. St. Paul: Minnesota Historical Society, 2002.

Taylor, Henry Louis, Jr., ed. *Race and the City: Work, Community, and Protest in Cincinnati, 1820–1970*. Chicago: University of Illinois Press, 1993.

Thornbrough, Emma Lou. *T. Thomas Fortune: Militant Journalist*. Chicago: University of Chicago Press, 1972.

Trotter, Joe William, Jr. *River Jordan: African American Urban Life in the Ohio Valley*. Lexington: University of Kentucky Press, 1998.

Walker, Clarence E. *A Rock in a Weary Land*. Baton Rouge: Louisiana State University Press, 1982.

Walker, David. *David Walker's Appeal: To the Coloured Citizens of the World*, Peter Hinks, ed. University Park: Pennsylvania State University Press, 2006.

Wallace, Maurice O. *Constructing the Black Masculine: Identity and Ideality in African American Men's Literature and Culture, 1775–1995*. Durham, N.C.: Duke University Press, 2002.

Ward, Gayle. *Crossing the Color: Racial Passing in the Twentieth-Century U.S. Literature and Culture*. Durham, N.C.: Duke University Press, 2000.

Ward, Geoffrey C. *Unforgivable Blackness: The Rise and Fall of Jack Johnson*. New York: Alfred A. Knopf, 2004.

Wendt, Lloyd. *Chicago Tribune: The Rise of a Great American Newspaper*. San Francisco: Rand McNally, 1979.

White, Graham, and Shane White. *Stylin': African American Expressive Culture From Its Beginnings to the Zoot Suit*. Ithaca, N.Y.: Cornell University Press, 1998.

Wiggins, David. *Glory Bound: Black Athletes in a White America*. Syracuse, N.Y.: Syracuse University Press, 1997.

Wignall, Trevor. *The Story of Boxing*. London: Hutchinson, 1923.

———. *The Sweet Science*. London: Chapman and Hall, n.d.

Wild, Mark. *Street Meeting: Multiethnic Neighborhoods in Early Twentieth Century Los Angeles*. Berkeley: University of California Press, 2005.

Wingerd, Mary Lethert. *Claiming the City: Politics, Faith, and the Power of Place in St. Paul.* Ithaca, N.Y.: Cornell University Press, 2001.

Wolseley, Ronald E. *The Black Press, U.S.A.,* 2nd ed. Ames: Iowa State University Press, 1990.

Woolridge, Clifton R. *The Devil and the Grafter: And How They Work Together to Deceive, Swindle and Destroy Mankind.* Chicago: Clifton R. Woolridge, 1907.

Works Project Administration. *Los Angeles: A Guide to the City and Its Environs.* New York: Hastings House, 1941.

Wyatt-Brown, Bertram. *Southern Honor: Ethics and Behavior in the Old South.* New York: Oxford University Press, 1982.

Young, Betty Lou. *Our First Century: The Los Angeles Athletic Club, 1880–1890.* Los Angeles: LAAC Press, 1979.

Young, R. J. *Antebellum Black Activists: Race, Gender, and Self.* New York: Garland Publishing, 1996.

JOURNALS AND MAGAZINE ARTICLES

Anderson, Jervis. "Black Heavies." *American Scholar* 47, no. 3 (Summer 1978): 387–95.

Best, Joel. "Looking Evil in the Face: Being an Examination of Vice and Respectability in St. Paul as Seen in the City's Press, 1865–83." *Minnesota Historian* (Summer 1987): 241–51.

Candela, Gregory. "We Wear the Mask: Irony in Dunbar's Sport of the Gods." *American Literature* 48, no. 1 (March 1976): 60–72.

Clymer, Jeffory A. "The Market in Male Bodies: Henry James's *The American* and Late Nineteenth Century Boxing," *Henry James Review* 25 (2004): 127–41.

De Graaf, Lawrence B. "The City of Black Angels: Emergence of the Los Angeles Ghetto, 1890–1930." *Pacific Historic Review* 39, no. 3 (August 1970): 323–52.

Donnan, Joseph. "Black Heroes in Sports from Jack Johnson to Muhammad Ali." *Journal of Popular Culture* 31, no.3 (1997): 115–35.

Farr, Finnis. "Black Hamlet of the Heavyweights." *Sports Illustrated,* June 15, 1959.

———. "Jeff It's Up To You." *American Heritage* 15, no. 2 (1964): 64–77.

Fisher, James A. "The Political Development of the Black Community in California, 1850–1950." *California Historical Quarterly* 3 (September 1971): 256–66.

Fradella, Sal. "Jack Johnson: The Dark Prince." *American Visions* 3, no. 5 (1988): 22–25.

Gaines, "Assimilationist Minstrelsy as Racial Uplift Ideology: James D Corrothers's Literary Quest for Black Leadership." *American Quarterly* 45, no. 3 (September 1993): 341–69.

Gilmore, Al-Toney. "Jack Johnson and White Woman: The National Impact, 1912–1913." *Journal of Negro History* 38, no. 1 (January 1973): 18–38.

———. "Jack Johnson: A Magnificent Black Anachronism of Early Twentieth Century." *Journal of Social and Behavioral Sciences* (Winter 1973).

———. "Jack Johnson The Man and His Times." *Journal of Popular Culture* 6, no. 3 (Spring 1973): 495–506.

Gray, Herman. "Black Masculinity and Visual Culture." *Callaloo* 18, no. 2 (1995): 401–5.

Griffin, James. "Blacks in the St. Paul Police Department: An Eighty-year Survey." *Minnesota Historian* (Fall 1975): 255–65.

Guzman, Jessie P. "Monroe Nathan Work and his Contributions: Background and Preparation for Life's Career." *Journal of Negro History* 34, no. 4 (October 1949): 428–61.

Haley, Melissa. "Storm of Blows." *Common Place* 3, no. 2 (January 2003): 1–17

Haller, Mark H. "Policy Gambling, Entertainment, and the Emergence of Black Politics." *Journal of Social History* 24, no. 4 (Summer 1991): 719–39.

Haywood, Robert C. "No Less A Man: Blacks in Cow Town Dodge City, 1876–1886." *Western Historical Quarterly* 19, no. 2 (May 1888): 161–82.

Hurd, Myles. "Blackness and Borrowed Obscurity: Another Look at Dunbar's the Sport of the Gods." *Callaloo* 11, no. 13 (February–October 1981): 90–100.

"Johnson vs. Christians." *California Cactus,* July 1910, 10.

Kaye, Andrew M. "'Battle Blind': Atlanta's Taste for Black Boxing in the Early Twentieth Century." *Journal of Sports History* 28, no. 2 (2001): 213–32.

Kilar, Jeremy W. "Black Pioneers in Michigan's Lumber Industry." *Journal of Forestry* 24, no. 3 (July 1980): 142–49.

Kramer, David J. "TKO in Las Vegas; Boosters as the Johnson-Flynn Fight." *New Mexico Historical Review* 61, no. 4 (1986): 301–18.

Kramer, William M, and Norton B. Stern. "San Francisco's Fighting Jew." *California Historical Quarterly* 53, no. 4 (1974): 333–46.

Marqusee, Mark. "Sport and Stereotype: From Role Model to Muhammad Ali." *Race and Class* 36, no. 4 (1995): 1–29.

McGehee, Richard V. "The Dandy and the Mauler in Mexico: Johnson, Dempsey, Et Al. And the Mexico City Press." *Journal of Sports History* 23 (1996): 20–33.

Meier, August. "Booker T. Washington and the Negro Press: With Special Reference to the Colored American Magazine." *Journal of Negro History* 38, no. 1 (January 1953): 67–90.

Moss, Rick. "Not Quite Paradise: The Development of the African American Community in Los Angeles Through 1950." *California History* 75, no. 3 (Fall 1996): 222–35.

O'Brian, Joseph. "The Business of Boxing." *American Heritage* 42, no. 6 (October 1991): 69–81.

O'Kelly, Charlotte G. "Black Newspapers and the Black Protest Movement: Their Historical Relationship, 1827–1945." *Phylon* (1960): 1–14

Roberts, Randy. "Heavyweight Champion Jack Johnson: His Omaha Image, A Public Relations Study." *Nebraska History* 57, no. 2 (1976): 226–41.

———. "Galveston's Jack Johnson: Flourishing in the Dark." *Southwestern Historical Quarterly* 87, no. 1 (July 1983): 37–56.

Schaeffer, Matt. "Boxing and Being a Man." *Iowa Heritage Illustrated* 80, no. 3 (1999): 98–107.

Stevens, Peter F. "Wyatt Earp's Word is Good with Me: In the ring the Gunman runs into Trouble." *American West* 25, no. 1 (1988): 44–47.

"The Story of Afro-Americans in the Story of Minnesota," *Gopher Historian* (Winter 1968–1969): 5–16.

Taylor, David Vassar. "John Quincy Adams: St. Paul Editor and Black Leader." *Minnesota Historian* (Winter 1973): 282–96.

"Tough Times: The Sometime Fortunes of Boxing in early Minnesota." *Ramsey Historical Society* (1977): 13–18.

Wamsley, Kevin B., and David Whitson. "Celebrating Violent Masculinities: The Boxing Death of Luther McCarty." *Journal of Sports History* 25 (1998): 419–31.

Wiggins, William H., Jr. "Jack Johnson as Bad Nigger: The Folklore of His Life." *Black Scholar* 2, no. 5 (January 1971): 34–46.

———. "Boxing's Sambo Twins: Racial Stereotypes In Jack Johnson and Joe Louis Newspaper Cartoons, 1908 to 1938." *Journal of Sports History* 15, no. 3 (1988): 242–54.

Wilson, Raymond. "Another White Hope Bites the Dust: The Jack Johnson Jim Flynn Heavyweight Fight in 1912." *Montana* 29, no. 1 (1979): 30–39.

Work, Monroe. "Crime Among the Negroes of Chicago. A Social Study." *American Journal of Sociology* 6, no. 2 (September 1900): 204–23.

Young, A. S. "Was Jack Johnson Boxing's Greatest Champion?" *Ebony,* January 1963.

———. "Why Do Boxers Go Broke?" *Negro Digest,* June 1962.

Young, Alexander J. R. "The Boston Tarbaby." *Nova Scotia Historical Quarterly* 4, no. 3 (September 1974): 277–98.

NEWSPAPERS

Black Newspapers

Baltimore Afro-American Ledger
Boston Guardian
Broad Ax (Chicago)
California Eagle (Los Angeles)
Chicago Conservator
Chicago Defender
Cleveland Gazette
Colored American Magazine
Frederick Douglass's Newspaper
Indianapolis Freeman
Liberator (Los Angeles)
New York Age
San Francisco Elevator
Western Appeal (St. Paul, Minn.)

White Newspapers

Baltimore American
Baltimore Sun
Boston Globe

Brooklyn Daily Eagle
Chicago Times
Chicago Tribune
Cincinnati Weekly Inquirer
Cleveland Leader
Cleveland Plain Dealer
Los Angeles Express
Los Angeles Herald
Los Angeles Times
Louisville Courier Journal
Marysville (California) *Daily Appeal*
Memphis Commercial Appeal
Memphis Scimitar
Minneapolis Tribune
National Police Gazette
New York Times
Sacramento Bee
Sacramento Star
Sacramento Union
San Francisco Call
San Francisco Chronicle
Santa Fe New Mexican
St. Paul Globe
St. Paul Pioneer Press
Washington Post

INDEX

LOUIS MOORE is associate professor of history at Grand Valley State University. He is the author of *We Will Win the Day: The Civil Rights Movement, the Black Athlete, and the Quest for Equality.*

SPORT AND SOCIETY

REPRINT EDITIONS
The Nazi Olympics   *Richard D. Mandell*
Sports in the Western World (2d ed.)   *William J. Baker*
Jesse Owens: An American Life   *William J. Baker*

The University of Illinois Press
is a founding member of the
Association of American University Presses.

University of Illinois Press
1325 South Oak Street
Champaign, IL 61820-6903
www.press.uillinois.edu

Printed by Printforce, United Kingdom